ANGLICAN LIFE AND WITNESS

A Reader for the Lambeth Conference of Anglican Bishops 1998

Foreword by
The Archbishop of Canterbury

Edited by
Vinay Samuel and Chris Sugden

First published in Great Britain 1997
SPCK
Holy Trinity Church
Marylebone Road
London NW1 4DU

By the same authors

Lambeth – A View from the Two Thirds World

(SPCK 1989)

British Library Cataloguing-in-Publication Data
CIP data for this book available from the British Library
ISBN 0–281–05099–6
Printed in Great Britain by
Arrowsmiths, Bristol

Contents

Contents

Part Two
Holding and Sharing the Faith

Part Three
Living as Anglicans
in a Pluralistic World

Contents

Foreword

This reader has been produced at the request of a number of bishops from Africa, Asia and Latin America, who are seeking resources so that they can be at the sharp end of the discussion on issues that critically affect the mission of the church in those parts of the world where many of the churches, including the Anglican church, are growing apace.

My own visits to so many countries encourage me to believe that as the bishops share their experiences and wisdom with one another at the Lambeth Conference in 1998, we shall have an unprecedented opportunity to recognise the work of the Holy Spirit through one part of the whole people of God as represented by the Anglican Communion.

Not everyone will agree with every position set out in the collection. The aim of the book is to stimulate debate and encourage people to bring their own perspectives and hear other voices in the fellowship of the communion. As such, it will be a most useful resource for us all, and especially as the official Lambeth documentation is produced and circulated.

I hope many people and not just bishops will read it.

George Cantuar   *Archbishop of Canterbury*

Authors

Dr Bernard Adeney is associate professor of Ethics and Cross-Cultural Studies at Satya Wacana Christian University, Indonesia.

The Rev Dr Kwame Bediako is director of the Akrofi-Kristaller Memorial Centre in Ghana and visiting lecturer in African Theology at the Centre for the Study of Christianity in the non-Western World, New College, Edinburgh.

The Rev Dr David Bennett is senior pastor of Mountain Park Church, Lake Oswego, Oregon, USA.

The Rev Gideon Byamugisha is a priest in the Church of Uganda.

Canon Professor Henry Chadwick is former Regius Professor of Divinity at the Universities of Oxford and Cambridge.

Dr Raja Chelliah is former fiscal adviser and Minister of State in the Ministry of Finance in the Government of India.

Dr Roger Griffin is principal lecturer in history at Oxford Brookes University, Oxford, UK.

The Rt Rev Richard Harries is the Bishop of Oxford, UK.

Dr Harriet Harris is lecturer in theology at the University of Exeter, UK.

The Rt Rev Emmanuel Kolini is Bishop of Shaba, Zaire.

The Rt Rev Dr Michael Nazir-Ali is Bishop of Rochester, UK.

Canon Dr Oliver O'Donovan is Regius Professor of Moral and Pastoral Theology in the University of Oxford, UK.

Dr Jean-Daniel Plüss is Chairman of the European Pentecostal Charismatic Association in Zurich, Switzerland.

The Rev Dr John Pobee is director of Ecumenical Theological Education of Unit 1 of the World Council of Churches, and a member of the Church of the Province of West Africa.

Canon Dr Vinay Samuel is executive director of the Oxford Centre for Mission Studies and of the International Fellowship of Evangelical Mission Theologians.

Dr Quentin Schultze is head of the department of communications at Calvin College, Grand Rapids, Michigan, USA.

The Most Rev Maurice Sinclair is Primate of the Anglican Province of the Southern Cone of Latin America.

The Rev Dr Christopher Sugden is Director of Academic Affairs at the Oxford Centre for Mission Studies.

The Rev Patrick Yu is Rector of St Theodore of Canterbury, Diocese of Toronto, Canada.

Copyrights

Introduction

The material in this reader in preparation for the Lambeth Conference of 1998 has been selected according to the following criteria and to fulfil the following requirements and needs.We have begun with the issues which the Lambeth design team has identified as those "we may need to consider, and in relation to which sound moral judgements have to be made".[1]

A recent international consultation of leaders in mission and development identified the following global trends:

- The global integration of economy.
- The breakdown of political machinery.
- The emergence of global communication and information network.
- Modern technological innovations and related knowledge.
- Increase in cases of AIDS, new clones of viruses and resistant bacteria and parasites.
- Environmental degradation.

The consequences of the above are:

- The widening gap between the rich and the poor.
- Movement of people for security and economic reasons.
- Diminishing sovereignty of the nation State.
- Marginalization of peoples and nations.
- Expectations being raised without real hope of fulfilment.
- Major economic decisions which affect the majority of people being made by the emerging global economy which is not accountable to governments nor the people.
- Increase in internal conflict, disintegration of communities and nations.
- The high cost and unavailability of health care.

In many of the marginalised countries, Christianity is also growing apace. However, such growth has not always been accompanied by the expression of integral Kingdom values.[2]

Therefore in the context of poverty, violence, the inability of states to guarantee rights, breakdown of family life, winners and losers in the market cultures, how should the church witness, what should the church uphold?

The articles have also been selected to highlight contentious issues, to reflect a "world church" rather than a denominational perspective, to have a bias to the two-thirds world, and to make available what is not readily available in published sources. A number of the articles are the reports or findings of international consultations. These consultations have all focused on issues with a special focus on the two-thirds world perspective. The production of theological writing in the two-thirds world tends to be a community and corporate process rather than a process of an individual contributor. Thus in many ways these consultations truly represent both the mind and the style of the two-thirds world church.

The Anglican Communion is in many ways a representation of the world church rather than of a denomination. While some church denominations focus on their distinctive traditions and history, where the church is growing the Anglican church behaves more like a global fellowship. This reader thus takes a global perspective in order to express that dimension that is reflected in the Anglican Communion.

We have taken soundings from gatherings of bishops in Asia, Africa and Latin America and in an international Anglican gathering in South Africa in preparing this material. All indicated that the critical issues for them were in sections I on "Called to Full Humanity" and II on "Holding and Sharing the Faith". These issues of witnessing to the gospel in the context of complex human situations are the priorities for the two-thirds world church in mission. This is therefore where we have concentrated our attention.

The first section is entitled *"Called to Full Humanity"*. What are the current threats to full humanity? It is the considered opinion of many that the direction of the world from centralised state structures to market dominated processes is set for at least a generation. In a market shaped culture there are two main concerns, security and identity. The quest for identity is critical in market shaped culture, since all the traditional sources of identity are marginalised and discounted by the market, be they traditional, religious, social or ascribed. None count in the market. Yet people cannot survive without identity. For many in the two-thirds world, the fundamental question is "What is the nature and basis of my human identity?" Is it to be found in a national and cultural assertion against the overwhelming presence of global economic and social forces which threaten to co-opt everyone? Is it to be found in a religious, economic or social identity? The issues that are noted by the design team are therefore not to be seen as isolated problems, but as part of a series of challenges to people's very identity. Our readings examine both the threats to humanity, and the searches that people undertake both to find their human identity, and having found it in Christ how they express it with integrity in cultures shaped by secular modern media or cultures of corruption.

The proud claim of indigenous Anglican Churches is that they are indigenous in the sense of national ownership and leadership of the church, particularly in its institutional forms. Indigeneity is also an issue of cultural identity with the increasing globalisation of culture. This becomes critical in Islamic contexts where it is not only the national leadership of the church that is likely to command respect, but the church's cultural identity as an indigenous religious institution. In our reflections on the Lambeth Conference of 1988 published as *Lambeth - a View from the Two Thirds World*, by Vinay Samuel and Chris Sugden (SPCK, 1989) we stressed the challenges that not only churches in two-thirds world cultures faced to express their Christian and Anglican identity within that culture in their worship, life and witness, but also the challenge to the communion as a whole to facilitate that process by respecting and valueing the contributions of each member church as the churches work together on mission, ministry and sharing around the word. Identity is found not in isolation but in communion.

The Lambeth design team notes the importance of ***Human dignity, rights and responsibilities and the risk of excessive individualism***. There has been a long struggle during this century between human rights defined as rights of the individual before the law, and human rights understood as the response of basic justice to the needs of a community. But as the millenium approaches there is a more fundamental problem. The collapse of enlightenment rationality, and in particular many accepted arguments for objectivity put at risk claims to their being objective, mandatory rights for human beings.

The Lambeth design team notes ***Racism, Tribalism, ethnicity and nationalism - positive and negative elements***. The source of identity for many is found in nationalism. Roger Griffin suggests in a reader on Fascism, that in the wake of "globalisation" in the twenty-first century, there will be a resurgence of nationalism, and religious renewal that is linked with nationalism.

In considering ***The family, its strengths and the causes of breakdown*** Vinay Samuel suggests that there is a temptation to an idolatry of the family, both in the west and also in two-thirds world societies where the family is the basis of society. Samuel suggests that Jesus relativised the family in the light of the kingdom of God. Family life is not an end in itself, it is to be in the service of the Kingdom.

A major issue in the current debate about ***Human Sexuality*** is whether our identity is to be found primarily in our sexual orientation[3]. Maurice Sinclair, the presiding bishop of the Southern Cone of Latin America, suggests that the current intense disagreement about the issue of homosexuality will be ignored at the expense a proper respect for the multi-cultural nature of the communion. The *St Andrew's Day Statement* issued in 1995 by a group of evangelical Anglicans in England at the request of the Church of England Evangelical Council offers an approach that puts the discussion on a theological footing. Patrick Yu from Canada gives a response and Oliver O'Donovan one of the authors of the statement provides a commentary on it. Gideon Byamugisha, an Anglican priest from Uganda with AIDS, asks that he be referred to as "living with AIDS rather than dying from AIDS".

Modern Technology: its life-enhancing and dehumanising possibilities brings with it a culture and values. These can undermine the cultures and values of vulnerable people and communities in the Two-Thirds World in the name of development and progress. Bernard Adeney reflects on this from Indonesia.

International debt, and the gap between the rich and poor both within and between nations sets the agenda for the life of many in the two-thirds world. The Oxford Conference on Christian Faith and Economics was an eight year international study process. It issued a Declaration in 1990 which identified some causes of poverty and the demands of justice. The United Nations Conference on Trade and Development (UNCTAD) Trade and Development Report in September 1996 includes their latest initiative on

International Debt. Raja Chelliah, former fiscal adviser and Minister of State in the Ministry of Finance in the Government of India, was the architect of India's financial reforms in the nineties. He examines the impact of market-based reforms on the poor of India.

Just as there are "business cultures" so there are cultures of corruption. We must identify the nature of these cultures and how they work, and how the church may promote covenant communities to address the problem of *Integrity and Corruption in Business and Public Life. Modern Mass Communication* is itself the product of a culture and the transmitter of culture, in particular the culture of modernity and modernisation.

Many approaches to *the world population* issue are based on "panic projections" of the future which require urgent measures to prevent population disaster. An international Christian consultation suggested that such approaches undermine people's cultures and values, and neglect the Christian perceptions that children are always welcome, and that obedience to God's will in the present will never jeopardise his blessing in the future. Harriet Harris provides a feminist perspective on the issue.

Section II is on *Holding and Sharing the Faith*. The gospel is good news of the Kingdom of God. So how does the Kingdom of God shape our understanding and presentation of the good news? An international study programme over six years of Christians from pentecostal, charismatic and evangelical perspectives issued "Kingdom Affirmations and Commitments."

Transmission of the gospel across cultures is a critically important issue, since part of the gospel is reconciliation between those of different cultures. A recent international consultation found that "Because western cultures, agencies and churches have networks that span the world, they often present their concerns as spanning the globe, and are perceived by others to be global agencies. This can produce a defensive reaction in two-thirds world people, (or minority groups in the north) who protect their own identity and contribution from being subsumed under others' powerful agendas and co-opted into a global operation over which they have no control by stressing the integrity of their own national identity. This can become a token nationalism in the face of a dominant supposed internationalism. It can misinterpret the present and misprescribe for the future on the basis of an idealised picture of a past that never was, also pitting the traditional against the modern. Thus for example local theologies are emphasised over against allegedly global theologies; and the contextual is seen as local and anti-global. However, western agencies and churches are just as local and contextual as two thirds world agencies and are just as shaped by their own local cultures. The global is not the preserve of one culture or agency. In the Christian sense the global is all kinds of locals comprising a family together. The global takes place at the intersection of two or more equally local cultures.

While a vision may be global, its outworking is always local. If any one local context sets itself up as global and claims to present a global content, then local contexts are weakened, and the content itself lacks substance. This colonial process continues to happen when the forces of modernity globalise all problems. This undermines the contextual shape of problems in each situation.

In every context the global and the local intersect. We need to look at the intersection of the global and the local rather than see them always as opposites: to see how the intersection of the global and local is also at the heart of a Christian understanding of the world where the gospel is universally valid and at the same time does not homogenise local cultures but rather transforms them and where necessary recovers them; to question whether the global is only owned by those who have economic power or whether a Christian understanding reinterprets the global in the light of spiritual realities of the existence and growth of the church globally, where God's work in power is discernible. Otherwise the definition of the global and the local will be shaped only by socio-political and economic understandings. There is an urgent need to reinterpret these terms from biblical and theological viewpoints.In these changing circumstances and especially in the face of the tendency of modernity to globalise, the role and level of partnership will need to be redefined".[4]

The relation of *gospel and culture* is critical in sharing the gospel. The Commission on World Mission and Evangelism of the the WCC is considering this issue at its conference in November 1996 in Brazil. Kwame Bediako suggests that in the engagement of Gospel and Culture the African Church will recover and highlight important aspects of the gospel and thus make an important contribution to the rest of World Christianity. There are cultures within cultures, and one important one is youth culture. By the year 2000 60% of the population of Nairobi will be under 21. An international report highlights the critical issues for *Ministry of youth and to youth*.

The issue of Christian identity, noted at the beginning of the introduction, is of crucial importance in considering the issue of the relationship of *Christianity and Other Faiths*. Michael Nazir Ali contributes his observations on "Dialogue in an Age of Conflict".

Lively worship and evangelism has an important place in *handing on the faith and in evangelism*. Jean-Daniel Plüss suggests that testimony is an important component in the worship of God. It also creates space for the contribution of the laity and thus contributes to the discussion of the relation between clergy and laity. Lively worship especially characterises World Christianity and Pluss suggests that testimony in worship is a component of this.

Henry Chadwick's article on *Reception* gives rooting in the bible, the fathers and historical theology for understanding a process that has come to be used as a means of enabling consensus to emerge in the Anglican Communion over matters of faith and conduct. Bishop Richard Harries of Oxford gives a case study of how this process worked out in the Anglican Communion with reference to contraception.

In Section III, *Living as Anglicans in a Pluralistic World*, most of the topics identified by the design team refer to the issue of *leadership*. This is indeed a crucial issue for the Anglican Communion. In some parts of South Asia it is clear that the model of episcopacy is failing as a pattern of leadership, while in East Africa episcopacy is a key to the powerful impact that the church is having on the society, enabling it to be in the words of a Kenyan Anglican research scholar Gideon Githiga "the bulwark of the people against oppression". Thus in this section our readings reflect on issues of leadership and in particular the leadership Bishop Emmanuel Kolini has given in bringing reconciation in Rwanda. John Pobee reflects on how an African understanding of authority in community can contribute to an understanding of episcopal leadership. David Bennett examines the implications of biblical themes for leadership in Christ's Church.

Section IV addresses the theme of *visible unity*. The question of unity is taking a different shape in an increasingly plural world. The Anglican Church in many situations has been closely allied to central state structures, and in some cases has been a form of religious civil service. The state and centralised structures are weakened and breaking down all over the world. The World Council of Churches for example recognises that it can only be one expression of ecumenical relating, and no longer the sole privileged example. The focus must be increasingly on koinonia rather than on structure. Can the Anglican Communion express koinonia in new ways that transcend the former expressions? In particular can it embrace and learn from the experience and growth of new movements to Christ, such as those represented by the Friends Missionary Prayer Band in India?

Finally, we are grateful to our good friends Bishop Michael Nazir-Ali and Professor Oliver O'Donovan for their observations and advice in putting this collection together; to the authors and publishers for their permission to include their work; to Paul Gordon Chandler, Lucy Gasson and SPCK for their encouragement and support for the project; and to Archbishop George Carey for contributing the foreword.

Oxford, All Saints Day 1996   Vinay Samuel and Chris Sugden

Notes

1   The four parts are those identified by the Lambeth Design Team. In this introduction the details of those parts are highlighted in bold type.
2/4 "Christian Relief and Development Agencies in the twenty-first century" in *Transformation* Volume 13 No 4 October 1996
3   See further on this issue Christl Ruth Vonholdt *Striving for Gender Identity – Homosexuality and Christian Counselling* (German Institute for Youth and Society, Schloss Reichenberg, D-64385 Reichelsheim, 1996) available from OCMS, PO Box 70 Oxford.

Part One

—

Called to
Full Humanity

I

Fascism and Nationalism

Roger Griffin

The idea that a 'nation' is an entity which can 'decay' and be 'regenerated' implies something diametrically opposed to what liberals understand by it. It connotes an organism with its own life-cycle, collective psyche, and communal destiny, embracing in principle the whole people (not just its ruling élites), and in practice all those who ethnically or culturally are 'natural' members of it, and are not contaminated by forces hostile to nationhood. In this way of conceiving the nation sometimes referred to by academics as 'integral nationalism', 'hypernationalism' or 'illiberal nationalism' it becomes a higher reality transcending the individual's life, which only acquires meaning and value in so far as it contributes directly to its vitality and well-being. Extensive study of the primary sources of Fascism and of other fascisms convinced me that at the core of its mentality was the *idée fixe* of devoting, and, if necessary sacrificing, individual existence to the struggle against the forces of degeneration which had seemingly brought the nation low, and of helping relaunch it towards greatness and glory. The fascist felt he (and it generally was a 'he') had been fatefully born at a watershed between national decline and national regeneration, a feeling that alchemically converted all pessimism and cultural despair into a manic sense of purpose and optimism. He knew himself to be one of the 'chosen' of an otherwise lost generation. His task it was to prepare the ground for the new breed of man, the *homo fascistus*, who would instinctively form part of the revitalized national community without having first to purge himself of the selfish reflexes inculcated by a civilization sapped by egotism and materialism.

Within fascist studies the recurrent obsession with national rebirth and the need for a 'new man' seemed to have been frequently noted without being recognized as a candidate for the 'fascist minimum'. A deliberate exercise in 'idealizing abstraction' turned this theme into fascism's sole necessary definitional trait. To sum up the mythic core in a single concept involved resuscitating what is an obscure and obsolescent word in English, 'palingenesis' (meaning rebirth), and coining the expression 'palingenetic ultra-nationalism'. The premiss of this chapter is thus that generic fascism can be defined in terms of this expression, or to repeat the formula expounded at length elsewhere (Griffin, The Nature of Fascism, Routledge, London 1993): *Fascism is a genus of political ideology whose mythic core in its various permutations is a palingenetic form of populist ultra-nationalism*. From this premiss about the matrix of fascist ideology, a number of features of generic fascism follow which have a profound bearing on how it operates in practice both as an opposition movement and as a regime.

Fascism is anti-liberal

Fascism's call for the regeneration of the national community through a heroic struggle against its alleged enemies and the forces undermining it involves the radical rejection of liberalism in all its aspects: pluralism, tolerance, individualism, gradualism, pacifism, parliamentary democracy, the separation of powers, the doctrine of 'natural rights', egalitarianism, the rectilinear theory of progress, the open society, cosmopolitanism, one-worldism, etc. The important proviso to this aspect of fascist movements is that, though they oppose parliamentary democracy and their policies would in practice inevitably lead to its destruction, they may well choose to operate tactically as democratic, electoral parties. Indeed, they may go to considerable lengths to camouflage the extent of their hostility to liberalism through euphemism and dishonesty, reserving their rhetoric of destruction of the 'system' and of revolution for the initiated.

Fascism is anti-conservative

The centrality to fascism of a myth of the nation's regeneration within a new order implies a rejection of illiberal conservative politics (for example, an absolutist system in which sovereignty is invested in a hereditary monarchy or oligarchy), as well as of liberal and authoritarian conservative solutions to the current crisis which imply a restoration of law and order that does not involve social renewal. In other words, in the context of fascism 'rebirth' means 'new birth, a 'new order', one which 'might draw inspiration from the past but does not seek to turn the clock back. However, two factors have obscured fascism's revolutionary, forward-looking thrust. First, in order to achieve power in the inter-war period fascism was forced to ally itself or collude with conservative forces (the Army, Civil Service, Church, industrialists, reactionary bourgeois, etc.) on the basis of common enemies (such as communism, cosmopolitanism) and common priorities (such as law and order, the family).

Second, fascist ideologues frequently attach great importance to allegedly glorious epochs in the nation's past and the heroes which embody them. They do so not out of nostalgia, but to remind the people of the nation's 'true' nature and its destiny to rise once more to historical greatness. In *The Eighteenth Brumaire of Louis Bonaparte* Marx expressed an insight into the readiness of Napoleon III's regime to use myths based on the past to enlist popular support for the Second Empire which is equally pertinent to fascism. He saw that the 'awakening of the dead [...] served the purpose of glorifying the new struggles, not parodying the old; of magnifying the given task in imagination, not fleeing from its solution in reality; of finding once more the spirit of revolution, not making a ghost walk around again'.

Fascism tends to operate as a charismatic form of politics

Since, to use Weberian terminology, fascism rejects both the traditional politics of the *ancien régime* and the legal-rational politics of liberalism and socialism, it follows that it is predisposed to function as a *charismatic* form of politics. This does not necessarily involve the epitome of such politics, the leader cult. Historically, some forms of fascism (for example Valois's *Le Faisceau*) have opted for a technocratic, managerial model of the planned society, while others (for example the French New Right) focus exclusively on the battle for cultural hegemony of ideas which would form the basis of a new order. In practice, though, there has been a marked tendency for fascist movements not to be containable within the framework of conventional party politics and to take the form of cadre or mass 'movements' with strong liturgical or cultic elements overtly appealing to highly charged collective emotions rather than to the individual's capacity for reasoned judgement.

All political ideologies are prone to assume a charismatic aspect when they operate as revolutionary forces – liberalism did, for example, in the French Revolution. It is significant, though, that fascism *remained* a charismatic form of politics in the two cases where it managed to install itself in power. Symptoms of this trait are the 'oceanic assemblies' and all-pervasive *littorio* (the *fasces*, or axe and rods carried as a symbol of power by lictors in ancient Rome) in the New Italy, and the Nuremberg rallies and the omnipresent *Hakenkreuz* (swastika) in the Third Reich. Both Fascism and Nazism as regimes were characterized by the centrality of the leader cult, the celebration of public over private space and time, and the constant attempt to use social engineering to regiment people into organizations with an ethos of activism and enthusiasm.

Such phenomena have often led specialists to use religious terminology in the analysis of fascism, claiming that it is a 'secular', 'civic', 'lay', or 'political' religion, replete with 'millenarian' or 'eschatological' energies. Such phrases are in order only so long as it is borne in mind that fascism sets out to operate on human society through human agency and within human history. It thus lacks a genuine metaphysical dimension and is the utter antithesis and destroyer of all genuine religious faith. Its compulsive use of the religious language of sacrifice, belief, resurrection, redemption, spirit, and its attacks on scepticism, doubt, materialism, consumerism, hedonism as the signs of moral decay are to be understood as the hallmarks of a modern political ideology seeking to offer a panacea to the malaise and anomie of contemporary society. They do not signify a literal regression to an earlier age of religious certainties (in which the nation as the focus of populist energies and the concept of the State as the creator of the ideal society did not exist).

Fascism is anti-rational

Consistent with its tendentially charismatic nature is fascism's frequent repudiation of rationalism and its overt celebration of myth. It is not so much irrational as anti-rational, seeing the most distinctive human faculty not in the reason celebrated in the Enlightenment, humanist, and positivist tradition, but in the capacity to be inspired to heroic action and self-sacrifice through the power of belief, myth, symbols, and *idées-forces* such as the nation, the leader, identity, or the regeneration of history. It should be stressed that fascism's anti-rationalism has not prevented it from producing a vast amount of highly articulate ideological writings, some of them displaying great erudition and theoretical verve, nor from turning selected components of the Western philosophical and scientific traditions into grist for its own mill.

Fascist 'socialism'

If it is the core mobilizing myth of the imminent (or, under a regime, ongoing) rebirth of the nation that forms the definitional core of fascism, it follows that the various fascist negations (anti-communism, anti-liberalism, etc.) are corollaries of this 'positive' belief, not definitional components. The same myth explains the recurrent claim by fascist ideologues that their vision of the new order is far from anti-socialist. Clearly it axiomatically rejects the internationalism and materialism of Marxism, but may well present the rejuvenation of the national community as transcending class conflict, destroying traditional hierarchy, expunging parasitism, rewarding all productive members of the new nation, and harnessing the energies of capitalism and technology in a new order in which they cease to be exploitative and enslaving. Indeed, in the inter-war period, when Bolsheviks were confident that their cause represented the next stage of human progress, many fascists made the counter-claim that their solution to the crisis of civilization embodied the only 'true' socialism, an assertion often associated with a commitment to corporate economics, national syndicalism, and a high degree of state planning.

Fascism's link to totalitarianism

Also implicit in fascism's mythic core is the drive towards totalitarianism. Far from being driven by nihilism or barbarism, the convinced fascist is a utopian, conceiving the homogeneous, perfectly co-ordinated national community as a total solution to the problems of modern society. Yet any attempt to expunge all decadence necessarily leads to the creation of a highly centralized 'total' State with draconian powers to carry out a comprehensive scheme of social engineering. This will involve massive exercises in regimenting people's lives, and the creation of an elaborate machinery for manufacturing consensus through propaganda and indoctrination combined with repression and terror directed against alleged enemies, both internal and external, of the new order.

In this way any regime's attempt to realize the fascist utopia would lead in practice to an Orwellian dystopia, though the actual scale of destruction and atrocities it caused would vary considerably according to how the ideal 'national community' was conceived and the degree of co-operation in the general public and crucial areas of State power that it could count on. As a result the 'totalitarian State' in Italy became a grim travesty of what Mussolini intended, namely a new order in which the individual's life was to be infused with moral purpose and heroism by becoming symbiotically linked to that of the State. The term thus acquired instead its chilling post-war connotations. It is worth remembering however, that modern society is intrinsically and irreducibly heterogeneous, and that no 'totalitarian' regime, fascist or not, has ever managed to stamp out elements of pluralism and polycentrism, no matter what lengths it has gone to.

Fortunately for humanity only two fascist movements have been in a position to attempt to implement their total solutions to society's alleged woes, namely Fascism and Nazism. All others have so far in one way or another been marginalized, emasculated, or crushed, though in the inter-war period some conservative authoritarian regimes (such as Franco's Spain or Antonescu's Romania) temporarily incorporated fascist movements, a ploy used by the Third Reich in several of its puppet states (for example, Norway and Hungary).

The heterogeneity of fascism's social support

The sociological implication of this ideal type of fascism is that it has no specific class basis in its support. If the middle classes were over-represented in the membership of Fascism and Nazism, this is because specific socio-political conditions made a significant percentage of them more susceptible to a palingenetic form of ultra-nationalism than to a palingenetic form of Marxism or liberalism. There is nothing in principle which precludes an employed or unemployed member of the working classes or an aristocrat, a city-dweller or a peasant, a graduate, or someone 'educationally challenged' from being susceptible to fascist myth. Nor is the fascist mentality exclusively the domain of men or the young, though its stress on heroism and the need for a new élite easily lends itself to militarism and hence to male chauvinism, especially when heroism is associated with physical courage, violence, war, and imperialism.

Fascist racism

By its nature fascism is racist, since all ultra-nationalisms are racist in their celebration of the alleged virtues and greatness of an organically conceived nation or culture. However, fascist ultra-nationalism does not necessarily involve biological or Social Darwinian concepts of race leading to eugenics, euthanasia, and attempted genocide. Nor does it necessarily involve anti-Semitism, or hatred directed against any particular group perceived as culturally or genetically different, or simply 'internal enemies' of the nation (such as Roma/Gypsies, Muslims, Hungarians, homosexuals, blacks). Obviously, if such elements of 'heterophobia', (fear and hatred of those felt to be 'different') are already present in the particular political culture of the nation where fascism arises, it is more than likely that they will be incorporated into its myth of national decadence and hence into the policies for creating the new order.

Fascism is also intrinsically anti-cosmopolitan, axiomatically rejecting as decadent the liberal vision of the multi-cultural, multi-religious, multi-racial society. However, this does not necessarily lead to a call for other races to be persecuted *per se*, but may express itself 'merely' in a campaign of propaganda and violence against their presence as 'immigrants' who have abandoned their 'natural' homeland. This type of fascism thus tends to produce an *apartheid* mentality calling for ethnically pure nation-states, for 'foreigners' to go back, or be returned, to 'where they belong', and a vitriolic hatred of 'mixed marriages' and cultural 'bastardization'.

Fascist internationalism

Fascism, though anti-internationalist in the sense of regarding national distinctiveness and identity as primordial values, is quite capable of generating its own form of universalism or internationalism by fostering a kindred spirit and bond with fascists in other countries engaged in an equivalent struggle for their own nation's palingenesis, often against common enemies (for example, liberals, communists, and, if they are white supremacists, non-white races). In Europe this may well lead to a sense of fighting for a common European homeland on the basis of Europe's alleged cultural, historical, or even genetic unity in contrast to non-Christian, non-Indo-European/Aryan peoples (for instance, Muslims, 'Asian' Soviet or Chinese communists) or degenerate ones (citizens of the USA or the 'Third World'). Within such a Europe, national or ethnic identities would, according to the fascist blueprint, be strengthened, not diluted. (The practical impossibility of realizing such a scheme does not worry fascists, since the nebulousness and impracticality of all their long-term goals is crucial to the mythic power they exert.)

Fascist eclecticism

Perhaps the most important corollary of our ideal type for the purpose of this chapter, however, is its suggestion that fascism pre-exists any particular externalization in the form of articulated or concretized thought. Inevitably each fascism will be made in the image or 'imagining' of a particular national culture, but even within the same movement or party its most influential ideologues will inevitably represent a wide range of ideas and theories, sometimes quite incompatible with each other *except at the level of a shared mythic core of palingenetic ultra-nationalism*. Fascism is thus inherently syncretic, bringing heterogeneous currents of ideas into a loose alliance united only by the common struggle for a new order. As a result there is in fascist thought a recurrent element of (and sometimes declared intention of) synthesis. This befits a latecomer to the European political scene which not only had to fight for its own political space against rival modern ideologies (liberalism, conservatism, socialism, communism), but legitimate itself ideologically in a culture teeming with well-established ideas and thinkers. What conditions the content and thrust of fascist eclecticism is the myth of national rebirth.

It is worth adding that, in its self-creation through synthesis, fascist ideology can draw just as easily on right-wing forms of thought (such as mutations of Christianity, racism, élitist and decadent aesthetics, Nietzscheanism, occultism, forms of illiberalism, integral nationalism, etc.) as on forms of left-wing thought (for example, derivatives of anti-materialist or utopian socialism, such as syndicalism). It is also implicit in what has been said that fascism is not necessarily confined to inter-war Europe, but can flourish wherever the stability of Western-style liberal democracy is threatened by a particular conjuncture of destabilizing forces.

If read in the light of the above considerations, many of the excerpts of fascist writings assembled in this volume will not appear simply as isolated samples of an aberrant genus of political thought. They should cumulatively acquire a deeper resonance as different products of the same ideological matrix, as permutations of the same rationale for a war of 'creative destruction' to be waged against a particular status quo. Within the shell of their utopianism lies the seed of a totalitaran nightmare for all those who in one way or other are not deemed to belong within the regenerated national community or fit into the new order. Whether their author is a lone dreamer, the mouthpiece of a purely 'cultural' think-tank, the spokesman of an activist paramilitary movement, the propagandist of a campaigning electoral party, the policy-maker of an organization within a fascist regime, or the charismatic leader himself, he is giving specific form to the latent mythic core which defines fascism and determines its various attributes in historical reality.

It is this mythic core which accounts for the sharp distinction which this volume implicitly draws between the fascist regimes in Italy and Germany bent on creating a revolutionary new social and ethical order on the basis of mass mobilization, and the many authoritarian right-wing regimes which have been spawned by the twentieth century whose fundamental aim is the reactionary one of using mechanisms of intensive social engineering and repression to maintain the social status quo. Many military dictatorships fit into this latter category, and are characterized by an absence of genuine ideology or myth of renewal: when they have recourse to a leader cult, appeal to populist nationalist sentiment, or stress traditional family or religious values, it is simply to manufacture consensus and conceal an ideological vacuum. In the inter-war period, however, a number of authoritarian regimes consciously adopted some of the trappings and style of Fascism or Nazism to generate an illusion of national rejuvenation while resolutely resisting any populist pressures to change the system from below. Examples are Salazar's Portugal, Franco's Spain, Pétain's 'Vichy' France, Dollfuss's Austria, Horthy's Hungary, Antonescu's Romania, Vargas's Brazil, and Tojo's Japan. The creation of a single-party state, the founding of a youth movement or a 'shirted' militia, and the rhetoric of national reawakening do not in themselves constitute fascism unless they are associated with a core ideology of rebirth which is as anti-conservative as it is anti-liberal or anti-Bolshevik, whatever compromises it has had to make with existing élites and institutions to achieve and retain power in practice. Such regimes I have termed elsewhere 'para-fascist'.

2

A Christian Perspective on the Family

Vinay Samuel

It is extremely difficult to find a universally valid definition of the family. The activities undertaken by members of 'families' which constitute family life range from marriage, reproduction, economic sharing to nurturing of members and socialization processes. Families live together in a house but a household is not the same as a family. People who regard themselves as members of one family may actually reside in different geographical locations.

Social science tends to have a static image of the family. It can identify an urban nuclear family, a Hindu joint family or an African polygynous household. In traditional societies of Asia and Africa a household even today can include three or four generations, usually with a patriarchal head. It is not a static situation. Young people get married, and move off to set up their own homes. As there are more layers in a traditional household such fission does not shrink the household significantly. Other children in the household grow up and fill the places of those who move out. A modern nuclear family is established by the union of two free adults, and the children born of that union. As children grow, marry and leave, it shrinks then finally disappears with the death of the elderly parents.

In the West, the Reformation (from 1517 onwards) entrenched in the Protestant mind the moral vision of a compact, socially responsible household. Marriage laws became simpler in contrast to traditional Catholic areas where celibacy and ecclesiastical interference in property and fertility were dominant. A new freedom and privacy came into the lives of the honourably married who had no sins to hide. "Most significantly," says Ozment, "home and family were no longer objects of widespread ridicule. Paternal authority was affirmed, but so too was the conjugal bond and the interdependence of man and wife in the domestic domain." According to Ozment, the home was a model of benevolent and just rule for the state to emulate.[1]

It is the Reformation which promoted and established the idea that family was the central unit of society. The Reformation continued to define the ethical nature of the State, Monarchy and Civil Society. The household was the focus for producing virtues that would uphold a responsible and civilized society. The household as family was to be morally stable and provide the moral foundation for society. This idea was more possible for the middle classes to practice as they lived off their capital but was far more difficult for the toiling rural and urban masses of the industrialized societies. Those who had a hand-to-mouth existence could rarely live up to that ideal, and they were not a minority in Europe even into the 19th century.

It is the Reformation image of the family, developed in Europe, shaped later by the industrial revolution, particularly by those who had the authority to define public institutions like the schools, universities, law courts, trading corporations, municipal authorities, parliament etc. that shaped the understanding of the family which was taught and promoted by western missionaries. Biblical and theological teaching was produced to demonstrate biblical authority for such a view. It is interesting to note that much of contemporary evangelical leadership in Asia and Africa continues to be a bearer and promoter of that image, in spite of the tensions and conflicts that have characterized Christian practice of family life in these contexts. It is essential to review the biblical material afresh against the background of such a Christian tradition about the family.

In the Old Testament, the word *mispaha* is used to denote an extended family, a clan or even a tribe. The *bethin* (the father's house) was the extended household and signified the identity of the members in terms of their lineage rather than the constitution of the family. Another word used for the family is *bayit*, which referred to a household as an extended family covering three or four generations. All three are mentioned in Joshua 7:14–16.

The New Testament uses 'patria' very few times for the family. Again it stresses origins and lineage through the father figure of the family (Acts 3:25); in Ephesians 3:14–15 all families in the world are described as having their origins in the Father. However the probable reference here is to nations not to extended families.

The words *oikos, oikia* are used more frequently. Families were seen as households. In Acts households were important bases for the Church (Acts 2:46; 10:7,24; 16:15,31,34). The household consisted of three or four generations and also included all who worked in the household and for the household. It was an indecisive term. Households were units of society in the New Testament times in Roman, Greek and Jewish cultures.

The Church is described as a household (Eph. 2:19) and ethical teaching was directed at the whole household, husbands and wives, parents and children, masters and slaves.

It is clear that biblical teaching has an inclusive definition of the family and does not confine it to a married couple and children which is seen as the norm in modernized western societies. We can continue to use family as long as we acknowledge that it is an inclusive term in the Bible. Biblical teaching on the nature of the family can be drawn out by using three biblical paradigms: Covenant, Sacrament and the Kingdom. I am using 'paradigm' to mean a framework which both explains and shapes something.

The Covenant Paradigm

In the Old and the New Testaments all lasting social relationships are seen as covenants. Malachi 2:13–16 appeals to the covenant between husband and wife as the basis of their commitment to each other. The relationship between parents and children is defined in covenant terms. The covenant paradigm stresses that all relationships in the family are to reflect the nature of God's covenantal relationship with his People. God's covenant is based on his character of Steadfast Love and Holiness. Faithfulness and permanency characterize God's covenant relationship. Christian families must enable such characteristics to undergird and shape all duties, responsibilities and privileges in the family. The understanding of family relationship as covenantal relationship shaped by God's covenantal dealings with us prevents legalism and inflexibility in family life and facilitates commitment to holiness of family and individual life.

Knowledge and love of God was to be at the centre of family life. Parents were responsible for the family's growth in the knowledge and love of God (Deut. 6:4–9). The parents partner each other in the discharge of their family responsibilities (Prov. 2:17). Children honour both parents. As families lived out their covenant obligations they built a strong nation (Deut. 5:16) and created a global family.

The Sacrament Paradigm

The Epistle of the Ephesians 5:21–6:9 presents the relationship between Christ and the Church as the model for the relationship between husband and wife in marriage. This places marriage, and by extension the family, in a sacramental paradigm. A sacrament highlights inward and spiritual dimensions of a relationship mediated by God's presence in grace. All relationships in the family between husband and wife, parents and children, head of the household and all other members of the household have an inward and spiritual dimension. That dimension must be shaped and nurtured by grace. The operation of God's grace in family life enables members to experience mutual submission. It is in the context of the operation of grace that submission is a fulfilling rather than degrading experience. The experience of 'one fleshness' in marriage shaped by grace transforms self- gratification to joyful self-giving. The family provides 'the other' and 'others' through which members shape and define their identity. God's grace enables encounters with the other in the family to be cleansing, sanctifying experiences which will lead to mutual upbuilding. Christ's sanctifying role with the Church is given as the model (Eph. 5:26–27) for marriage and family. Each member sacrifices and strives to present the other holy and blameless before God. Each member seeks the wholeness of the others.

The Kingdom Paradigm

Jesus' teaching recorded in the Gospel places all human relationships in the context of the Kingdom of God. God's rule synonymous with His Kingdom defines all relationships. The family is defined by the Kingdom in inclusive terms. Jesus defined his family as all who do the will of the Father (Matt. 12:50). In the Kingdom it is the people of God who constitute the family. The tribe, clan and extended family are replaced by the Church. The Church is the household of God: the family of God. The God of the Kingdom is described as the Father. Instead of the Church modelling the family, it is the family which must model its life on the Church with its inclusive loving relationships. Single people, fragmented families, all are included in the family of the Church. The family is not defined in such a way as to exclude them or make them feel unwhole or inadequate. This inclusiveness extended to economic sharing in the New Testament community as it sought to practise the principles of the Kingdom.

Family in the Kingdom is not defined by its boundaries but by its centre in the Lordship of Christ. This Lordship is demonstrated in all areas of life. Families in the Kingdom paradigm demonstrate the Lordship of Christ in all their relationships - social, economic and political.

The Kingdom paradigm provides a warning to families where family life has become an idol. Families live for their security, welfare and fulfilment. Family life becomes an end. Jesus' teaching on the conflict of interest between family obligation and Kingdom service is clear. "No one," said Jesus, "who puts his hand to the plough and looks back is fit for service in the Kingdom of God" (Lk. 10:62). The service of the Kingdom is to be the goal of family life. Self-fulfilment and family wholeness and happiness are to be fruits of such service.

The Kingdom paradigm also places the family in an eschatological context. The future of the family in its final form is in the consummated Kingdom. Jesus' teaching has no place for marriage in Heaven. While God's Fatherhood continues in the fulfilled Kingdom, it is clear that the family as we know it on earth will not exist in Heaven. Family life on earth must take this dimension seriously and recognize that building the Kingdom is the best way of ensuring the wholeness of family on earth. Desperate measures to preserve an unchanging family model do not reflect the way the Kingdom redefines and reshapes human models of family.

Conclusion

Contemporary families face many pressures. Western societies have moved largely from the focus on household to families to individuals. It is individual rights which occupy the central place in society. Morality is primarily a matter of individual conscience. In the Protestant west the responsibility of nurturing and teaching individual consciences was assigned primarily to the family with support from the local church. This model of the family as the focus for moral nurture was promoted by western missions and remains an important conviction among evangelical Christians in the two-thirds world. Such a view of the family places the emphasis on individual responsibility which a family must nurture and support. The individual needs take priority over family needs. The social vitality of the family is neglected in the commitment to promote individual fulfilment and responsibility.

As individual autonomy dominates in such families, the understanding and relation to any authority gets shaped by individual needs and rights. As relationships between generations disintegrate during one's lifetime in such an understanding of family, commitment to generational continuity is abandoned in the interests of the maximum freedom for a generation. Children are no longer a part of the marriage commitment. They belong to a family as an institution which they will leave by their choice.

In the two-thirds world 'traditional' understanding of authority within the family, the priority of family over the individual and commitment to generational continuity are still dominant in the shaping of family life. It is here that biblical Christians in the two-thirds world need to read the Bible afresh and discover its teaching on the family. Biblical material needs to be related to the cultural perspectives of the family and appropriate Christian understandings of family life developed in African, Asian and Latin American contexts. This is a neglected area for two-thirds world mission theologians and activists and it is time for change.

Notes

1   Robertson A.F., *Beyond the Family*, Oxford 1991, p.111–113.
     This section draws heavily from the above work.

3

Why Questions of Gospel and Culture must be included in the Preparations for Lambeth '98

Maurice Sinclair

Through the growth of the Anglican Church in Africa, Asia and Latin America the cultural diversity of our Communion has increased progressively in recent decades. Although English continues to be of great importance as a medium of communication between our churches, this language ceases to be the mother tongue of the majority of Anglicans and not even a second language for many. With good reason Archbishop Keith Rayner, the President of the Design Group for Lambeth, concludes a preliminary report by saying: *'In worship as in all other respects the Design Group is very conscious of the need to recognize the multilingual and multicultural nature of our Communion'*.

The cultural mix should be seen as a source of great encouragement in that it reflects evangelistic advances in different parts of the world. In addition the growing Anglican cultural diversity can help us in a new way to understand the profundity of the Gospel of God, enflesh this Gospel in the different cultures represented, and reduce the cultural distortions of the Gospel that all of us are guilty of making. Arguments in favour of an inter-cultural theology could appear to be of only specialist interest: something for armchair discussion. On the contrary I maintain that this matter has practical, universal and urgent applications.

We live at a time when the cultures of the world are in crisis. With accelerating urbanization and massive increases in the movement of refugees, people of different cultures are thrown together as never before. With the rapid pace of change regional and national societies find difficulty in organizing themselves on the basis of the new pluralism, which ideally should give just and adequate space for expression of the different cultures. Instead of benefiting from mutual enrichment, all sub-groups tend to manifest their more aggressive or even violent characteristics.

But not all cultures have the same advantages of power. Through its technology, its communication media, and its economic resources the western culture dominates to the extent that parallel with a process of pluralism we see the homogenization of culture. Tragically, this superculture also de-humanizes the human family. Through its pervasive world-wide influence the modern and post-modern culture represents an immense challenge to the World Church and the Anglican Communion within it.

Of course the Gospel affirms the good in every culture and judges and denounces the bad. It is essential the Church learns and re-learns how to discern between the two. The part of the Church most strongly exposed to a particular culture can be expected to see clearly some of its defects but not all. Almost certainly it will have its blindspots. It will need correction from brothers and sisters from other cultural backgrounds.

Unfortunately, this process of mutual correction still has not functioned adequately either in the Anglican Communion or in other branches of the Church. The Moderator of the World Council of Churches in his report to the Central Committee in September '95 underlined the crisis of cultures. He asked: '*How can the various cultural expressions of Christian faith enter into dialogue with each other?*' Then he comments: '*The church has suffered enormously for not having been able to develop a creative dialogue among the various expressions of the one Gospel*'.

A specific example of the need for inter-cultural correction concerns the Gospel and sexuality. Obviously attitudes to sex and sexual behaviour and ethics play a major role in all cultures, and without doubt the Gospel can and must transform sexual relationships in each of them. What would happen though if the representatives of a dominant culture, pressing for their preferred teachings on sex, will not listen to the warnings of Christian brothers and sisters from other cultural backgrounds? Almost certainly these doctrines will turn out to have some valuable insights but also some dangerous blindnesses.

Isn't it true that we could fall into precisely this trap in Lambeth 98?. Already it is anticipated that homosexuality will figure prominently in the debates. If all effective influence remains with those participants whose cultural formation is exclusively Western, one may guess what will be the emphasis of the recommendations. They will focus upon what they see as the fulfilment and satisfaction of the individual. They will seek a pastoral sensitivity, but will neutralize the biblical texts which run counter to the powerful cultural pressures consciously or unconsciously driving the innovators.

For a particular reason Christians from the dominant culture need to be guided by their counterparts from the more traditional world. This great modern culture even though in part a product of the Gospel also fundamentally denies the Gospel. This opposition is not always open but rather hidden. However, what some cannot see others can. Thus if we achieve an effective inter-cultural dialogue before and during the Lambeth Conference we have, under the guidance of the Holy Spirit, the opportunity to offer sound leadership to our churches. We will be able to combine pastoral sensitivity, contemporary relevance, and doctrinal orthodoxy.

With this goal in mind I insist again that we must promote this inter-change of cultural perspectives as we prepare for Lambeth. The process already set in hand with its regional consultations favours this dialogue. In our encounters we will identify critical questions which will certainly not be limited to sexuality. We must make the fullest use of our confessional and ecumenical resources for cross-cultural communication and research. They are excellent and we have no excuse for remaining with our cultural blinkers. As an example the School of Mission in Selly Oak and the Centre for Anglican Communion Studies have expressed interest in pursuing any matter which arises needing further study.

I conclude then that if we do not apply the multi-cultural wisdom available in our Communion we are in danger of being exposed to distortions of the Gospel and precipitate decisions which will divide our church. In contrast, with the desired communication and mutual respect we can anticipate something infinitely better: *'Power to grasp with all the saints how wide and long and high and deep is the love of Christ'*.

4

An Examination of the Theological Principles affecting the Homosexuality Debate
The St Andrew's Day Statement

Michael Banner et al

INTRODUCTION

Faced with practical questions which arouse strong and conflicting passions, the church has only one recourse: to find in the Gospel a starting-point of common faith from which those who differ can agree to proceed in their discussions. Such a question now before the Church of England is how we should respond to those, including clergy, seeking to live in quasi-marital relations with a partner of the same sex. The purpose of the following statement is to provide some definition of the theological ground upon which the issue should be addressed and from which any fruitful discussion between those who disagree may proceed.

By defining its fundamental agreements more clearly, the church may lighten the weight which is at present laid upon a practical question not without importance in its own right but in danger of being over-freighted with symbolic resonances. This in turn may create a context for principled pastoral care which is more responsive to particular individual circumstances and less to political meanings that can be read into them. That the issue should have become so highly dramatized calls for repentance on the part of all members of the church. It suggests that the Gospel has not been directing the acts, words and thoughts of Christians on this subject.

To emphasize its purpose the statement is in two parts, the first an affirmation of credal principles, the second an application of these principles to the question of homosexuality as it presents itself to the church today. It is not indeed to cover every issue that must be considered in this context, and nothing should be inferred from what the statement does not say. If its assertions prove susceptible of being accommodated within more than one interpretation of present disputes, that will be an advantage, since it hopes to include all who do not intend a decisive break with orthodox Christianity. Of those who, nevertheless, find that they cannot agree, it is asked only that they should be precise about their disagreements, so that the extent of common ground available to the church may become clear.

Principles

1   Jesus Christ is the one Word of God. He came in human flesh, died for our sins and was raised for our justification. In the flesh he lived for us a life of obedience to the will of God; on the cross he bore God's judgement on our sin; and in his resurrection our human nature was made new. In him we know both God and human nature as they truly are. In his life, death and resurrection we are adopted as children of God and called to follow in the way of the cross. His promise and his call are for every human being: that we should trust in him, abandon every self-justification, and rejoice in the good news of our redemption.

2   The Spirit of Jesus Christ bears witness to the Gospel in Holy Scripture and in the ministry of the people of God. He directs us in the task of understanding all human life and experience through the Scriptures. And so, guided by the Spirit of God to interpret the times, the church proclaims the Word of God to the needs of each new age, and declares Christ's redeeming power and forgiveness in mutual encouragement and exhortation to holiness.

3   The Father of Jesus Christ restores broken creation in him. For he himself is its fulfilment: in him the church learns by its life and witness to attest to the goodness and hope of creation. The Spirit gives us strength and confidence to live as men and women within the created order, finding peace and reconciliation and awaiting the final revelation of the children of God.

Application

I. "In him" – and in him alone – "we know both God and human nature as they truly are"; and so in him alone we know ourselves as we truly are. There can be no description of human reality, in general or in particular, outside the reality in Christ. We must be on guard, therefore, against constructing any other ground for our identities than the redeemed humanity given us in him. Those who understand themselves as homosexuals, no more and no less than those who do not, are liable to false understanding based on personal or family histories, emotional dispositions, social settings, and solidarities formed by common experiences or ambitions. Our sexual affections can no more define who we are than can our class, race or nationality. At the deepest ontological level, therefore, there is no such thing as "a" homosexual or "a" heterosexual; there are human beings, male and female, called to redeemed humanity in Christ, endowed with a complex variety of emotional potentialities and threatened by a complex variety of forms of alienation.

"Adopted as children of God and called to following the way of the cross", we are summoned to various forms of self-denial. The struggle against disordered desires, or the misdirection of innocent desires, is part of every Christian's life, consciously undertaken in baptism. In any individual case, the form which this struggle takes may be determined by circumstances (wealth or poverty, illness or health, educational success or failure). Often these are not open to choice, but are given to us as a situation in which we quickly and triumphantly resolved, nor even that it will be successful at every point along the way; only that it will be crowned at last by a character formed through patience to be like Christ's.

II. The interpretation of homosexual emotion and behaviour is a Christian "task", still inadequately addressed. "Guided by God's Spirit", the church must be open to empirical observation and governed by the authority of the apostolic testimony. According to this testimony the rebellion of humankind against God darkens our mind and subverts our understanding of God and Creation (Acts 26:18; Rom. 1:19–32; Eph. 4:17–19). For the biblical writers the phenomena of homosexual behaviour are not addressed solely as wilfully perverse acts but in generalized terms, and are located within the broader context of human idolatry (Rom. 1:26–27 with 1:19–31; 1 Cor. 6:9–10 with 6:12–20).

Many competing interpretations of the phenomena can be found in contemporary discussion, none of them with an unchallengeable basis in scientific data. The church has no need to espouse any one theory, but may learn from many. To every theory, however, it must be the question whether it is adequate to the understanding of human nature and its redemption that the Gospel proclaims. Theories which fail this test can only imprison the imagination by foreclosing the recognition of emotional variety and development. To "interpret the times" in the midst of this theoretical confusion, the church must avoid being lulled by the vague idea that there is a transparent and necessary progress of thought working itself out in history, with which it has only somehow to keep abreast. It must search for conceptual and theological clarification. Without this there are dangers in a wide-ranging programme of discussions which, with insufficient support from the church's teaching, may serve merely to amplify the Babel of confused tongues.

The primary pastoral task of the church in relation to all its members, whatever their self-understanding and mode of life, is to re-affirm the good news of salvation in Christ, forgiveness of sins, transformation of life and incorporation into the holy fellowship of the church. In addressing those who understand themselves as homosexual, the church does not cease to speak as the bearer of this good news. It assists all its members to a life of faithful witness in chastity and holiness, recognizing two forms or vocations in which that life can be lived: marriage and singleness (Gen. 2:2–24; Matt. 19:4–6; 1 Cor. 7 passim). There is no place for the church to confer legitimacy upon alternatives to these. Pastoral care, however, needs a certain flexibility, taking note of the circumstances which make each individual case different from each other, and discerning ways in which the Gospel touches people in different situations. The church, then, will give constant encouragement in following Christ not only to those who conform to one of these two vocations, but to all who seriously intend discipleship in fellowship with the body of the church. It is in this sense that the Bishops' Statement (*Issues in Human Sexuality*, 1991) is to be understood when it speaks of "respecting the integrity" (cf. 5:21) of those who conscientiously dissent from the biblical teaching as the church understands it. While this teaching applies to all - for the priesthood of believers consecrates all Christians to a life of holiness - the Bishops have Scripture on their side in arguing that special considerations affect the behaviour of the clergy who have a particular commission to expound and exemplify the teaching of the church (cf. 1 Tim. 3:11–13; 4:12–13; 5:19–20; Tit. 1:5–9; Jas. 3:1; 2 Pet. 2:2).

III. The "fulfilment" of all creation is found in Christ (Eph. 1:23; Col. 1:15–19). Our own fulfilment, therefore, is not merely a private one but a communal, even a cosmic one. Both marriage and singleness in their different ways point forward to this fulfilment in the fellowship of God with his redeemed creation. In neither vocation, then, does fulfilment require or allow the exercise of every power or the satisfaction of every desire that any individual may reasonably have: a life may be fulfilled without occasion to employ the power of sexual expression, just as it may have occasion to exploit the potential for education, parenthood or mobility.

Both vocations in their different ways give equal expression to the blessing of human friendship which is sanctified by Christ who calls us his friends (John 15:13–15; cf. Isa. 41:8) and elevated in him to become the "fellowship of the Holy Spirit" (2 Cor. 13:14). Every aspect of our common life in Christ, friendship included, has a properly exploratory character: understanding our humanity in him, we are freed from human constructs to search out and discover the richness of creation that is opened to us by God's redeeming work. This search finds its fulfilment as it is directed by the hope for the final appearing of Jesus the Son obedient to the Father who will put all things in subjection to him.

For the grace of God has appeared, bringing salvation to all, training us to renounce impiety and worldly passions, and in the present age to live lives that are self-controlled, upright, and godly, while we wait for the blessed hope and the manifestation of the glory of our great God and Saviour, Jesus Christ. He it is who gave himself for us that he might redeem us from all iniquity and purify for himself a people of his own who are zealous for good deeds. Declare these things; exhort and reprove with all authority. Let no one look down on you. (Titus 2.11–15)

Michael Banner
F.D. Maurice Professor of Moral and Social Theology, King's College, London
Markus Bockmuehl
University Lecturer in Divinity and Fellow of Fitzwilliam College, Cambridge
Timothy Bradshaw (Chairman)
Dean of Regent's Park College, Oxford
Oliver O'Donovan
Regius Professor of Moral and Pastoral Theology, Oxford
Ann Holt
Director of Care for Education
William Persson
Formerly Bishop of Doncaster
David Wright
Senior Lecturer in Ecclesiastical History, University of Edinburgh

St Andrew's Day 1995.

This theological work group met in response to the request
of the Church of England Evangelical Council.

5

A Response to the St Andrew's Day Statement

Patrick Yu

Upon reviewing the current debate in the church on homosexuality, one is struck by the great differences, not only in the positions of the various factions but also in the kinds of arguments being used. It seems at times that the debaters share hardly any common ground at all. Into this situation, the writers of the St. Andrew's Day Statement have set as their goal "to find in the gospel a starting-point of common faith from which those who differ can agree to proceed in their discussion."

This is a refreshing approach in that it does not start with the concrete issues which have brought the church to its present impasse: Namely, the blessing of same sex unions and the ordination of practicing homosexuals. A discussion too closely tied to these symbolic actions quickly becomes "over-freighted". Instead, the tack which these authors have followed has been to hold their conclusions lightly and to insist on some fundamental starting points for all Christians.

This exercise is also ambitious. If the church could define the legitimate starting points of the discussion which the authors insist must originate in the Gospel, the logic of theological discourse could lead to a range of conclusions which ought to be acceptable to the whole Church. It is also an inclusive move, inviting into the exercise "all who do not intend a decisive break with orthodox Christianity." As such it is an irenic gesture, one that is still hopeful of agreement in principle, without engaging in the language of compromise which often suggests a surrender of any such possibility.

The Statement begins with three fundamental assertions which are indeed basic. The first touches on Christian anthropology, the second on Revelation and the third on the Christian understanding of creation which the authors consider in conjunction with salvation history. We are part of the created order which is nevertheless fallen. The way we relate to creation is to accept it as fundamentally good but incomplete. As gospel people we live in hope of its fulfilment.

The first principle challenges the root cause of alienation experienced by the homosexual. There is an understanding about, often held by homosexuals themselves, that they are fundamentally different from all other human beings. Christian anthropology sees the whole of humanity "in Christ." This immediately relativizes the "we-they" attitude so prevalent in the debate. If all are judged and forgiven, there is no cause to treat the homosexual person as a particularly loathsome sinner or to consign his struggles as his solitary burden. To emphasize humanity's solidarity in Christ also addresses the paradoxical feeling among many homosexuals of wanting to be included in the mainstream while claiming an exclusive ownership of the issue, to the extent that their own experience becomes the critical factor in determining credibility.

Understanding our common humanity in Christ makes the question of homosexuality our common concern. At the same time it insists that homosexual persons are also called to discipleship. Their struggles are unique but, nevertheless, part of the calling of all Christians to follow Jesus "in the way of the cross." The statement is prudently silent as to the exact nature of that discipleship, leaving it as a matter of pastoral discretion.

If the Church takes this first principle seriously, the discussions around the issue would not be carried out in different communities of discourses, as is largely the case today. There is much distrust and fear to overcome, but what we should be looking for is an ownership of the question by the whole Church, a movement away from discussions among those who already agree with each other to conversations where all are truly involved and truly free to speak. A practical move on the part of those who consider themselves in the mainstream would be to invite gays and lesbians as full partners in any discussions on the issue, with a clear affirmation of their identity in Christ, but without giving up the mutual challenge to discipleship which is common to all who confess Jesus as Lord.

The second principle deftly addresses the most serious dispute regarding the role of Scripture and the role of experience. According to the Statement, the experience which is used by the Spirit is not just an human experience but the experience of God's people engaging in ministry in obedience to the Spirit, a context in which the Scripture is a living voice for today. The Statement advocates a dynamic use of scripture which does not isolate such deliberations from ministry, or, as it becomes clear in the application, from the proper and wider inquiry into the phenomenon of homosexuality. Its approach to scripture is *prima scriptura*, rather than *sola scriptura*.

In the application of the second principle, the authors address many pitfalls which exist in this debate. Their treatment of scripture is nuanced, and draws back from a simple and legalistic use of the texts. They warn that the final word has not been said in the sciences. They have a mild rebuke for those who frame the question according to a superficial theory of progress. By avoiding a static faith-science dilemma, they refuse to subject scriptural declarations about human nature to any current scientific theory.

This is a caution which cuts across many parties in the debate. We have exaggerated claims from both the nature and nurture schools of thought. Despite exaggerated claims, the question of determinacy of sexual orientation has not been settled. Those who believe that change is possible however, should have a healthy scepticism about claims of cure or change. All are subject to further scientific investigation and clinical results. If the Church continues to engage in active ministry among homosexuals which holds together compassion, realism and hope, its own praxis will be a source of significant pastoral insights rather than the stereotypical portrayals of homosexual lifestyles which all too often pass as descriptions.

Going further in specifics than the introduction suggests, the authors hold up marriage and singleness as the only Christian vocations. They refuse to legitimize any other. At the same time they urge the Church to be pastorally flexible for those whose lives do not conform to these two vocations. This counsel is a continuation of the historical development which Philip Turner observed in his Toronto address, that the Church has modified its pastoral practice while insisting on its teaching on sexual behaviour[1]. In other words, the authors would withhold any symbolic legitimization of homosexual unions such as the blessing of such unions or ordination of practising homosexuals, while urging all Christians to be truly understanding and supportive of individual circumstances.

The third is the shortest but also the most condensed point in that it combines the concept of creation with salvation history. Placing the discussion of sexuality within the doctrine of creation runs counter to the privatistic understanding of sexuality which sees it as a matter of individual fulfilment, "a basic human right" as it is often put. Rather, the Statement presents our sexuality as subject to God's order and invites all people to regard it in the context an overarching order which is fundamentally a gift of God. How we live sexually is not only a matter for the individual, it is not even limited to the parties involved in the sexual relationship. In the Christian understanding, sexuality is part of a greater design in how society is ordered, perhaps even how creation is ordered.

To consider our sexual fulfilment in terms of salvation history in this way, that is, acknowledging its goodness, confessing its brokenness, and awaiting its fulfilment in glory, is a direct contradiction of theories like those of James Nelson who, in his book "*Embodiment*"[2], argues that sexual expression is a necessary part of being human. In contrast to the modern trend of sexualizing all human relationships, the authors elevate friendship as a more lasting understanding of human relating which, like love, will not fade away.

The statement is a bold and generous attempt to set the discussion on its proper theological footing. Nevertheless I believe that, even proceeding from this starting point, one will not go along the road too far before having to face the difficult choices in application. For example, should the Church support alternatives to sexual abstinence for those people for which marriage is not a possibility, but who struggle against seemingly hopeless odds to be continent?

What would such support look like for relatively stable homosexual relationships? Where is the fine line between a course of action that is pastorally prudent and one which is symbolically scandalous? We have long since passed the point where pastoral counsel can be strictly a private affair. They will soon be proclaimed from the media roof tops.

In any case, the authors seem to have declared their intention to be as inclusive, as understanding and as generous as possible under the constraint of the gospel. It is important to insist on this pro-active approach which, nonetheless, keeps the important points of the discussion theological. However, in areas where the issue has already been politicized one has to acknowledge that the kind of discussion envisaged by the authors will meet with much opposition. Most likely it will need to take place with new players. It will also take considerable leadership, well, churchmanship, to carve out a space for this most important task to take place.

Notes

1 Philip Turner, *Homosexuality and the Churches*, Toronto, Fidelity, 1994, p.1.
2 James Nelson, *Embodiment*, N.Y: Pilgrim Press, 1978, p. 144.

6

Reading the St Andrew's Day Statement

Oliver O'Donovan

The St. Andrew's Day Statement (named from the date of its publication in 1995) is a contribution to a heated debate in the Church of England about "how we should respond to those, including clergy, seeking to live in quasi-marital relations with a person of the same sex." This debate, which had been a feature of church life for a decade or more, was given a new impetus in 1991 by a statement from the House of Bishops, *Issues in Human Sexuality*, which held that someone living in such a relation should not be ordained, and that an ordained priest or deacon should not live in such a relation. The debate assumed an embittered and confrontational tone, fanned by a great deal of publicity; and it was dismay at this situation, as well as dissatisfaction with the theological weakness of much that was being said on either side, that led the authors to undertake their work. They believed that a new approach and new theological perspectives needed to be brought to bear upon the question. So, then, the Statement does not present itself as the work of a "representative" group, if by that is meant a group in which all shades of existing opinion are represented at the start. They speak for a point of view of their own, one which they think has been crowded out by the polarised alternatives of a polemical debate. In another sense, however, they are not *unrepresentative* of the church as it now is, and bring quite a variety of personal and pastoral experience to bear on the problem - more than might appear from the list of signators which excludes some who wished to safeguard their anonymity. They conceived their work as the beginning of a process, which must continue by way of careful and sympathetic dialogue with representatives of the polarised blocs of opinion.

This commentary on the Statement is intended to help the reader appreciate both its strategy and the nature of the contribution to the debate it intends to make. Like all commentaries, it has only the authority of its own author; others might well have drawn attention to different things in the Statement, or explained certain points differently. Still, it will have some use, I hope, in showing what one of the Statement's authors thought the Statement achieved and why he thought the enterprise important.

The most important thing, perhaps, comes right at the beginning, where it is all too easy to overlook. There, under the heading "Introduction", the authors of the Statement describe the approach to the question of homosexuality which they recommend to the church and which they propose to follow themselves. They invite the church to define its "fundamental agreements". These agreements are to be theological; that is to say, they concern the way Christian faith views human nature and its powers, including sexual powers. If these agreements can be brought to the fore, the authors argue, then the range of controversial issues, theoretical and practical, with which the gay consciousness has presented us, can be discussed in a better atmosphere and on a stronger foundation. They don't suggest that the church should *avoid* discussing these controversial issues. It is simply that they must first be set in the context of common Christian faith if progress is ever to be made with them.

In other words, the church must decide afresh what its *starting* certainties are. For when it rushes headlong into debate with every kind of unexamined and conflicting presupposition, it ends up, as we have seen, with a confused battle which is given virulence by mutual suspicions about how the Gospel is understood on either side. Worse: the battle is fought out over particular pastoral decisions which ought to be taken with some flexibility, responding to the needs of each particular case, and ought to be protected by a measure of confidentiality. These decisions, then, can never be made or evaluated on the right criteria, but always end up being read as programmatic statements in a partisan cause. And so the church becomes divided in reproach and recrimination. Only an assertion of Gospel truths held in common, so the authors hold, can change the way in which these differences are seen. It is, of course, a classic ecumenical strategy; but it has been strikingly absent from the debate so far.

The Statement sets out to follow the same course that the Introduction recommends to the church. It is organised in two parts: a credal-type statement which asserts the theological principles in a trinitarian pattern, followed by an "Application" of this statement to the issues in debate. The comparative brevity of the Statement is significant. There is, of course, a great deal more to be said about the subject than is said here; but as a matter of policy the authors left the greater part of what they had to say on the cutting-room floor, because they wanted to confine themselves to those front-rank, "fundamental" points which they urge the church to concentrate on first. They wanted their Statement to be one on which people with differing opinions about many other matters could find agreement on the central matters. So the first thing we must make up our minds to as we read the Statement is not to "read between the lines", filling in all the things we imagine the authors were "really" meaning to say. If they didn't say them, they meant not to say them. Not because they thought that "they" – whatever they are - could or should never be said; but because they thought they didn't have a place here, among the things that must be said to hold the church together in the unity of faith. Their lines are meant, as it were, to have empty spaces between them, spaces for the reader's own views, not spaces for the reader to project back views which they are supposed to have implied without saying.

The second thing we must make up our mind to is not to apply the "shibboleth-test": have they or have they not said the one all-important thing which *I* always say? The authors do not expect to say just what their readers always say; they expect their readers to say it for themselves in the space which the authors have left them. So we must get over our initial disappointment that "it" – whatever it is – is not there; and we must look rather hopefully to see whether and how it can comfortably be put in. But what if there is not space for it? What if the authors have squeezed it out, by denying something that is essential to it or saying something that excludes it? Then, of course, we have a real disagreement with them; but even at this point our responsibility to them does not come to an end. They have, slightly unusually, addressed a request to readers who reach this position. They have asked them to be "precise" about the scope of their disagreement – that is to say, to indicate *how little adjustment* in the Statement would suffice to allow them to say what they think must be said. The constructive reader, then, into whose hands they hope the Statement will come, is the reader who is prepared to cut the disagreements down to size and look for ways in which disagreements can be situated within agreements. Needless to say, the authors of the Statement would be delighted to hear from readers who wish to communicate with them on these lines; but whether or not they do so, being "precise", letting the disagreement deflate to its proper size, is the way that the peace of the church and the truth of the Gospel demands.

Another formal feature of the Statement that may strike us, besides its structure and its brevity, is its cool, even detached manner, that may seem hardly in keeping with a subject so inevitably steeped in human emotion. Here, too, it is a matter of deliberate policy. Rhetorical flamboyance is an indulgence that nobody can afford when the peace of the church is threatened. But avoiding it means more than avoiding words of overt suspicion or contempt. Part of the trouble is that people do not always know when they are being rhetorically flamboyant. Loose categories and inept paradigms can build up a style of rhetoric that suggests sweepingly that everything is perfectly clear and that one must be disingenuous or a fool to deny it. Two examples suggest themselves from current rhetorical fashions: the rhetoric of "nature" and the rhetoric of "liberation". Now, of course, both these terms have a responsible and illuminating use. The question of how and where they belong within the discussion of homosexuality is one that any serious discussion has to explore. But precisely for that reason one cannot simply deploy either of those notions as though there were nothing to be explored. No interest of those who understand themselves as gay can possibly be served by a rhetoric of liberation that wraps up everything in a carpet-bag category of "blacks, women and gays" without the slightest interest in what makes the gay experience distinctive. To elucidate the truth of the gay experience in the light of the truth of the Gospel: that is the cause for which the gay Christian struggles. Even a rhetoric deployed supposedly in his interest, insofar as it violates the truth of the experience, violates him.

The charge is commonly made, to be sure, that credal language, too, fails to pay sufficient attention to experience. The authors do not share this view. They believe that a disciplined and discriminate deployment of credal categories does, in fact, illumine complex areas of human experience. For them, as for the tradition of the church which has used creeds and confessions in baptism, the importance of the creed is as an initiatory and pedagogical resource, a light to shine in on a dark and confused area of experience and make exploration possible. That is their theological stance; obviously, it can only be tested in life itself, by actually living through experience under the light of the wisdom of the Gospel. This in different ways different members of the group have done and do do, so that their creed, too, has experience behind it, both their own experience and that of others to which they have attended. But they do not think that the church's understanding can simply begin and end with their, or other people's, experience, moving, as it were, in a closed circle. They have used the credal formulation as a starting-point from which experience, which never comes self-interpreted, can be interpreted out of the Word of God in Christ.

There is, of course, no one single experience. Even within the compass of a single person's life, the experience of emotion and of sexuality is very varied; and when the experiences of different people are put in play, they often challenge and contest one another. The only possible outcome, then, of a discourse founded wholly on experience is unresolved conflict. Nothing is gained by appealing to experience if only one kind of experience is to be admitted - for this would not really be an appeal to experience at all, since the ground on which the privileged experience was selected would not itself be a part of experience, but merely an idea which had, as it were, selected the experience to confirm itself. Nor is anything gained if we insist that two conflicting kinds of experience should be considered - a "majority" experience alongside a "minority" experience. There can be no majorities and minorities in this field; reality is too complex for such simple- minded partitions. There may be, of course, those who are quite prepared to conduct a discourse on the basis of a single privileged experience that is not their own - either because their own experience frightens them, or perhaps because it bores them. But this strategem, too, in whatever interest it is deployed, is in bad faith and will lead nowhere. For the search for an understanding of homosexuality is a search for the understanding of our common humanity itself. None of us can engage in it with the comfortable feeling that we are only doing it for the sake of other people. It concerns us all alike.

There are two reasons why the Statement proper begins with the question of "identity" - i.e. what we know ourselves to be. The first is that it gives priority to the theological assertion that is central to the discussion: Jesus Christ is the disclosure of all true humanity. But it also allows the authors to attend immediately to the way the gay movement presents itself: as a form of identity and as a suffering identity. They have no preamble, then, about what they take the problem of homosexuality to be, what the phenomena are, what is said about it in Scripture etc. etc. These issues are to be touched on later, after they have addressed the point at which the gay self-consciousness is engaged by the central point of the Christian self-consciousness.

We ask ourselves, "who or what am I?" And the way in which we set about answering determines everything that follows. For the St. Andrew's Day Statement self-knowledge is a gift of divine grace in Jesus Christ. "There can be no description of human reality, in general or particular, outside the reality of Christ." If we accept this starting-point, we will accept, too, that we always stand in danger of *mis*understanding ourselves. The deliveries of our self-consciousness enjoy no infallibility; we may read our identities in ways that do not find their ground where God has provided it, in the humanity created and redeemed in Christ. What, then, of a statement such as, "I am a homosexual"? What status can such a claim to self-knowledge have? Clearly, we can't exclude it; we may come to understand elements in our emotional disposition that are properly, even necessarily, formulated in such a claim. But it has to be surrounded by a caution: such a claim can never be foundational or definitive. It may tell us something that is true about ourselves, but it cannot close the book on our self-discovery. It cannot protect itself against further questions and further answers. A knowledge of ourselves derived from our patterns of emotional response can only be a provisional knowledge. It is part of the evidence; it tells us just so much, not the whole; and so it must be held in an open-ended way. By implication the Statement criticises an attitude, characteristic of some homosexual identity – claims which, having been wrung from a hard struggle, come out brittle and defiant, daring anyone to raise a question or suggest a qualification. "Affective fundamentalism" is a name that has been given, not unsuitably, to this attitude.

Yet the Statement by no means suggests that this temptation is unique to homosexual identity-claims. It mentions several other kinds of self-definition which people may assume out of "personal and family histories...social settings and solidarities". "I am English", "I am an intellectual", or "I am working-class" can be quite as destructive and falsifying of our identity before God. But then, equally, these assertions can be used innocently and helpfully. It all depends on the place they hold in our hierarchy of self-interpretations and on the use we put them to in opening up or closing off relations with others. And the same can be said of "I am a homosexual". When the Statement says, "there is no such thing as 'a' homosexual or 'a' heterosexual", it does not mean that there can be no use for such a term, but that "at the deepest ontological level" this distinction is not a determinant of personal identity. If one is conscious of homosexual or of heterosexual responses to other people, or, indeed, of both, that consciousness discloses a *quality*, like other qualities, of the person one knows oneself to be in Christ. It tells us "what am I like?" , "in what ways do I function?", not, "*what* am I?". We are warned against *reifying* the homosexual-heterosexual distinction.

It would be quite wrong to think that this warning is meant to be heeded only by those who speak for the gay consciousness. It is meant at least as much for other participants in the debate, who may find it quite convenient for the purposes of dogmatic clarity to divide the human race into two opposed and exclusive "sexual orientations". It is like the reified party-consciousness which Gilbert mocked in Victorian England: "Every boy and every gal That's born into the world alive, Is either a little Liberal Or else a little Conservative." It is essentially a mythical construction, this Either-Or. Certainly it owes nothing to such empirical evidence as is available, all of which points to a spectrum of emotional attraction in which there is more weight in the centre than at either end. But it suited the purposes of nineteenth-century psychiatrists, who wanted to categorise the "true" homosexual, just as it now suits the purposes of lawyers who want some clear-cut notion of "discrimination on the basis of sexual orientation". The real complexity of the emotional responses that any human being may experience is all too easily lost sight of.

It will become apparent in the second section of the Statement how concerned the authors are about the effect of such simplistic and rigid categories, which "imprison the imagination by foreclosing the recognition of emotional variety and development." The Either-Or locks people in, "heterosexuals" so-called as well as homosexuals, to refusing emotional ambiguity and growth. It also pronounces a terrible verdict against the inappropriately named "bisexual", for whom ambiguity is a constant feature of emotional experience. One example of the distorting effect of this theoretical strait-jacket is to be found in *Issues in Human Sexuality*, where the Bishops offer such people the preposterous advice that they should seek counselling, "to discover the truth of their personality"! That is to say: ambiguity and diversity of emotional response cannot be the truth; only something monochrome and uniform will do!

The Statement then turns to the question of emotional struggle. Once again, there are two reasons: one is to pursue the Christological form of human existence, "following in the way of the cross"; the other is to attend to the gay self-consciousness. They mention two aspects of the struggle, subjective and objective. The essence of struggle is subjective - "against disordered desires or the misdirection of innocent desires"; the objective factors, "wealth or poverty, illness or health, educational success or failure", determine the form which the subjective struggle may take. It is left almost entirely up to the reader to decide how this general observation applies to the special form of struggle which is part of the gay self-consciousness. It is another example of the authors' deliberate reticence, and one which certainly exposes them to unsympathetic interpretation on the basis of a hasty reading.

It would be possible, for example, to conclude that the "disordered desires" which they think it our vocation to struggle against are, quite simply, impulses of homosexual attraction, no more and no less. Possible, but very unfriendly. For there is actually no ground in the Statement even for thinking that *sexual* desires in general are what is primarily meant. The description serves perfectly well for the struggle of a Christian who, say, has constant difficulty making ends meet and is consumed by the desire for more money; or of one who encounters persistent hostility and has to struggle with resentment, anger and a desire to quit the battle instead of struggling on. These struggles against "disordered desires" are just as much "part of every Christian's life", common to the experience of discipleship. It is reasonable to attribute to the words the widest reference they will bear. On the other hand, there is no point in them unless they also refer to some aspect of the homosexual disposition. (The phrase "disordered desires" echoes a phrase used of homosexual acts in the Vatican document *Personae Humanae*, "intrinsically disordered", and the echo may have some significance.) Their point, then, is that the emotional life of homosexual Christians cannot be excluded from the general confession of affective disorder which all Christians believe they have to make. It is as though they were saying to the advocate of gay-consciousness, who might bridle at the idea that homosexual affections were disordered: Can you accept that disorder is no less a feature of the homosexual situation than of the affective life of human beings in general? While to the un-gay Christian who might be prepared to regard that description complacently, simply as an account of the homosexual dilemma, the question is put: Why do you not see your own position, too, described in these terms?

The experience of struggle against emotional disorder ought to lead us to moral solidarity with one another. If it does not, the reason is suggested in the words from the Principles section: "that we should trust in him, abandon every self-justification, and rejoice..." A sense of struggle may lead us to get bogged down in "self-justification"; and when it does so, as the Book of Job unforgettably illustrates, it evokes a retaliatory self-justification in response. And that is one reason why homosexuality has become a controversial issue: accusations, reproaches, defences are the stuff of this supposed debate. They spring from the acute self-consciousness we all feel when the integrity of our instinctual reactions is put in question. But Christians are supposed to have learned that they *must* be put in question, all of them, all the time. If we had grasped the truth expressed in the phrase "justification by faith", and had come to know ourselves frankly as sinners living under grace, our disagreements would lack that bitterness which comes from an outrage at feeling somehow accused.

Only at this point, when it has spoken of identity and struggle, does the Statement discuss the question of homosexuality as such and what the church should be saying to homosexuals in its midst. Here again it begins with a word of caution: the church should not pretend to be too knowing. There are "phenomena", plenty of them, including accumulated observations of sexual behaviour and instinct that have been systematically acquired and tested, the "scientific data", but also, as should not be forgotten, many informal observations, not least those relating to the cultural and social dynamics of our own civilisation. There are also "interpretations" of the phenomena; these are multiple and conflicting, and often fail to accommodate all the phenomena sufficiently. In other words, the discussion has to proceed in an open theoretical field. There is no "science" of homosexuality which we can all simply take as read. Some may regret this, some be glad of it; but it requires care on the part of the church not to wed its reflections to a theory that seems to have plausibility and may have acquired some currency, but which may quite well be discredited in a couple of decades. Naturally, this should not discourage Christian thinkers and investigators from advocating theoretical approaches they think fruitful. It is simply that fruitful lines of thought are one thing, presumed knowledge is another.

The church, too, has an interpretative rôle and this is the "Christian task" which it needs to address more adequately. The Statement does not accept the view that there is nothing new to be thought or proposed on this subject, all that is needed being to reiterate traditional moral teaching. The traditional moral teaching has its importance for the authors, as we shall see; but in the Principles they speak of the guidance of the Holy Spirit in "interpreting the times" and "the needs of each new age", while in the Application the church's interpretation is not only to be "governed by the authority of the apostolic testimony" but "open to empirical observation". There is, I think, at least a suggestion here that the phenomena are not simply the same from one age to the next, but evolve. However, none of this implies that the meaning of the times and the needs of the age can simply be read off the course of history "transparently". They criticise the naive view that the church has only to "keep abreast" of the times, floating downstream, as it were, on the current of ideas. Far from it: interpreting the times requires "clarification"; that is to say, boundaries must be drawn, distinctions made, and (though this is not said) dangers warned against, confrontations risked. The church has to offer a wisdom that is not simply lying there on the surface of the culture; its task is described in the Application as a "teaching" task, and in the Principles as "proclaiming the Word of God".

The bearing of the New Testament on our contemporary debates has been extensively discussed, and a wide range of hermeneutic strategies followed. At one extreme only a very general set of normative principles are accepted, and all the specific references to homosexuality are excluded as culturally conditioned; at the other minute investigations of the precise sense of such words as *arsenokoites*; and many proposals fall somewhere in between. The authors had some difficulty in deciding just how much they needed to say on this topic. There was plenty they could have said; but their approach encouraged them to leave as much width for varying interpretations as would be responsible rather than advancing a favoured interpretative strategy of their own. They contented themselves finally with two observations, each of them especially relevant to Romans 1, the locus classicus, but borne out, as they indicate, by other texts too.

In the first place, the human condition that gives rise to homosexual behaviour is seen by the New Testament authors as a *failure to understand* God and his world. This, not arbitrary and wilful disobedience, is at the heart of the N.T. doctrine of human sinfulness. In the second place, it follows that homosexual behaviour is "located within" the broader context of idolatry, and is not simply a matter of "wilfully perverse acts". This reading pits the Statement against a view popularised a generation or so ago by D.S. Bailey and still much held, that the biblical condemnation of homosexual acts is concerned only with wilfully perverse engagement in them on the part of those whose emotional dispositions were otherwise. It is, of course, impossible to imagine Saint Paul actually making the distinction between "inverts" and "perverts" (to use the now old-fashioned language that Bailey deployed); but it is also hard to imagine that he *would* have built on this distinction *had* he known it, since for him the nub of the issue was the cultural misconstrual of the world out of which cultural homosexuality arose. Homosexuality is not condemned as one might condemn someone who could have been a fine composer but spent his life writing popular scores for Hollywood. It is more like someone who might have been a philosopher devoting himself to black magic. Yet, by the same token, the apostles are not especially concerned to condemn homosexual persons or acts when it is, all the time, the *culture* that they have in their sights, a culture of idolatry which they share with everybody else. The culpability of the individual is irrelevant: it is the culture that has, to pursue the analogy, substituted black magic for philosophy. There is nothing in the Statement to exclude the suggestion, made recently by some gay Christian apologists, that to begin with the morality of particular acts is simply to begin in the wrong place.

Attention now switches from the interpretative to the pastoral task of the church. First, the pastoral task in general, "in relation to all its members", is to "reaffirm" the Good News in a particular address to particular people with particular needs. Nothing is different in principle when the addressee is a self-defined homosexual living with a partner. Here, too, the word that the church has to speak is a word of evangelical encouragement. No distinction is made between an "evangelistic" word addressed to those who are actually or morally outside the church and a "pastoral" word addressed to members in good standing; whatever the usefulness of that distinction in other contexts, it is not invoked here. The homosexual member of the church is not treated as actually or morally outside the church, but as a serious follower of Jesus Christ like any other. Throughout this section of the Statement the best-case scenario is assumed. That is appropriate, because it is the scenario on which the claim for recognition of homosexual partnerships is based. There is no point in insisting that many homosexuals do not conform to this scenario, any more than there is in objecting to church marriage on the ground that most married couples do not attend church.

The faithful homosexual Christian, however, is in a situation which the church cannot recognise as one of "two forms or vocations" within which a "life of faithful witness in chastity and holiness can be lived." As it stands, the claim that there are two and only two such forms, though well supported, as the authors think, from Scripture, is not directly a biblical one but claims the authority of unbroken church tradition. If that tradition were shown to be essentially defective (i.e. without the supposed support of Scripture) or (less implausibly) to be more accommodating than has been thought (e.g. including homosexual unions as a valid variant of marriage), then, of course, there would be no general difficulty. But that supposes a radical development in the church's understanding of the tradition. The Statement does not rule such a development out a priori; in principle, no Anglican who believed, as Anglicans are supposed to believe, in the corrigibility of tradition *could* rule it out a priori. Yet the authors do not entertain the suggestion that such a development is in train or can be anticipated, and so they conclude: "there is no place for the church to confer legitimacy upon alternatives", i.e. to marriage and singleness.

This phrase has been read as saying rather more than it does. It is the *conferral of legitimacy*, i.e. by implication some kind of ceremonial endorsement, which it rules out. Relationships may have moral integrity in varying degrees without the church's formal authorisation. The integrity that is claimed for some homosexual unions does not depend on any ceremony. Indeed, when, in the ordinary course of events, the church solemnizes a marriage, it is not purporting to pronounce on the moral quality of the relationship involved. It is shaping the expectations of the community and conferring evangelical authorisation on the *form* which the relationship takes. Something similar can be said about vows of celibacy. It is this formal function which the authors think inappropriate in the case of a homosexual partnership, given the church's understanding of the two alternative vocations. Yet the church member in this generally irregular situation is to be "assisted" and "encouraged" in discipleship; in any personal counsel that is offered, due weight is to be given to "the circumstances which make each individual case different from every other". This is the "flexibility" which the Statement claims for personal practice. It means the freedom to begin from the needs of *this* person in *this* situation, and from what the Holy Spirit is saying to him or her at *this* point. And it means being able to treat different people differently, responding to their different capabilities, receptivities, patterns of responsibility and obligation, curves of moral and spiritual development.

Let us entertain an analogy, which may seem far-fetched at first glance but which has some illumination to offer: how the church addresses capitalists, of whom it has a number (and once had rather more) among its members. A virtually unanimous church tradition from the early period to the Reformation held that wealth was to be devoted to the needs of the poor, and should not be lent at interest. The member of the congregation, then, who earns a living on the Stock Exchange is apparently in a doubtful position vis-à-vis the church's tradition of moral teaching. But that does not mean the pastor must belabour him or her with exhortations to repent at every opportunity. It does mean, however, that at some point in a programme of pastoral care a thoughtful discussion is in place about what it means for those who work in the financial industries to serve God rather than Mammon. In the course of that discussion challenges from the tradition will quite naturally be heard and taken up. Here, however, the analogy goes further, and may point to a way in which the dialogue with gay Christians could develop. For the church has more to offer the capitalist Christian than a simple repetition of the economic doctrines of the pre-industrial era. Its sustained wrestling with the acquisitive impulses of industrial society over the past two centuries has left a deposit of insight into how capitalist structures can be made susceptible of socially responsible development. Questions about ethical patterns of investment, responsible industrial decision-making and employment terms and so on, all arise out of this ongoing dialogue between Christian charity and the logic of industrial enterprise, and they constitute an authentic extension of the church's moral tradition into which the contemporary investor can be, and needs to be, introduced.

Can we imagine something similar happening in the realm of sexual ethics? Well, a development of the tradition cannot take place just by announcing that it is going to. It is the result of a deepening understanding on the part of the whole church, the outcome of serious and prolonged engagement with theoretical questions, practical problems and successful and unsuccessful experiments. It is not simply a matter of Bishops or Synods deciding that they will change their line. On the other hand authentic developments cannot be ruled out; and we can learn to conduct our dialogue in such a way that, if and as new understanding does offer itself, we will be open to it. Borrowing a phrase from *Issues in Human Sexuality*, the Statement speaks of "respecting the integrity" of members of the church who "conscientiously dissent" (i.e. reflectively and with careful thought) from the church's teaching. That is to say, the church can recognise the seriousness of the stance these members are taking, want to engage equally seriously with them, acknowledge that such an engagement may have the long-term effect of developing the tradition of church-understanding (though nobody is in a position to say how and to what extent), all without thinking that its advocacy of the traditional view is, as such, mistaken.

It is worth pausing here to measure the width of the space between the lines; that is to say, how much the authors of the Statement have felt it safe to leave open as the subject for constructive disagreement. On the one hand, what they have said is compatible with the view that the serious gay Christian is simply mistaken; his or her position rests on a misunderstanding; the gay consciousness is a blind alley, with which the church simply has to be patient. Provided there is no attempt to stir up conflict, the church can respect the good faith of those who are mistaken, discuss the issues in a relaxed way as they arise, and wait for light to dawn. On the other hand, it is also compatible with the view that the serious gay Christian is a kind of prophet, acting in the loneliness of faith by stepping self-consciously and deliberately outside the church's tradition to point in a new direction that God is opening up and which the church will come to recognise in time. Precisely the seriousness of such an act rules out the hope for cheap or easily won concessions. Like certain Roman Catholic couples who, though using contraceptives themselves, resist the idea of a change in the church's teaching because they don't think such a step should be taken lightly, so, on this account, gay Christians would accept a minority stance for as long as it takes for the testing and appropriation of their insight. These two outlooks, the authors imply, can exist together and argue their differences fruitfully. Neither believes the church's understanding can be lightly set aside; both believe the situation requires patience and attention to God's voice.

In this context the Statement accepts the distinction that the Bishops made between what is acceptable among the laity and what is acceptable among the clergy. The clergy have "a particular commission to expound and exemplify the teachings of the church". They are by their office advocates of the tradition. The prophetic charism, if such it is, naturally takes its stand in distinction to the official ministry. The Bishops propounded a disciplinary rule that clergy might not live in homosexual partnerships. The Statement offers no verdict on this rule as such; it may be wise, or it may be unwise. But it does think it is morally intelligible to make a distinction within church order between what is demanded of clergy and laity; and it draws attention to New Testament precedents for this. One might add that there are many Anglican precedents, too. The 1969 Canons of the Church of England, for example, forbade anyone to be ordained who had remarried and had a former partner living, or who was married to someone who had a former partner living. It is probably quite inevitable that some such distinction should be made in any church which has an ordained ministry at all, so that only Plymouth Brethren can reject the idea with complete consistency!

The third section completes the trinitarian structure of the Statement by turning from the Son, the source of our human self-knowledge, and from the Spirit, the source of the church's interpretation and ministry, to the Father. Here the authors wish to speak about fulfilment and satisfaction. The logic of this progression is drawn from 1 Corinthians 15:27f., where the work of redemption is completed in the final sovereignty of God the Father, who shall be "all in all". Once again the theological structure casts light on the crisis of the times, a crisis by no means limited to sexual, let alone homosexual preoccupations. What is the relation of God's call to fulfilment to the restless search for satisfaction which causes us to make love and break up the relationship, have children and forsake them, make money and squander it, settle down and uproot ourselves, set our ambitions on some appointment and then, when we have it, look out for another?

Two images of the self and its fulfilment are contrasted. One sees the self as "private", and its fulfilment as a perfect act of self-expression, like a bunch of flowers in which all the blooms open. The other sees it as destined to make a contribution to a larger whole; its fulfilment is like that of a well-pruned branch which has been trained straight and strong to make the whole tree shapely. We are invited to see our lives in the latter way: fulfilled through participation in the fulfilment of God's creation. When we speak of being "fulfilled" in marriage or singleness, we do not mean simply that we find our state of life inherently satisfying; that may or may not be the case. We mean that it "points forward" to that further goal, taking us beyond ourselves. In doing this our state of life will realise some aspects of our personal endowment and leave others unrealised; only as it does so do we cease to be a set of open possibilities and become *something*, making the unique contribution that we are called to make. The moment of denial is essential to the process of fulfilment. There were ways I might have gone; powers I might have developed; but only by closing them off could I go the way I have gone, develop the powers that I have developed. Accepting the call that God has given means accepting the closures which that call demands.

The idea of vocation includes a great deal more than the alternative of the married and single states of life, but these are aspects of our individual vocations, and impose their own logic of denial and growth upon them. The single life does not offer an exclusive, intimate and permanent relationship at the centre of our network of relationships. The lack of this may have its own distinctive timbre of poignancy, especially when it catches up with us in middle age; but essentially it is to be viewed in the same way as other denials, including those that marriage imposes. The authors do not say that all who understand themselves as homosexual are called to do without such a relationship. Some readers will draw this inference, others may not. What they do say, however, is that a vocation to do without such a relationship can coincide with a "desire that (one) may reasonably have" for one. The "reasonable desire" is not a sufficient ground for a reasonable expectation.

There is, however, something which one may not only reasonably desire but form a reasonable expectation of, and that is friendship. This is a "blessing" which we can know our vocation, whether we are married or single, is to include. For friendship is the natural form of what, touched by Christ, becomes the "fellowship of the Holy Spirit". And because it is capable of this transformation, it has, the authors claim, a "properly exploratory character". That is to say, in making and deepening friendships in the context of the Christian life, we are discovering something of what God intends for ordinary human relations in the Kingdom of God. Here a warning may be necessary; there is danger, as well as hope, in the eschatological openness of human nature to transformation. If exploration guided by the Spirit of Christ expands the horizons of mutual confidence, exploration guided by the Spirit of Antichrist may expand very different possibilities: domination and exploitation, for instance. Yet the authors still feel compelled to say that the forms authentic friendship takes can be unconventional and unexpected – "freed from human constructs", as they put it, meaning patterns of expectation which inhibit the imagination from grasping possibilities God is preparing us for. Some gay apologists have suggested that homosexual relations are properly to be understood as experimental forms of deeper friendship. The authors of the Saint Andrew's Day Statement do not accept this contention, but neither do they rule it out a priori. They leave it to be proven to the church, by those who make such claims for homosexual friendships, that they are in fact "directed by the hope for the final appearing of Jesus".

In conclusion we may briefly ask ourselves how the debate on homosexuality would look and sound different if the principles which the Statement proposed were observed on all sides. There would, of course, still be a debate; there would still be disagreements. But their focus would be, as suggested by the text from Titus 2 which the authors placed at the end of their Statement, questions of Christian authenticity and holiness. "Rights" is a term one might expect not to hear in it; and it would not buzz so insistently around the status-honeypot of holy orders or hover over the power-switch, forbidden/allowed. It would be far more a lay debate, clearly about and for the sake of lay Christian living, concerned to identify what is admirable, impressive, authentically Christ-like. And let us not miss hearing the text's emphasis on "waiting". A debate conducted on these lines would have to be less impatient: waiting on experience, waiting on understanding, waiting on the manifestation of Christ which heralds the transformation of all things.

7

Living with
HIV/AIDS
A Personal Testimony

Gideon B Byamugisha

*The Rev Gideon Byamugisha is an ordained minister in Uganda. He is
thirty-six years old. In 1992 tests confirmed that he was HIV positive.*

INTRODUCTION

This paper is adapted from the presentation made by Gideon Byamugisha
during the Oxford conference *A Christian Response to Population Issues* in
January 1996. It is an account of the challenges faced by Uganda and its
Christian community in addressing the complex problems of widespread
HIV/AIDS infection, an account informed by the special understanding of a
person who will have to confront the issues in his own life as an infected
individual. The paper therefore includes biographical material which gives
force to statistics, background and predictions.

Gideon Byamugisha began and concluded his presentation to the
workshop with some reflections on his own future and present as a person
living with the knowledge that he is HIV+.

THE AUTHOR'S TESTIMONY

I could say that you are blessed with my presence here. I am a symbol of what
AIDS has done to humankind: I am living with HIV/AIDS infection. This
may be shocking news to some people who meet me but for me it is reality, it
is something which has happened to my life. When others speak about the
personal tragedy of HIV/AIDS I think about my own life. I should now be
finishing my PhD with the University of Wales but once I was told that I was
HIV+ I had to reconsider my position. Why should I study if I am going to die
tomorrow? I know I cannot hope for a future. I think of my family: sometimes
I could cry when my six-year-old daughter Patience says "Daddy, I want to
grow up very fast and the reason why I want to grow up very fast is that I am
going to grow up and wash for you.' I know that by the time she grows up I
will probably be dead. Sometimes I wonder whether I should try to explain
that, but more often I just cry and leave it at that. This is what 'personal
tragedy' means.

THE ROOTS OF THE HIV/AIDS SITUATION IN UGANDA

Many who discuss the present Ugandan situation see the 'fundamental factors' and 'co-factors' in reverse from the way I see them. The Ugandan experience shows that the co-factors are actually the fundamental causes and the fundamental factors are the co-factors. This paradoxical view I have comes from the fact that infection with HIV/AIDS by sexual contact does not begin with the act of intercourse. That is the end of a series of many events which have occurred against a complex social, economic and religious background. All these add up and prepare the ground for a person to become infected with HIV/AIDS.

The research results are evidence that this is true. Africa holds 70% of all the HIV/AIDS infection in the world; 80% of all the infected women of the world are living in Africa. However, people have sexual contact and produce babies all over the world. Why then is it that part of the world has very little HIV/AIDS while another has so high a proportion of the total infection? If it were right to focus on the act of sexual intercourse this would not be the case. Rather it is because of what I believe to be the fundamental factors: poverty, behaviour patterns, the spiritual outlook on life, and one more: character of the individual. Personality is a direct result of how you are brought up. Sadly I have found out in Uganda that it is the 'good' obedient girls who are dying of HIV/AIDS. The aggressive assertive ones are relatively safe.

'SAFE SEX'

Present sex education is very inadequate as a means to stop the spread of HIV/AIDS. Sadly, our churches are particularly weak: their message is simply that if people do not stop having sexual contact they will contract HIV/AIDS. The moral inadequacy is obvious. Does this mean that if there were no HIV/AIDS risk it would be acceptable to be promiscuous?

THE LEVEL OF HIV/AIDS INFECTION IN UGANDA

Uganda has become notorious for the high level of HIV/AIDS infection. The reputation is somewhat misleading: it is true that surveys show many are infected, but it is partly because the government has pursued a policy of openness about the subject. People are encouraged to come out into the open about their infection; the government discusses the national problem with the result that it appears as if everyone in Uganda is dying.

TABLE 1:

POPULATION SUMMARY OF HIV/AIDS INFECTION IN UGANDA

Numbers infected	**1.5 million**
Rising infection in women in urban areas	
Affected age groups	
children (less than 15 years)	8.2%
young people (16-40 years)	80%
adults over 40 years	11.8%

The implications of the statistics in Table 1:

- Uganda's young population has a limited future.
- Although the present high proportion of urban infection (25% of the population is infected in major urban areas) is decreasing in the urban areas, levels are increasing in rural areas. The causes are complex; one is lack of appropriate information.
- The projection is that by the year 2000 there could be 2 million infected people in the country.

THE UGANDAN RESPONSE TO THE HIV/AIDS PROBLEM

A three-fold response

1 The creation of awareness through education and training for prevention. The Church of Uganda has a good record. The slogan is 'Help stop AIDS *chusa*'. *Chusa* means 'Change your behaviour' in the local language. The Church has trained more than 500 church leaders in HIV/AIDS prevention and about 100 trainers. There are approximately 20,000 community health educators who go around sharing information about HIV/AIDS.

2 HIV/AIDS care and counselling.

3 Research into drugs, vaccines and in nutrition.

What groups have responded?

1 **The government** has responded effectively using a multi-sectoral approach which recognizes that HIV/AIDS is not only a health problem: it is a social, spiritual and economic problem. The Uganda AIDS Commission is an umbrella organization which co-ordinates and registers all projects when they are established.

2 **Local and international non-governmental organizations (NGOs)**. I am proud to say that the newly-formed UN organization in response to HIV/AIDS, UNAIDS, is based on the Ugandan model for a multi-sectoral approach.

3 **The religious community**. As well as churches, mosques are active. The Islamic Medical Association is the equivalent to the Christian response.

4 **The media** takes up HIV/AIDS issues and reports abuse. It also reflects the mood of the country.

5 **Individuals** all react in their own way: Ugandan doctors have been responsible for discovering some of the new drugs on the market. The ethical problem is that they are too expensive for most to afford. I began treatment but was forced to abandon it after two treatments. Now I rely on God's mercy.

6 **People living with HIV/AIDS**. Remember that the person to 'respond' first to HIV/AIDS is the person who is told that he or she is infected. We believe we should not be passive victims. We would rather stand up and enjoy the work for HIV/AIDS prevention and care and its benefits.

The National Guidance and Empowerment Network of People Living with HIV/AIDS in Uganda of which I am the leader was recently formed to encourage as many infected people as possible to admit their problems and help others in a similar situation: either by counselling or sharing information.

THE IMPACT OF HIV/AIDS INTERVENTION

a. Prevention

There have been reductions in infections in the project areas. After two years of activity by the church we have reduced the number of sexual partners by a high percentage, increased abstinence levels and also have raised the use of condoms by marriage partners from 9% to 12%. This small difference is understandable in the context of religious acceptance of condoms.

The general level of infection is still increasing:

i at a reduced rate in the urban areas
ii at an increasing rate in the rural areas

Awareness is now high but has not been matched by behavioural changes.

b. Research

i there is no cure or vaccine in sight
ii there are some drugs but their efficacy is not proved and their costs are prohibitive
iii TB management has become more effective.

c. Care, counselling and orphan support

Many people living with HIV/AIDS and orphans have been helped by various intervention groups but the need is still great. Those who have been helped are fewer than those who have not been helped. A recent Tear Fund study came to that conclusion. The problem is not that the projects are not working but that the demand is overwhelming.

A CHRISTIAN'S RESPONSE TO HIV/AIDS

We must continue with these for the most part successful responses, but seek new responses to meet the shortcomings. My intention in this section is not a general narrative of what is happening in Uganda, but to highlight some points which have arisen from my own personal experience and activity in the field of HIV/AIDS and which I believe are areas for further research and action:

1. Development of a theological and ethical framework

So far no clear policy on HIV/AIDS has emerged amongst the churches: responses are ad hoc. Policy must be developed to cope with many themes: prevention, care, widowhood, loneliness, etc. I focus here on three in particular:

a. Prevention: There is a problem which needs addressing even before we can start to formulate a coherent policy. It lies in the answer to the question 'Why should HIV/AIDS be prevented anyway?' Some churches use HIV/AIDS infection as a warning to prove that their traditional teaching on behaviour and morality is correct. On the other hand, some churches approach the issue from the angle that Christian teaching can prevent HIV/AIDS. There is a clear conflict here.

b. Widowhood: In Uganda there are now 600,000 widows: most are very young, between 14 and 25 years of age. I personally have had to grapple with the problem in my own life. I could almost call the pressure which I faced as a young pastor from women who wanted to marry me sexual harassment. I now live with a very young widow who is 23 years old. She is also HIV/AIDS infected. We are trying to live positively.

c. Loneliness: The church needs to enter the lives of people with the positive message that they may be lonely but they are not alone. We know that Christ is our redeemer but lonely people need to have that brought to them. What is the Christian answer to the question posed in the title of a very popular song, 'Sing alone and frightened'?

2. Development of appropriate language on HIV/AIDS prevention and care

Vocabulary is important. 'AIDS victim' is not a helpful term. For myself, I may be a victim of circumstances, of social conditions, of my own personality, but it is no longer helpful to be labelled that. I need to be empowered. We are people living with HIV/AIDS, not people dying with HIV/AIDS. You might also like to think about the current use of the word 'client'. Is it appropriate, does it empower a person to live with AIDS and face his problem?

3. Challenge the relevance and usefulness of the popular debates which divert and drain our energy for action

For example, the condom debate: I feel that undue emphasis is given to the question of condom use. Condoms are a must for every act of sexual intercourse to prevent the birth of children destined to suffer in the world and to prevent the acceleration of the death of the partners. However it is not adequate to concentrate on advocating condom use. It is not even enough to develop a culture of abstinence and faithfulness without realizing that there is a problem beyond this. The church must ask why people continue to have unprotected sexual contact despite the evidence of the suffering and early death caused by HIV/AIDS.

4. Inquiry into just resource distribution

Africa has 70% of the AIDS/HIV infection of the world, yet it only has 13% of the resources available to fight AIDS. This is unjust and an infringement of the human rights of African people.

5. Challenge traditional African concepts especially where they are a barrier to understanding the HIV/AIDS question

Witchcraft and the spirit world are an inadequate response to AIDS. There are three major types of learning: intuition, tuition and experience. Intuition is stultifying and hinders original thought. Tuition is education, which is not affordable for most Africans so the information they might have is beyond their reach. In practice today most Africans are left with experience. Used well, experience is the best teacher, but in the HIV/AIDS context experience is dangerous. Ugandans and Africans, like all other people must have tuition: education and information.

6. Improve the information flow network

However good services or education are, they must be widely available and people must know where to find them. We must improve the network.

7. Empowerment of people living with HIV/AIDS as participants in prevention and care activities

Who is better placed to be a partner in care and action? If my doctor asks me where my pain is I will immediately point to the place which hurts most. All people living with HIV/AIDS are well-placed to be incorporated in the HIV/AIDS campaign, not as clients but as partners in HIV/AIDS prevention and care.

8. Teach that a community right to avoid infection must be accompanied by community responsibility

No individual who does not behave or act responsibly should be surprised when they become infected. Communities too should realize that they must participate in examining and revising community attitudes responsible for the conditions which bring a high incidence of HIV/AIDS. As we discuss the individual so we must also discuss the community.

A PERSONAL CONCLUSION

My HIV/AIDS infection is a burden to me. I have the problem of being infected and meeting people who do not know this and are probably not infected. Do I keep quiet as a Christian? So far I have told few people about my condition. Before presenting this paper I was asked to introduce myself. First I shared the truth with two Christian friends. It is the strength of their prayers for and with me which has given me strength to present my life and the problems we have in Uganda to you. I think we should encourage this shared responsibility: the burden for us all could be reduced.

8

The Dark Side
of Technology

Bernard Adeney

THE SWEETNESS AND DANGER OF TECHNOLOGY

Many people in developing countries are fascinated by modern technology. Technology means the bright and shiny wonders that characterize the "modern" world. Technology is perceived as the sweet fruit of globalization, the tool of development and the sign of progress. Technology is a symbol of hope; hope in a wonderful future of security, prosperity and freedom. Technology is also a symbol of status and power. Those who possess the latest gadgets are the new elite. Those who cling to the old ways are destined to be left behind.

Since moving to Indonesia I have found that, while many Indonesians would like to taste the mysterious fruit of technology, most Indonesians know very little about it. Most live in villages which have yet to receive electricity. Some have never seen a car. Many live their lives without reference to a clock. Jakarta, with its soaring creations of steel and glass and marvellous highways choked with expensive cars is like a foreign country to those who have never left the village. Even a well-educated graduate student was heard to remark during a trip to Jakarta, "This is not Indonesia!".

That comment expresses a deep ambivalence felt by many young, educated people in developing countries, about their future. On the one hand, they are hungry for the freedom and prosperity of "modern" life. On the other hand, technology not only signifies prosperity, but also inequality and injustice. Technology often seems to benefit the few at the expense of the many. Some Indonesians fear the rapid change and the loss of traditional values that seems to accompany modern urban culture. As a neighbour of mine commented, "It seems that as people become more prosperous, they also become more individualistic and the spirit of mutual, harmonious cooperation decreases."

The government of Indonesia recognizes these dangers, perhaps in part because its members are at the top of the new urban elite and have personally tasted the sweetness and bitterness of technological culture. Almost daily there are speeches by high officials urging the people to hang on to their traditional Indonesian and religious values. In particular, it is common to appeal to religion to provide the moral resources people need to adapt to a technological society without losing their soul. "Western" values of individualism, materialism and capitalism are to be avoided, while Indonesian values of mutual and co-operative labourare to be elevated.

Within this context, the role of Christian faith is seen as a conservative force to protect moral values without in any way threatening the process of development and progress. Christian faith certainly must help preserve moral values in the midst of technological change. But Christian values must also interpret the meaning of technology and expose its dark side. Hope in the Kingdom of God is a source of values that transcend and sometimes oppose the values of technology. Technology can easily become an idol - a false god which does not save, but becomes a slave master. This article will try to expose the dark side of technology.

IS TECHNOLOGY MORALLY NEUTRAL

Technology is often perceived as morally neutral. An automobile, for example, is a morally neutral tool which may be used for good or for evil. A car may be used to rush a sick child to the hospital to save his life, or it may be used as a weapon to run over an enemy. Good or evil, from this perspective, reside not in the car, but in its application. Thus it is logical to think that the crucial place for Christian faith is in restraint of the bad uses of technology and promotion of its good uses. In other words, Christian ethics is concerned with the application of technology. Technology itself is good or neutral. Technology used for injustice and oppression is bad, while technology used to feed children and bring prosperity is good. The use of a knife in a gang fight is bad, while the use of the same knife to cut up a mango is good. The knife itself remains morally neutral.

The above reasoning seems self-evident, but reality is much more complex. Technology is never morally neutral, but almost always both good and evil. The structure of technological tools both reflects the values of a society and changes those same moral values. Technology, by its very existence, changes the world. It is inherent in the structure of a knife, that it can both cut up mangoes and kill another person. The invention of knives changed human life. Killing became easier. Some of the changes were good and some evil. Most of us believe that the majority of changes, in the case of a knife, were good. The changes created in human society by gunpowder, bombs and nuclear reactions, on the other hand, seem to have resulted in more fear and suffering than prosperity and justice.

These observations about technology apply not only to weapons, but to all tools created by humankind. For example, the speed and comfort of travel was revolutionized by the automobile. But the internal combustion engine created a society in which air pollution, traffic accidents, oil spills, cement cities, traffic congestion, environmental degradation, social inequality, changed perceptions of time, parking problems and a host of other effects are commonplace. An Indonesian friend remarked that he pitied the village person who had never seen a car. But a harried office worker trying to cross Jakarta, or a grieving mother of a child killed in an accident, or a grief-stricken husband whose wife died a torturous death from cancer caused by pollution, might envy the simple villager. Less dramatically, more than one long-time resident of the town I live in has remarked to me on how much cooler, cleaner, less congested and noisy Salatiga was before buses and trucks filled the roads.

Recently as I was driving from Jakarta to Salatiga, an old farmer made a sudden right turn into my path on the highway. As I slammed on my brakes and skidded around him, I reflected that only a few years ago, he would not have had narrowly to face instant death on his way to market. Nor would I have had to face the possibility of killing an innocent man as I hurried home. The internal combustion engine made my trip possible and even brought me to this beautiful land. But it is also changing this country at a rate that is frightening and dangerous.

Thirty or forty years ago the big lie was that science and technology could solve all human problems. Now it is recognized that technology creates problems as quickly as it solves them. Today the great new lie in the Third World countries is that universal prosperity derived from unlimited production and growth is the goal of human life. The collapse of socialism, with its vision of an egalitarian society, has given way to a faith in capitalistic development as a rapid route to prosperity for all. It is this faith that needs to be demythologized.

THE DANGERS OF DEVELOPMENT
AND ECONOMIC GROWTH

There are three major problems with putting faith in unlimited economic growth as the goal of life. One is that *such growth leads to the rapid destruction of the environment and the depletion of natural resources*. By squandering the riches of nature in the interests of short-term prosperity, we threaten not only the beauty of our world, but also the long-term survival of life on this planet. As E.F. Schumacher remarked, "If we squander our fossil fuels, we threaten civilization; but if we squander the capital represented by living nature around us, we threaten life itself."[2] The rich countries of the world, and the wealthy elites of the developing countries are rapidly stripping the world of non-renewable cheap and simple fuels.[3]

Secondly, while rapid technological economic growth is an effective way to create wealth, *such growth primarily benefits a small elite*. Even in the few countries where all seem to benefit, the gap between the rich and the poor tends to increase. As Gandhi remarked, "Earth provides enough to satisfy every man's need, but not for every man's greed."

Thirdly, *even those who apparently benefit from unlimited growth do not thereby achieve a fully human, satisfying life*. In my own country, the United States, there is a malaise, a weakness and a lack of happiness today that belies the abundant prosperity attained. The very qualities which are cultivated in the process of rapid economic growth undermine the human community. Greed and envy destroy the ability of people to see what really matters in life. By the process of becoming rich in material things, people are impoverished in their spirits. As Schumacher says,

> the foundations of peace cannot be laid by universal prosperity, in the modern sense, because such prosperity, if attainable at all, is attainable only by cultivating such drives of human nature as greed and envy, which destroy intelligence, happiness, serenity, and thereby the peacefulness of man.[5]

Technology, growth, development, progress, globalization: these words represent realities which will not disappear through moral argument. Religious faith cannot simply reject them as if that would make them go away. Technology has great potential for good as well as evil. We cannot go back or simply strive, like a romantic anthropologist, to preserve pre-modern ways of life. On the other hand, Christians must reject the tendency of "progress" to become a new religion. Christians in developing countries are sometimes the most susceptible to incorporating "progress" into their own faith. Western technology and unlimited material prosperity somehow become confused with Christian hope. Sometimes this confusion is received directly from missionaries from the West. As H. Richard Niebuhr observed,

> Christianity, democracy, Americanism, the English language and culture, the growth of industry and science, American institutions - these are all confounded and confused. The contemplation of their own righteousness filled Americans with such lofty and enthusiastic sentiments that they readily identified it with the righteousness of God ... the Kingdom of the Lord ... is in particular the destiny of the Anglo-Saxon race, which is destined to bring light to the gentiles by means of lamps manufactured in America.[6]

It is not enough to strive for moral values in the process of development. Development itself must be demythologized. It must be criticized. For those who worship at the altar of globalization, moral platitudes about justice, or the environment are just nice words with no power to affect empirical reality. We must look with clarity at the dark side of technology.

E.F. Schumacher argues against Marx that the problems of industrial society are not caused by the private ownership of the means of production, but by the structural degradation of work by the demands of complex technology. Schumacher suggests that the four great evils of industrial society are: 1. its vastly complicated nature, 2. its continuous stimulation of, and reliance on the deadly sins of greed, envy and avarice, 3. its destruction of the content and dignity of most forms of work and 4. its authoritarian character, owing to organization in excessively large units.

> Mechanical, artificial, divorced from nature, utilizing only the smallest part of man's potential capabilities, it sentences the great majority of

> workers to spending their working lives in a way that contains no worthy challenge, no stimulus to self-perfection, no chance of development, no element of Beauty, Truth or Goodness. The basic aim of modern industrialization is not to make work satisfying but to raise productivity.[7]

While Schumacher is a vigorous critic of capitalism, he argues that the basic problem is not the superstructure of the economic system, but the totalitarian nature of large-scale technologies. Highly complex technologies demand a division of labour in which only a very small elite can understand or control the machines. All society must be reorganized to meet the requirements of technology. Most human beings are reduced to servants of a technology that is beyond their understanding or control. Those who cannot adapt to technological requirements are simply shoved out of the way and often deprived of their traditional means of livelihood.[8]

Schumacher argues that the best way to change the system is to change the technologies that organize our lives. If our tools are to serve people they must be on a scale that can be controlled by the people they serve. "Appropriate technologies", according to Schumacher, are those which give power and relative independence to the people who use them. In contrast, one of the great problems of technology transfer to developing nations is that it increases the power of the donor and fosters dependence. A simple machine, designed for the needs of its user, which can be locally maintained, is vastly superior to a complex technology which serves the interests of an absentee elite. Schumacher's ideas have become basic axioms of development and relief workers all over the world. By focusing on technology, rather than politics or economics, he set in motion grass-roots changes that can be practically introduced immediately. In Indonesia many positive and negative examples prove his point.[9] The smaller the technology, the greater the local control. Not only does this reduce dependence on foreign experts, it requires less bureaucracy, less money and results in more of the benefits of the technology remaining in the community that needs it most.

Schumacher was a Christian who assumed that the purpose of technology was to serve human need, not human greed, or the demands of production. Because technology is not morally neutral, bigger, more expensive, and more complex technology that increases production is not necessarily better. The critical standard is not the amount of wealth produced, but the long-term impact on real human communities.

The weakness in Schumacher's work is its idealism. The forces of globalized development are far more powerful than the well-meaning few who are striving to build self-sustaining communities with appropriate technology. The problem lies not merely in the inappropriate scale of some technologies, but in the power of the bureaucratic elites who control the dissemination of technology. To analyze the political and economic forces which largely control the application of technology today is a far greater task that can be attempted in this article. Instead we will briefly consider why the institutions which control technology so often end up as oppressors of the poor.

INSTITUTIONS THAT CONTROL TECHNOLOGY: MOTIVATED BY POWER AND PROFIT

Ivan Illich suggests that technological invention begins as a powerful tool to solve specific human problems. But invariably, the experts who control technology develop social institutions which channel the tendency for the wholesale exploitation of society. Large-scale technology requires vast investment and sophisticated experts. Only large corporations or governments have the resources needed. It is the search for power and profit which motivates such large enterprises. The purpose of the technology is thus subverted from the enhancement of human life. Instead it comes to serve the greed of a powerful elite. Like Schumacher, Illich tacitly locates the origin of the problem in the immense scale of technology. But unlike Schumacher, Illich focuses on the institutional systems human beings create which restructure and transform technology into an instrument of oppression.

Illich believes there is a natural scale. When enterprises which channel technology pass a certain size, they first frustrate the original purposes of the technology, then rapidly become a positive threat to society. Thus he observes,

> society can be destroyed when further growth of mass production renders the milieu hostile, when it extinguishes the free use of the natural abilities of society's members, when it isolates people from each other and locks them into a man-made shell, when it undermines the texture of community by promoting extreme social polarization and splintering specialization, or when cancerous acceleration enforces social change at a rate that rules out legal, cultural and political precedents as formal guidelines to present behaviour.[10]

Illich, with characteristic exaggeration, suggests that all the Western social agencies reorganized according to scientific principles in the last 150 years have passed the second watershed and become a threat to society. Unlike Schumacher, Illich does not suggest a grass-roots development of appropriate technology as the solution, but rather calls for "new political arrangements" which will enforce structures for a radical redistribution of power. The power of technology must pass from the control of tiny institutional elites, or experts, into the hands of the people. Illich's proposals for an individualistic "convivial society" in which the power structures of all major social institutions are overthrown verges on anarchy and is unrealistic anywhere, let alone in developing countries. Nevertheless, his analysis helpfully highlights the power and motives of the institutions which control technology. Religious and traditional values will be powerless to affect the application of technology if it is controlled by institutions devoted to their own wealth and power. Moral statements then become masks which hide the true purposes of "development". Technology remains a tool of exploitation.

As in the case of technology, megacorporations and huge government bureaucracies are required to sustain the complexity of the tools we now possess. Nor are such institutions inherently capitalistic. The fragmentation of the Soviet Union and Eastern Europe illustrates what can happen when government institutions of power become so corrupt and inefficient that they are intolerable to the people.

RELIGION AND THE CONTROL OF POWER

Even if we agree with Schumacher, Gandhi and Illich, that "small is beautiful", it remains true that at this moment in history, large is necessary. Large and powerful organizations will remain a reality for the foreseeable future. Wherever power and wealth are concentrated there is great potential for oppression and injustice. Socialism prefers to see such power monopolized by the state. Capitalism claims it is safer in private hands. Indonesia, because of the necessities of competing in the global market- place, seems to concentrate power in a coalition of government, military and private enterprise. Such power is not "safe" anywhere. But the greatest hope for its subordination to the needs of the people lies in the movement towards increasing democracy.

Gandhi well understood the dangers of power. One of his disciples once asked him what he would do if he were given the power to change anything in the world. Gandhi thought for a long time while his disciples waited with bated breath. Finally he looked up and answered, "I would immediately pray for the strength to reject such power." Gandhi knew that power was dangerous, even in his own humble hands.

Reinhold Niebuhr, in reflecting on the Christian doctrine of the universality of sin said, "There is no one good enough or wise enough to be completely entrusted with the destiny of his fellow men."[11]

Christian institutions can certainly promote the use of appropriate technology after the model of Schumacher. That may take unusual courage in the face of the powerful elites who favour large-scale development projects with their greater opportunities for corruption and profit. Christians who work for the government, or for large corporations can certainly use their limited influence to promote the use of technology for the good of the community. Governments and corporations are often the source of great good as well as great evil.

Beyond that, Christian institutions must find ways to become advocates for individuals and communities that are oppressed by institutions which seek their own enrichment. Community organizing that gives power to the poor is one means to this end. Above all, the Church must not fall into the trap of becoming like the institutions they oppose. Christians are not immune from the temptation to use their power for the glorification of their own elite.[12]

We have passed from the industrial revolution to the information revolution. With the advent of the microchip, the whole world is being changed, not primarily through the production of things, but through the exchange of information. The primary symbol of this revolution is the computer. But telephones, faxes, satellites and televisions are equally important. Information has become the world's greatest industry. It is information, not technological products, that is making the biggest impact on Indonesia. The most significant result of the information revolution is not the exchange of "facts" but changes in the way of thinking and the way of seeing the world.

It is commonplace in Indonesia to decry the influx of Western sexual values, individualism and materialism through television and film. But less recognized, and far more serious is the inundation of technological ways of thinking. This influence is primarily limited to the educated classes. Yet its power to change all of society is enhanced by the fact that hardly anyone recognizes it as a danger.

In 1954, a French sociologist/theologian, Jacque Ellul, published a book on the dangers of technological thinking. His warnings are overgeneralized and oversimplified, but his argument has proved prophetic. Ellul's most penetrating insight is his distinction between technologies per se and the mentality, or world view, or ethos that makes them possible in the modern world. Ellul calls this ethos "Technique".

> Technique is the totality of methods rationally arrived at and having absolute efficiency in every field of activity.[13]

Technique is the scientific process, or way of thinking which makes technology possible. It is a way of thinking that subordinates all values to the value of efficiency and utility.

TECHNIQUE

According to Ellul, technique is characterized by rationality. All methods are chosen in keeping with judgements from the logical, rational dimension alone. All that is spontaneous, emotional, or irrational is excluded. Secondly, technique is artificial. It is opposed to nature. "It destroys, eliminates, or subordinates the natural world."[14] Thirdly, technical choices are automatic. There is no real choice between alternatives. "The one best way" is the rule of technique.

> When everything has been measured and calculated mathematically so that the method which has been decided upon is satisfactory from the rational point of view, and is the most efficient, then the technical movement becomes self-direction.[15] In the modern world everything may be called into question except technical progress.

Self-augmentation is Ellul's fourth category. Technique finds more and more areas to conquer such that its growth is virtually unlimited. Technical progress is irreversible and grows according to a geometric progression. Each new discovery provokes other discoveries. The impact of technology is felt in other fields in a way that is unpredictable. Technique creates more technical problems which can only be solved by more technique which in turn creates its own problems, etc.

Fifthly, a technical way of thinking unites all the different kinds of technique. It is impossible to separate the good uses of technique from the bad uses because all technologies operate by the same rule: What is most efficient and useful? Different techniques correspond to different necessities, not to moral judgements. Ellul's sixth category is an extension of the fifth. Different technologies are linked together. You cannot pick and choose between them except by technical reason. Ellul says,

> Every successive technique has appeared because the ones which preceded it rendered necessary the ones which followed.[16]

Technique is, seventhly, characterized by geometric and qualitative universalism. Technique is rapidly spreading all over the world, both as an ideology and as a product. In fact we might say that globalization and technique are the same thing. War and commerce are its main carriers. In order to survive in the world, both economically and physically, nations are impelled to adopt technique. But technique does not confine itself to instruments of war and economics.

> It is totalitarian in message, methods, field of action, and means ...
> Technique can leave nothing untouched in a civilization. Everything is its concern.[17]

Finally, technique is autonomous. It operates according to the rules of necessity and tolerates no judgement on itself outside of utility. Ellul insists that it is impossible to apply moral criteria to utility or technique. Technique demands all or nothing. If you accept it you must play by its rules. Technique is one of the two modern "sacreds" (the other is politics).

Nothing is sacred before it. It invades every area of life. Yet the operations of technique are mysterious and sacred. The technicians in white coats are the new high priests who will save humanity through the power they mediate. Ellul sees the world which technique is creating as "Hell organized upon earth for the bodily comfort of everyone."[18]

Most two-thirds world countries are far from being enslaved by technique. We might even say most need more technique: more efficiency, more rationality, more scientific thinking. Not only are most people in the developing countries uneducated in strictly rational, scientific thinking, even those who are educated are also influenced by other values than efficiency. Community values, status considerations, ethnic commitments, nationalism and religious values are still powerful motivations which undermine efficiency as a value in and of itself. Scientific thinking can serve a useful function by uniting representatives from diverse ethnic communities to work for common, utilitarian goals. Technique, or scientific thinking transcends cultural or ethnic boundaries.

Science is not a god that can save us. But technical reason as defined by Ellul, is also a serious danger in Indonesia. In some ways it is even a greater danger here than in the West. Because the West has had greater experience with the failures of technology, scientific reasoning has lost some of its aura of infallibility.

Articulate critics of "progress" are quick to point out the dangers of new applications of technology. For example, in North America, public criticism of nuclear power has grown so strong that no new nuclear power plants have been built or planned for years. In spite of the backing of huge corporations, nuclear power is seen as too dangerous and too expensive. In contrast, Indonesia is proceeding with plans to build a new, untested nuclear power plant in highly populated Central Java.

Technique, or scientific reason, is a powerful tool which must always be subordinated to human values that are greater than efficiency or "progress". Science is not a god that can save us. Like fire, its power to destroy is as great as its power to create. Like a false god it seeks worshippers. Like a fire it seeks to spread into every area of life. Jurgen Habermas points out that in the West the techniques of money and power have sought to take over the "life world" of human relationships. Technical reason is only one part of human reason and should not be allowed to dominate areas of life which are greater than its competence. We cannot prevent technique and its material applications from changing our world - for good and evil. But Christians can reject its tendency to become the god of the modern world.

SUMMARY: THE DARK SIDE OF TECHNOLOGY

The positive importance of technology is well recognized in the two-thirds world. There is a dark side of technology which needs equal attention. This dark side of technology may be summarized as follows:

1 Technology is often the tool of inequality and injustice. Therefore Christians must always ask how development affects the poor of the community.

2 Technology is often the vehicle of greed and envy which destroys the ability to see the wholeness of life. A simple villager may be more happy than a harried executive who drives a BMW. Therefore we must beware of the god of Mammon.

3 Technology is never morally neutral but always brings good and evil. Therefore we must face rapid social change with realism and seek ways to minimize the evil of our new world.

4 Technology has a tendency to destroy nature. Therefore we must limit its effects and reverence the earth which ultimately belongs to God.

5 Complex technology that is bigger, more efficient and more profitable usually benefits a small, educated elite. Therefore we must favour "appropriate technology" that increases the power and independence of the majority of people who are most affected.

6 Communities should work for the decentralization and democratization of power so that local communities can enjoy the fruit of technology.

7 Scientific reasoning is a powerful tool that tends to exclude all values except utility and efficiency. Therefore we must resist its deification and make it subservient to Christian values.

Notes

1   Among Indonesians "capitalism" is often considered a synonym for greed, corruption, decadence and oppression. Its actual definition remains vague.

2   E.F. Schumacher, *Small is Beautiful*, (New York: Harper and Row, 1973), p.17.

3   See the Brandt Commission, *Common Crisis*, (New York: 1983). For example, a multinational mining company purchased 20 years' mining rights in a very rich area in exchange for 10% of the profit. A likely result is that after 20 years the valuable metals will all be depleted and sent to the West, a few of the national elite will be very rich, the environment degraded, and the majority of poor who actually live in the area, worse off than they were before.

4   The evidence for this is admittedly ambiguous. In some countries, such as Brazil, it is clear that as GNP has risen, the actual living conditions of the majority of poor people has deteriorated. On the other hand, the economic "miracles" of countries like Singapore, S. Korea and Taiwan provide counter-examples.

5   *Small is Beautiful*, p.32.

6   H. Richard Neibuhr, *The Kingdom of God in America*, (New York: 1937), p.242.

7   E.F. Schumacher, *Good Work*, (New York: Harper and Row, 1979), p.27.

8   There are many examples of this process in Indonesia. For example, traditional farmers in the Molucus, who could not adapt to the plywood industry, simply lost their land and means of support with very little reimbursement.

9   For example, a development project in Salatiga designed to improve the dairy industry proved a dismal failure, in part because the animals and equipment provided were too costly and complex to be maintained by uneducated farmers.

10   Ivan Illich, *Tools for Conviviality*, (New York: Harper and Row, 1973), p.xi.

11   Reinhold Niebuhr, *Christian Realism and Political Problems*, (New York: Charles Scribner's Sons, 1953), p.10.

12   For example, one church in a two-thirds world country attracted widespread criticism after it became an agent for the farmers in its congregation to sell their produce with the result that the poor farmers in the congregation became even poorer while church officials began driving expensive cars.

13   Jacques Ellul, *The Technological Society*, (New York: Vintage Books, Random House, 1964), p.xxv.

14   Ibid., p.79.

15   Ibid., p.80.

16   Ibid., p.116.

17   Ibid., p.125. This is illustrated by the fact that there are technical books on how to pray, how to have sex, how to save your marriage, how to get a divorce, how to raise your kids, etc.

18   Jacques Ellul, *The Presence of the Kingdom*, (New York: Seabury Press, 1967), p.41.

9

The Oxford Declaration on Christian Faith and Economics

Preamble

This Oxford Declaration on Christian Faith and Economics of January 1990 is issued jointly by over one hundred theologians and economists, ethicists and development practitioners, church leaders and business managers who come from various parts of the world. We live in diverse cultures and subcultures, are steeped in differing traditions of theological and economic thinking, and therefore have diverse notions as to how Christian faith and economic realities should intersect.[1] We have found this diversity enriching even when we could not reach agreement. At the same time we rejoice over the extent of unanimity on the complex economics of today made possible by our common profession of faith in our Lord Jesus Christ.

We affirm that through his life, death, resurrection, and ascension to glory, Christ has made us one people (Galatians 3:28). Though living in different cultures, we acknowledge together that there is one body and one Spirit, just as we are called to the one hope, one Lord, one faith, one baptism, and one God and Father of us all (Ephesians 4:4).

We acknowledge that a Christian search for truth is both a communal and also an individual effort. As part of the one people in Christ, each of us wants to comprehend the relevance of Christ to the great issues facing humanity today together "with all the saints" (Ephesians 3:18). All our individual insights need to be corrected by the perspectives of the global Christian community as well as Christians through the centuries.

We affirm that Scripture, the word of the living and true God, is our supreme authority in all matters of faith and conduct. Hence we turn to Scripture as our reliable guide in reflection on issues concerning economic, social, and political life. As economists and theologians we desire to submit both theory and practice to the bar of Scripture.

Together we profess that God, the sovereign of life, in love made a perfect world for human beings created to live in fellowship with God. Although our greatest duty is to honour and glorify God, we rebelled against God, fell from our previous harmonious relationship with God, and brought evil upon ourselves and God's world. But God did not give up on the creation. As

Creator, God continues patiently working to overcome the evil which was perverting the creation. The central act of God's redemptive new creation is the death, resurrection, and reign in glory of Jesus Christ, the Son of God, and the sending of the Holy Spirit. This restoration will only be completed at the end of human history and the reconciliation of all things. Justice is basic to Christian perspectives on economic life.

Justice is rooted in the character of God. "For the Lord is righteous, he loves justice" (Psalm 11:7). Justice expresses God's actions to restore God's provision to those who have been deprived and to punish those who have violated God's standards.

CREATION AND STEWARDSHIP

God the Creator

1 . From God and through God and to God are all things (Romans 11:36). In the freedom of God's eternal love, by the word of God's omnipotent power, and through the Creator Spirit, the Triune God gave being to the world and to human beings which live in it. God pronounced the whole creation good. For its continuing existence creation is dependent on God. The same God who created it is present in it, sustaining it, and giving it bountiful life (Psalm 104:29). In Christ, "all things were created … and all things hold together" (Colossians 1:15-20). Though creation owes its being to God, it is itself not divine. The greatness of creation – both human and non-human – exists to glorify its Creator. The divine origin of the creation, its continued existence through God, redemption through Christ, and its purpose to glorify God are fundamental truths which must guide all Christian reflection on creation and stewardship.

Stewardship of Creation

2. God the Creator and Redeemer is the ultimate owner. "The earth is the Lord's and the fullness thereof" (Psalm 24:1). But God has entrusted the earth to human beings to be responsible for it on God's behalf. They should work as God's stewards in the creative, faithful management of the world, recognising that they are responsible to God for all they do with the world and to the world.

3. God created the world and pronounced it "very good" (Genesis 1:31). Because of the Fall and the resulting curse, creation "groans in travail" (Romans 8:22). The thoughtlessness, greed, and violence of sinful human beings have damaged God's good creation and produced a variety of ecological problems and conflicts. When we abuse and pollute creation, as we are doing in many instances, we are poor stewards and invite disaster in both local and global eco-systems.

4. Much of human aggression toward creation stems from a false understanding of the nature of creation and the human role in it. Humanity has constantly been confronted by the two challenges of selfish individualism, which neglects human community, and rigid collectivism, which stifles human

freedom. Christians and others have often pointed out both dangers. But only recently have we realised that both ideologies have a view of the world with humanity at the centre which reduces material creation to a mere instrument.

5. Biblical life and world view is not centred on humanity. It is God-centred. Non-human creation was not made exclusively for human beings. We are repeatedly told in the Scripture that all things – human beings and the environment in which they live – were "for God" (Romans 11:36; 1 Corinthians 8:6; Colossians 1:16). Correspondingly, nature is not merely the raw material for human activity. Though only human beings have been made in the image of God, non-human creation too has a dignity of its own, so much so that after the flood God established a covenant not only with Noah and his descendants, but also "with every living creature that is with you" (Genesis 9:9). Similarly, the Christian hope for the future also includes creation. "The creation itself will be set free from its bondage to decay and obtain the glorious liberty of the children of God" (Romans 8:21).

6. The dominion which God gave human beings over creation (Genesis 1:30) does not give them licence to abuse creation. First, they are responsible to God, in whose image they were made, not to ravish creation but to sustain it, as God sustains it in divine providential care. Second, since human beings are created in the image of God for community and not simply as isolated individuals (Genesis 1:28), they are to exercise dominion in a way that is responsible to the needs of the total human family, including future generations.

7. Human beings are both part of creation and also unique. Only human beings are created in the image of God. God thus grants human beings dominion over the non-human creation (Genesis 1:28-30). But dominion is not domination. According to Genesis 2:15, human dominion over creation consists in the twofold task of "tilling and taking care" of the garden. Therefore all work must have not only a productive but also a protective aspect. Economic systems must be shaped so that a healthy ecological system is maintained over time. All responsible human work done by the stewards of God the Sustainer must contain an element of cooperation with the environment.

Stewardship and Economic Production

8. Economic production results from the stewardship of the earth which God assigned to humanity. While materialism, injustice, and greed are in fundamental conflict with the teaching of the whole Scripture, there is nothing in Christian faith that suggests that the production of new goods and services is undesirable. Indeed, we are explicitly told that God "richly furnishes us with everything to enjoy" (1 Timothy 6:17). Production is not only necessary to sustain life and make it enjoyable; it also provides an opportunity for human beings to express their creativity in the service of others. In assessing economic systems from a Christian perspective, we must consider their ability both to generate and to distribute wealth and income justly.

Technology and its Limitations

9. Technology mirrors the basic paradox of the sinfulness and goodness of human nature. Many current ecological problems result from the extensive use of technology after the onset of industrialisation. Though technology has liberated human beings from some debasing forms of work, it has also often dehumanised other forms of work. Powerful nations and corporations that control modern technology are regularly tempted to use it to dominate the weak for their own narrow self-interest. As we vigorously criticise the negative effects of technology, we should, however, not forget its positive effects. Human creativity is expressed in the designing of tools for celebration and work. Technology helps us meet the basic needs of the world population and to do so in ways which develop the creative potential of individuals and societies. Technology can also help us reverse environmental devastation. A radical rejection of modern technology is unrealistic. Instead we must search for ways to use appropriate technology responsibly according to every cultural context.

10. What is technologically possible is not necessarily morally permissible. We must not allow technological development to follow its own inner logic, but must direct it to serve moral ends. We acknowledge our limits in foreseeing the impact of technological change and encourage an attitude of humility with respect to technological innovation. Therefore continuing evaluation of the impact of technological change is essential. Four criteria derived from Christian faith help us to evaluate the development and use of technology. First, technology should not foster disintegration of family or community, or function as an instrument of social domination. Second, persons created in the image of God must not become mere accessories of machines. Third, as God's stewards, we must not allow technology to abuse creation. If human work is to be done in cooperation with creation then the instruments of work must cooperate with it too. Finally, we should not allow technological advancements to become objects of false worship or seduce us away from dependence on God (Genesis 11:1-9). We may differ in what weight we ascribe to individual criteria in concrete situations and therefore our assessment of particular technologies may differ. But we believe that these criteria need to be taken into consideration as we reflect theologically on technological progress.

11. We urge individuals, private institutions, and governments everywhere to consider both the local, immediate, and the global, long-term ecological consequences of their actions. We encourage corporate action to make products which are more "environmentally friendly". And we call on governments to create and enforce just frameworks of incentives and penalties which will encourage both individuals and corporations to adopt ecologically sound practices.

12. We need greater international cooperation between individuals, private organisations, and nations to promote environmentally responsible action. Since political action usually serves the self-interest of the powerful, it will be especially important to guarantee that international environmental agreements

are particularly concerned to protect the needs of the poor. We call on Christians everywhere to place high priority on restoring and maintaining the integrity of creation.

WORK AND LEISURE

Work and Human Nature

13. Work involves all those activities done, not for their own sake, but to satisfy human needs. Work belongs to the very purpose for which God originally made human beings. In Genesis 1:26–28, we read that God created human beings in his image "in order to have dominion over ... all the earth." Similarly, Genesis 2:15 tells us that God created Adam and placed him in the garden of Eden to work in it, to "till it and keep it." As human beings fulfil this mandate, they glorify God. Though fallen, as human beings "go forth to their work" (Psalm 104:23) they fulfil an original purpose of the Creator for human existence.

14. Because work is central to the Creator's intention for humanity, work has intrinsic value. Thus work is not solely a means to an end. It is not simply a chore to be endured for the sake of satisfying human desires or needs, especially the consumption of goods. At the same time, we have to guard against over-valuation of work. The essence of human beings consists in that they are made in the image of God. Their ultimate, but not exclusive, source of meaning and identity does not lie in work, but in becoming children of God by one Spirit through faith in Jesus Christ.

15. For Christians, work acquires a new dimension. God calls all Christians to employ through work the various gifts that God has given them. God calls people to enter the kingdom of God and to live a life in accordance with its demands. When people respond to the call of God, God enables them to bear the fruit of the Spirit and endows them individually with multiple gifts of the Spirit. As those who are gifted by the Spirit and whose actions are guided by the demands of love, Christians should do their work in the service of God and humanity.

The Purpose of Work

16. In the Bible and in the first centuries of the Christian tradition, meeting one's needs and the needs of one's community (especially its underprivileged members) was an essential purpose of work (Psalm 128:2; 2 Thessalonians 3:8; 1 Thessalonians 4:9–12; Ephesians 4:28; Acts 20:33–35). The first thing at issue in all fields of human work is the need of human beings to earn their daily bread and a little more.

17. The deepest meaning of human work is that the almighty God established human work as a means to accomplish God's work in the world. Human beings remain dependent on God, for "unless the Lord builds the house, those who build it labour in vain" (Psalm 127:1a). As Genesis 2:5 suggests, God and human beings are co-labourers in the task of preserving creation.

18. Human work has consequences that go beyond the preservation of creation to the anticipation of the eschatological transformation of the world.

They are, of course, not ushering in the kingdom of God, building the "new heaven and a new earth." Only God can do that. Yet their work makes a small and imperfect contribution to it – for example, by shaping the personalities of the citizens of the eternal kingdom which will come through God's action alone.

19. However, work is not only a means through which the glory of human beings as God's stewards shines forth. It is also a place where the misery of human beings as impeders of God's purpose becomes visible. Like the test of fire, God's judgement will bring to light the work which has ultimate significance because it was done in cooperation with God. But it will also manifest the ultimate insignificance of work done in cooperation with those evil powers which scheme to ruin God's good creation (1 Corinthians 3:12-15).

Alienation in Work

20. Sin makes work an ambiguous reality. It is both a noble expression of human creation in the image of God, and, because of the curse, a painful testimony to human estrangement from God. Whether human beings are tilling the soil in agrarian societies, or operating high-tech machinery in information societies, they work under the shadow of death, and experience struggle and frustration in work (Genesis 3:17–19).

21. Human beings are created by God as persons endowed with gifts which God calls them to exercise freely. As a fundamental dimension of human existence, work is a personal activity. People should never be treated in their work as mere means. We must resist the tendency to treat workers merely as costs or labour inputs, a tendency evident in both rural and urban societies, but especially where industrial and post-industrial methods of production are applied. We encourage efforts to establish managerial and technological conditions that enable workers to participate meaningfully in significant decision-making processes, and to create opportunities for individual development by designing positions that challenge them to develop their potential and by instituting educational programmes.

22. God gives talents to individuals for the benefit of the whole community. Human work should be a contribution to the common good (Ephesians 4:28). The modern drift from concern for community to preoccupation with self, supported by powerful structural and cultural forces, shapes the way we work. Individual self-interest can legitimately be pursued, but only in a context marked by the pursuit of the good of others. These two pursuits are complementary. In order to make the pursuit of the common good possible, Christians need to seek to change both the attitudes of workers and the structures in which they work.

23. Discrimination in work continues to oppress people, especially women and marginalised groups. Because of race and gender, people are often pushed into a narrow range of occupations which are often underpaid, offer little status or security, and provide few promotional opportunities and fringe benefits. Women and men and people of all races are equal before God and should, therefore, be recognised and treated with equal justice and dignity in social and economic life.

24. For most people work is an arduous good. Many workers suffer greatly under the burden of work. In some situations people work long hours for low pay, working conditions are appalling, contracts are non existent, sexual harassment occurs, trade union representation is not allowed, health and safety regulations are flouted. These things occur throughout the world whatever the economic system. The word "exploitation" has a strong and immediate meaning in such situations. The God of the Bible condemns exploitation and oppression. God's liberation of the Israelites from their oppression served as a paradigm of how God's people should behave towards workers in their midst (Leviticus 25:39–55).

25. Since work is central to God's purpose for humanity, people everywhere have both the obligation and the right to work. Given the broad definition of work suggested above (cf. para 13), the right to work here should be understood as part of the freedom of the individual to contribute to the satisfaction of the needs of the community. It is a freedom right, since work in its widest sense is a form of self-expression. The right involved is the right of the worker to work unhindered. The obligation is on every human being to contribute to the community. It is in this sense that Paul says, "if a man will not work, let him not eat."

26. The right to earn a living would be a positive or sustenance right. Such a right implies the obligation of the community to provide employment opportunities. Employment cannot be guaranteed where rights conflict and resources may be inadequate. However the fact that such a right cannot be enforced does not detract in any way from the obligation to seek the highest level of employment which is consistent with justice and the availability of resources.

Rest and Leisure

27. As the Sabbath commandment indicates, the Biblical concept of rest should not be confused with the modern concept of leisure. Leisure consists of activities that are ends in themselves and therefore intrinsically enjoyable. In many parts of the world for many people, life is "all work and no play." While masses of people are unemployed and thus have only "leisure" millions of people - including children - are often overworked simply to meet their basic survival needs. Meanwhile, especially in economically developed nations, many overwork to satisfy their desire for status.

28. The first pages of the Bible tell us that God rested after creating the universe (Genesis 2:2-3). The sequence of work and rest that we see in God's activity is a pattern for human beings. In that the Sabbath commandment interrupted work with regular periods of rest, it liberates human beings from enslavement to work. The Sabbath erects a fence around human productive activity and serves to protect both human and non-human creation. Human beings have, therefore, both a right and an obligation to rest.

29. Corresponding to the four basic relations in which all people stand (in relationship to non-human creation, to themselves, to other human beings, and to God), there are four activities which we should cultivate in leisure

time. Rest consists in the enjoyment of nature as God's creation, in the free exercise and development of abilities which God has given to each person, in the cultivation of fellowship with one another, and above all, in delight in communion with God.

30. Worship is central to the Biblical concept of rest. In order to be truly who they are, human beings need periodic moments of time in which God's commands concerning their work will recede from the forefront of their consciousness as they adore the God of loving holiness and thank the God of holy love.

31. Those who cannot meet their basic needs without having to forego leisure can be encouraged by the reality of their right to rest. The right to rest implies the corresponding right to sustenance for all those who are willing to work "six days a week" (Exodus 20:9). Modern workaholics whose infatuation with status relegates leisure to insignificance must be challenged by the liberating obligation to rest. What does it profit them to "gain the whole world" if they "forfeit their life" (Mark 8:36)?

POVERTY AND JUSTICE

God and the Poor

32. Poverty was not part of God's original creation, nor will poverty be part of God's restored creation when Christ returns. Involuntary poverty in all its forms and manifestations is a result of the Fall and its consequences. Today one of every five human beings lives in poverty so extreme that their survival is daily in doubt. We believe this is offensive and heart breaking to God.

33. We understand that the God of the Bible is one who in mercy extends love to all. at the same time, we believe that when the poor are oppressed, God is the"defender of the poor" (Psalm 146:7-9). Again and again in every part of Scripture, the Bible expresses God's concern for justice for the poor. Faithful obedience requires that we share God's concern and act on it. "He who oppresses a poor man insults his maker, but he who is kind to the needy honours Him" (Proverbs 14:31). Indeed it is only when we right such injustices that God promises to hear our prayers and worship (Isaiah 58:1-9).

34. Neglect of the poor often flows from greed. Furthermore, the obsessive or careless pursuit of material goods is one of the most destructive idolatries in human history (Ephesians 5:5). It distracts individuals from their duties before God, and corrupts personal and social relationships.

Causes of Poverty

35. The causes of poverty are many and complex. They include the evil that people do to each other, to themselves, and to their environment. The causes of poverty also include the cultural attitudes and actions taken by social, economic, political and religious institutions, that either devalue or waste resources, that erect barriers to economic production, or that fail to

reward work fairly. Furthermore, the forces that cause the perpetuate poverty operate at global, national, local and personal levels. It is also true that a person may be poor because of sickness, mental or physical handicap, childhood, or old age. Poverty is also caused by natural disasters such as earthquakes, hurricanes, floods, and famines.

36. We recognise that poverty results from and is sustained by both constraints on the production of wealth and on the inequitable distribution of wealth and income. We acknowledge the tendency we have had to reduce the causes of poverty to one at the expense of the others. We affirm the need to analyse and explain the conditions that promote the creation of wealth, as well as those that determine the distribution of wealth.

37. We believe it is the responsibility of every society to provide people with the means to live at a level consistent with their standing as persons created in the image of God.

Justice and Poverty.

38 Biblical justice means impartially rendering to everyone their due in conformity with the standards of God's moral law. Paul uses justice (or righteousness) in its most comprehensive sense as a metaphor to describe God's creative and powerful redemptive love. Christ, solely in grace, brought us into God's commonwealth, who were strangers to it and because of sin cut off from it (Romans 1:17-18, 3:21-26; Ephesians 2:4-22). In Biblical passages which deal with the distribution of the benefits of social life, in the context of social conflict and social wrong, justice is related particularly to what is due to groups such as the poor, widows, orphans, resident aliens, wage earners and slaves. The common link among these groups is powerlessness by virtue of economic and social needs. The justice called forth is to restore these groups to the provision God intends for them. God's law expresses this justice and indicates its demands. Further, God's intention is for people to live, not in isolation, but in society. The poor are described as those who are weak with respect to the rest of the community; the responsibility of the community is stated as "to make them strong" so that they can continue to take their place in the community (Leviticus 25:35-36). One of the dilemmas of the poor is their loss of community (Job 22:5; Psalm 107: 4-9, 33-36). Indeed their various needs are those that tend to prevent people from being secure and contributing members of society. One essential characteristic of Biblical justice is the meeting of basic needs that have been denied in contradiction to the standards of Scripture; but further, the Bible gives indication of how to identify which needs are basic. They are those essential, not just for life, but for life in society.

39. Justice requires special attention to the weak members of the community because of their greater vulnerability. In this sense, justice is partial. Nevertheless, the civil arrangements in rendering justice are not to go beyond what is due to the poor or to the rich (Deuteronomy 1:17; Leviticus 19:15). In this sense justice is ultimately impartial. Justice is so fundamental

that it characterises the personal virtues and personal relationships of individuals as they faithfully follow God's standards. Those who violate God's standards, however, receive God's retributive justice, which often removes the offender from society or from the divine community.

40. Justice requires conditions such that each person is able to participate in society in a way compatible with human dignity. Absolute poverty, where people lack even minimal food and housing, basic education, health care, and employment, denies people the basic economic resources necessary for just participation in the community. Corrective action with and on behalf of the poor is a necessary act of justice. This entails responsibilities for individuals, families, churches, and governments.

41. Justice may also require socio-political actions that enable the poor to help themselves and be the subjects of their own development and the development of their communities. We believe that we and the institutions in which we participate are responsible to create an environment of law, economic activity, and spiritual nurture which creates these conditions.

Some Urgent Contemporary Issues

42. Inequitable international economic relations aggravate poverty in poor countries. Many of these countries suffer under a burden of debt service which could only be repaid at an unacceptable price to the poor, unless there is a radical restructuring both of national economic policies and international economic relations. The combination of increasing interest rates and falling commodity prices in the early 1980s has increased this debt service burden. Both lenders and borrowers shared in creating this debt. The result has been increasing impoverishment of the people. Both lenders and borrowers must share responsibility for finding solutions. We urgently encourage governments and international financial institutions to redouble their efforts to find ways to reduce the international indebtedness of the Third World, and to ensure the flow of both private and public productive capital where appropriate.

43. Government barriers to the flow of goods and services often work to the disadvantage of the poor. We particularly abhor the protectionist policies of the wealthy nations which are detrimental to developing countries. Greater freedom and trade between nations is an important part of reducing poverty worldwide.

44. Justice requires that the value of money be reliably known and stable, thus inflation represents poor stewardship and defrauds the nations' citizens. It wastes resources and is particularly harmful to the poor and the powerless. The wealthier members of society find it much easier to protect themselves against inflation than do the poor. Rapid changes in prices drastically affect the ability of the poor to purchase basic goods.

45. Annual global military expenditures equal the annual income of the poorest one-half of the world's people. These vast, excessive military expenditures detract from the task of meeting basic human needs, such as

food, health care, and education. We are encouraged by the possibilities represented by the changes in the USSR and Eastern Europe, and improving relations between east and west. We urge that a major part of the resulting "peace dividend" be used to provide sustainable solutions to the problems of the world's poor.

46. Drug use and trafficking destroys both rich and poor nations. Drug consumption reflects spiritual poverty among the people and societies in which drug use is apparent. Drug trafficking undermines the national economies of those who produce drugs. The economic, social, and spiritual costs of drug use are unacceptable. The two key agents involved in this problem must change: the rich markets which consume drugs and the poorer countries which produce them. Therefore both must urgently work to find solutions. The rich markets which consume drugs must end their demand. And the poorer countries which produce them must switch to other products.

47. We deplore economic systems based on policies, laws, and regulations whose effect is to favour privileged minorities and to exclude the poor from fully legitimate activities. Such systems are not only inefficient, but are immoral as well in that participating in and benefitting from the formal economy depends on conferred privilege of those who have access and influence to public and private institutions rather than on inventiveness and hard work. Actions need to be taken by public and private institutions to reduce and simplify the requirements and costs of participating in the national economy.

48. There is abundant evidence that investment in small scale enterprises run by and or the poor can have a positive impact upon income and job creation for the poor. Contrary to the myths upheld by traditional financial institutions, the poor are often good entrepreneurs and excellent credit risks. We deplore the lack of credit available to the poor in the informal sector. We strongly encourage governments, financial institutions, and Non-Governmental Organisations to redouble their efforts to significantly increase credit to the poor. We feel so strongly about this that a separate statement dedicated to credit-based income generation programmes has been issued by the conference.

FREEDOM, GOVERNMENT, AND ECONOMICS

The Language of Human rights

49. With the United Nations declaration of Human rights, the language of human rights has become pervasive throughout the world. It expresses the urgent plight of suffering people whose humanity is daily being denied them by their oppressors. In some cases rights language has been misused by those who claim that anything they want is theirs "by right". This breadth of application has led some to reject rights as a concept, stating that if everything becomes a right then nothing will be a right, since all rights imply corresponding responsibilities. Therefore it is important to have clear criteria for what defines rights.

Christian Distinctives

50. All human interaction is judged by God and is accountable to God. In seeking human rights we search for an authority or norm which transcends our situation. God is that authority; God's character constitutes that norm. Since human rights are a priori rights, they are not conferred by the society or the state. Rather, human rights are rooted in the fact that every human being is made in the image of God. The deepest ground of human dignity is that while we were yet sinners, Christ died for us (Romans 5:8).

51. In affirmation of the dignity of God's creatures, God's justice for them requires life, freedom, and sustenance. The divine requirements of justice establish corresponding rights for human beings to whom justice is due. The right to life is the most basic human right. God created human beings as free moral agents. As such, they have the right to freedom - e.g., freedom of religion, speech, and assembly. Their freedom, however, is properly used only in dependence on God. It is a requirement of justice that human beings, including refugees and stateless persons, are able to live in society with dignity. Human beings therefore have claim on other human beings for social arrangements that ensure that they have access to the sustenance that makes life in society possible.

52. The fact that in becoming Christians we may choose to forego our rights out of love for others and in trust of God's providential care does not mean that such rights cease to exist. Christians may endure the violation of their rights with great courage but work vigorously for the identical rights of others in similar circumstances. However it may not be appropriate to do so in some circumstances. Indeed this disparity between Christian contentment and campaigning on behalf of others in adverse situations is a witness to the work and love of God.

53. All of us share the same aspirations as human beings to have our rights protected - whether the right to life, freedom, or sustenance. Yet the fact of sin and the conflict of competing human rights means that our aspirations are never completely fulfilled in this life. Through Christ, sin and evil have been conquered. They will remain a destructive force until the consummation of all things. But that in no way reduces our horror at the widespread violation of human rights today.

Democracy

54. As a model, modern political democracy is characterised by limited government of a temporary character, by the division of power within the government, the distinction between state and society, pluralism, the rule of lawn, institutionalisation of freedom rights (including free and regular elections), and a significant amount of non-governmental control of property. We recognise that no political system is directly prescribed by scripture, but we believe that Biblical values and historical experience call Christians to work for the adequate participation of all people in the decision-making processes on questions that affect their lives.

55. We also recognise that simply to vote periodically is not a sufficient expression of democracy. For a society to be truly democratic economic power must be shared widely and class and status distinctions must not be barriers preventing access to economic and social institutions. Democracies are also open to abuse through the very chances which make them democratic. Small, economically powerful groups sometimes dominate the political process. Democratic majorities can be swayed by materialistic, racist, or nationalistic sentiments to engage in unjust policies. The fact that all human institutions are fallen means that the people must be constantly alert to and critical of all that is wrong.

56. We recognise that no particular economic system is directly prescribed by scripture. Recent history suggests that a dispersion of ownership of the means of production is a significant component of democracy. Monopolistic ownership, either by the state, large economic institutions, or oligarchies is dangerous. Widespread ownership, either in a market economy or a mixed system, tends to decentralise power and prevent totalitarianism.

The Concentration of Economic Power

57. Economic power can be concentrated in the hands of a few people in a market economy. When that occurs political decisions tend to be made for economic reasons and the average member of society is politically and economically marginalised. Control over economic life may thus be far removed from a large part of the population. Transnational corporations can also wield enormous influence on some economies. Despite these problems, economic power is diffused within market-oriented economies to a greater extent than in other systems.

58. In centrally planned economies, economic decisions are made for political reasons, people's economic choices are curtailed, and the economy falters. Heavy state involvement and regulation within market economies can also result in concentrations of power that effectively marginalise poorer members of the society. Corruption almost inevitably follows from concentrated economic power. Widespread corruption so undermines society that there is a virtual breakdown of legitimate order.

Capitalism and culture

59. As non-capitalist countries increasingly turn away from central planning and towards the market, the question of capitalism's effect on culture assumes more and more importance. The market system can be an effective means of economic growth, but can, in the process,cause people to think that ultimate meaning is found in the accumulation of more goods. The overwhelming consumerism of Western societies is testimony to the fact that the material success of capitalism encourages forces and attitudes that are decidedly non-Christian. One such attitude is the treatment of workers as simply costs or productive inputs, without recognition of their humanity. There is also the danger that the model of the market, which may work well in economic transactions, will be assumed to be relevant to other areas of life, and people may consequently believe that what the market encourages is therefore best or most true.

The Role of Government

60. Government is designed to serve the purposes of God to foster community, particularly in response to our rebellious nature (Romans 13:1, 4; Psalm 72:1). As an institution administered by human beings, government can exacerbate problems of power, greed, and envy. However, it can, where properly constructed and constrained, serve to limit some of these sinful tendencies. Therefore it is the responsibility of Christians to work for governmental structures that serve justice. Such structures must respect the principle that significant decisions about local human communities are usually best made at a level of government most directly responsible to the people affected.

61. At a minimum, government must establish a rule of law that protects life, secures freedom, and provides basic security. Special care must be taken to make sure the protection of fundamental rights is extended to all members of society, especially the poor and oppressed (Proverbs 31:8-9; Daniel 4:27). Too often government institutions are captured by the economically or socially powerful. Thus, equality before the law fails to exist for those without power. Government must also have regard for economic efficiency and appropriately limit its own scope and action.

62. The provision of sustenance rights is also an appropriate function of government. Such rights must be carefully defined so that government's involvement will not encourage irresponsible behaviour and the breakdown of families and communities. In a healthy society, this fulfilment of rights will be provided through a diversity of institutions so that the government's role will be that of last resort.

Mediating Structures

63. One of the phenomena associated with the modern world is the increasing divide between private and public sectors. The need for a bridge between these two sectors has led to an emphasis on mediating institutions. The neighbourhood, the family, the church, and other voluntary associations are all such institutions. As the early Church did in its context, these institutions provide citizens with many opportunities for participation and leadership. They also provide other opportunities for loyalty in addition to the state and the family. Their role in meeting the needs of members of the community decreases the need for centralised government. They also provide a channel for individuals to influence governments, business, and other large institutions. Therefore Christians should encourage governments everywhere to foster vigorous voluntary associations.

64. The future of poverty alleviation is likely to involve expanded microeconomic income generation programmes and entrepreneurial development of the so-called "informal sector" as it becomes part of the transformed formal economy. In this context, there will not likely be an even greater role for Non-Governmental Organisations. In particular, church bodies will be able to make a significant and creative contribution in partnership with the poor, acting as mediating institutions by virtue of the churches' longstanding grass-roots involvement in local communities.

Conclusion

65. As we conclude, we thank God for the opportunity God has given us to participate in this conference. Through our time together we have been challenged to express our faith in the area of economic life in practical ways. We acknowledge that all too often we have allowed society to shape our views and actions and have failed to apply scriptural teaching in this crucial area of our lives, and we repent.

We now encourage one another to uphold Christian economic values in the face of unjust and subhuman circumstances. We realise, however, that ethical demands are often ineffective because they are reinforced only by individual conscience and that the proclamation of Christian values needs to be accompanied by action to encourage institutional and structural changes which would foster these values in our communities. We will therefore endeavour to seek every opportunity to work for the implementation of the principles outlined in this declaration, in faithfulness to God's calling.

We urge all people, and especially Christians, to adopt stewardship and justice as the guiding principles for all aspects of economic life, particularly for the sake of those who are most vulnerable. These principles must be applied in all spheres of life. They have to do with our use of material resources and lifestyle as well as with the way people and nations relate to one another. With girded loins and burning lamps we wait for the return of our Lord Jesus Christ when justice and peace shall embrace.

Notes

* The Oxford Declaration was first published in *Transformation*, April/June 1990, pp.1-8. It has been republished in Christianity and Economics in the Post-Cold War Era: The Oxford Declaration and Beyond, edited by Herbert Schlossberg, Vinay Samuel and Ronald J Sider (Grand Rapids, Eerdmans, 1994).

1 In January 1987, 36 Christians from all continents and a broad range of professions and socio-political perspectives came together at Oxford to discuss contemporary economic issues in a way that was both faithful to the scriptures and grounded in careful economic analysis. (The papers from that conference were published in *Transformation* 4 [1987], nr. 3.4.) They authorised a three-year process to attempt to draft a comprehensive statement on Christian faith and economics. In this project, groups of economists and theologians met all over the world in regional conferences and addressed issues under four headings: Stewardship and Creation; Work and Leisure; The Definition of Justice and Freedom; Government and Economics. A separate paper on micro-enterprise was also undertaken. These regional discussions and studies were then drawn together to form the issues for analysis and debate at the Second Oxford Conference on January 4-9, 1990.

IO

Trade and Development Report 1996

UNCTAD, Geneva

EDITORS' INTRODUCTION

The 1988 Lambeth Conference spoke of International Debt in its section report on Christianity and the Social Order (Section 73):

"Crippling levels of debt - amounting to some $1000 billion - which add intolerable burdens to the poorer nations of our world, raise sharp moral questions. Debt of this nature creates unhealthy dependencies of the weak upon the powerful, leads to the breakdown of the life of poor communities and threatens the relationships of international politics and finance. It is urgent to find new ways of relieving the problem without crippling the world economy. The practice of borrowing at this level needs boundaries set by moral values. Christians need to recall the meaning of forgiveness and those parts of their history where the Church has sought to protect the poor from exploitation by the rich in matters of debt".

Resolution 36 of the Conference stated:

"This Conference

1   Calls attention to the life and death urgency of the problems of world poverty.

2   Salutes the courage and solidarity of poor people, who at great personal cost, are struggling to achieve their own liberation from poverty and oppression.

3   Calls for an international, co-operating settlement, negotiated by both industrial and developing countries, that will establish policies to reduce interest charges and the level of indebtedness, based on shared responsibility for the world debt and in accordance with Christian and humanitarian principles of economic justice and social and ecological interdependence.

4   Calls on national governments, transnational corporations, the International Monetary Fund and the World Bank together, to re-examine all principles governing trade relationships, the transfer of technology and resources and all loan and aid policies in order to improve the economic

viability and local autonomy of developing countries.
5   Requests these bodies to consider these and other creative ways of involving the global economy over time by
(a) (i) correcting demand imbalances
     (ii) reducing protectionism
     (iii) stabilising exchange rates
     (iv) increasing resource transfers
(b) offering relief from debt incurred with commercial banks in ways that will not leave debtor economies vulnerable to foreign manipulation, by
     (i) lending directly to developing countries at reduced and subsidised interest rates
     (ii) improved rescheduling of existing debt repayments
     (iii) debt conversion arrangements
     (iv) establishing a multilateral body to co-ordinate debt relief
(c) offering relief from official debts incurred with the World Bank and the International Monetary Fund through
     (i) improved rescheduling of existing debt repayment
     (ii) lending on conditions oriented to development objectives
     (iii) refraining from making demands on debtor countries which would endanger the fabric of their national life or cause further dislocation to their essential human services."

The Most Rev Njongonkulu Ndungane in his enthronement sermon as Archbishop of Cape Town in September 1996 proposed that the Church of the Province of Southern Africa add its voice to those calling for the year 2000 to be the year of Jubilee which entails the cancellation of the international debt and redressing the imbalances in the World Economic Order. He said: "There is the awesome burden of the repayment of the international debt which makes it difficult in the extreme for governments to engage in human development programmes. The 1996 United Nations Human Development Report states that between 1990 and 1993, debt servicing costs Sub-Saharan Africa about $13 billion annually - considerably more than its combined spending on education and health. If a question were to be asked as to what use African governments could have made of that $13 billion, the answer would be: it could have been used to meet basic human needs such as health, education, nutrition and reproductive health for everyone in Sub-Saharan Africa whose total annual cost is around $9 billion."

He continued: "In South Africa, the total debt is approximately R311 billion. 20% of South Africa's budget is spent on servicing this debt. This is the second largest national expenditure item on the budget, the first being education. It is clear as daybreak that the South African government's programme of reconstruction and development is being seriously hampered by the servicing of this debt which it has inherited from the apartheid regime.

It is considerations such as these as well as the demands of responsible stewardship of the resources that God has made available to us in this world, that I propose that the Church of the Province of Southern Africa add its voice to those calling for the year 2000 to be the year of Jubilee which entails the cancellation of the international debt and redressing the imbalances in the World Economic Order. Such an action will enable Africa, a continent of ancient ruins, to have an opportunity to make new beginnings for the general well-being of humanity."

We are grateful to the United Nations Conference on Trade and Development for making available to us the latest statement from those in a position to affect the problems of international debt which we reproduce here. This document provides factual information and perspectives which could form the basis for discussion and proposals at the Conference.

1   From *The Truth Shall Make You Free: The Lambeth Conference 1988* (Anglican Consultative Council, 1988).

OFFICIAL DEBT

The severe difficulties that heavily indebted poor countries (HIPCs)[43] continue to experience in servicing their debt and the perception that the debt overhang poses a serious impediment to growth and development have thrust the multilateral debt issue into prominence. Debt owed to multilateral institutions accounts for an important and rising portion of total indebtedness and an even larger share of total debt service for these countries. It has become increasingly clear that existing debt relief mechanisms will not suffice to bring the debt burden of a significant number of these countries to a sustainable level. It is now generally agreed that a lasting solution to their debt problems requires a comprehensive and coordinated approach, involving stronger measures and a sharing of the burden among all creditors, including multilateral financial institutions (MFIs). The framework for action to resolve the debt problems of HIPCs, which was proposed by IMF and the World Bank and welcomed by both the Interim Committee and the Development Committee at their spring 1996 meetings, is an official recognition of the need for a comprehensive debt strategy and represents a commitment to act decisively to ease the burden of multilateral debt. It addresses the concerns of the 29 debt-distressed LDCs which are categorized by IMF/World Bank as HIPCs. The proposal offers hope for LDCs and other poor countries with a proven track record of economic reform and structural adjustment to attain debt sustainability. It is in the interest of all parties concerned that growth in these countries be resumed as rapidly as possible.

Multilateral debt

(a) Recent developments regarding the multilateral debt of HIPCs

In 1994, the total multilateral debt of HIPCs amounted to around $62 billion, of which almost 70 per cent was concessional. With multilateral debt accounting for the bulk of new loans, its share continued to rise, reaching over 25 per cent of the total external debt of $241 billion in 1994. Multilateral debt service in that year amounted to over $4 billion, representing over 46 per cent of total debt service (see table 19), or about 9 per cent of exports of goods and services.

The grave difficulties which these countries continue to encounter in servicing their debt are reflected in actual debt service payments to all creditors, amounting in 1994 to just over one third of debt service due.[44] As a result, arrears continued to mount, reaching $74 billion by the end of that year. However, since priority has been given to the servicing of multilateral debt, the problem of arrears is relatively much greater for bilateral debt. Although practically all HIPCs registered arrears, those with protracted arrears (i.e. of six months or more) with the World Bank and IMF number only four. As shown in table 19, debt profiles vary considerably among countries, with multilateral debt accounting for over 50 per cent of total debt in 13 cases.

As for the structure of multilateral debt by source, the World Bank was the largest creditor in 1994, accounting for 55 per cent of the total; followed by the regional development banks (22 per cent) and IMF (12 per cent).[45] Net transfers from multilateral financial institutions to the group as a whole have consistently been positive and substantial, totalling over $2 billion in 1994.

(b) Current policies affecting the burden of multilateral debt[46]

Three MFIs - the World Bank, IMF and the African Development Bank - dominate the multilateral debt scene. Together, they accounted for over 82 per cent of the multilateral debt of HIPCs in 1994, so that action taken on their debt would be critical to the resolution of the multilateral debt problem. In addition to measures by MFIs, an innovative scheme entirely financed by bilateral donors was recently established in Uganda, involving the creation of a multilateral debt fund (see box 1).

(i) Increased concessionality of debt

The soft windows of MFIs were established to support the development efforts of low-income countries. The debt crisis reinforced the importance of and the need for providing financial support, on terms more closely suited to debtors' capacity to pay, not only for development projects but also for implementing policy reforms and overcoming chronic balance-of-payments difficulties. This is a good preventive approach, and for those countries already encountering serious debt-servicing problems improving the concessionality of debt has eased their burden, as it led in effect to implicit refinancing of loans contracted on near-commercial terms with funds secured on softer terms. This was the basic strategy adopted by the Bretton Woods institutions to provide debt relief.

The International Development Association (IDA), the soft window of the World Bank, is the most important channel for providing highly concessional financing to low-income countries. In 1994, it accounted for 44 per cent of the multilateral debt of HIPCs. The cessation of non-concessional IBRD lending in almost all of these countries and the sustained rise in IDA disbursements have resulted in significant positive net transfers from the Bank. Net transfers from the World Bank rose sharply (by 78 per cent) in 1994, reaching $1.4 billion.

DEBT STATISTICS FOR HEAVILY INDEBTED POOR COUNTRIES, 1994
(Millions of dollars and percentage shares)

Country	Debt			Debt Service					Net transfers on debt-creating cash flows	
	Total	Multilateral	% share of multilateral	Total	Multilateral	% share of multilateral	Debt service due	Arrears	Total	Multi-lateral
All HIPCs	240725	62157	25.8	9085	4223	46.5	28654	74017	2370	2174
Angola	10609	159	1.5	74	-	-	1085	4747	69	33
Benin	1619	856	52.9	41	22	53.7	52	42	86	94
Bolivia	4749	2539	53.5	343	215	62.7	426	137	131	128
Burkina Faso	1126	927	82.3	44	37	84.1	43	47	100	88
Burundi	1126	937	83.2	41	30	73.2	41	13	16	19
Cameroon	7275	1664	22.8	374	237	63.4	1068	883	88	71
Central African Republic	891	632	70.9	23	20	87.0	80	65	20	38
Chad	816	633	77.6	15	11	73.3	25	49	55	60
Congo	5275	717	13.6	655	174	31.4	1524	1076	-262	85
Côte d'Ivoire	18452	3695	20.0	1274	606	47.6	2144	3646	-919	154
Equatorial Guinea	291	120	41.2	2	2	75.0	22	110	15	5
Ethiopia	5059	2196	43.4	92	50	54.3	414	1022	178	216
Ghana	5389	3370	62.5	343	165	48.1	322	150	182	27
Guinea	3104	1376	44.8	97	36	37.1	244	559	77	115
Guinea-Bissau	816	369	45.2	7	4	57.1	69	222	19	9
Guyana	2038	787	38.6	97	66	68.0	165	148	-51	-20
Honduras	4418	2171	49.1	433	283	65.4	468	217	36	-88
Kenya	7273	3159	43.4	888	251	28.3	1356	100	-597	-62
Lao People's Dem. Rep.	2080	576	27.7	20	7	35.0	20	-	56	59
Liberia	2056	768	37.4	15	15	100.0	160	1469	-14	-15
Madagascar	4134	1683	40.7	60	49	81.7	419	1425	-	21
Mali	2781	1340	48.2	130	61	46.9	196	406	21	94
Mauritania	2326	916	39.4	105	70	66.7	188	364	42	60
Mozambique	5491	1266	23.1	91	36	39.6	361	1159	191	226
Myanmar	6502	1458	22.4	173	35	20.2	577	1778	-111	-23
Nicaragua	11019	1363	12.4	183	70	38.3	1463	5816	-65	132
Niger	1570	688	56.6	66	31	47.0	242	65	7	49
Nigeria	33485	4807	14.4	1916	812	42.4	5799	10238	-1818	-201
Rwanda	964	762	79.9	6	6	85.9	32	70	-18	14
Sao Tome and Principe	252	167	66.3	3	2	85.2	9	58	7	12
Senegal	3678	2075	50.4	197	154	78.2	465	289	-74	28
Sierra Leone	1392	479	34.4	148	124	84.9	186	90	38	71
Somalia	2616	938	35.9	-	-	-	171	1519	-	-
Sudan	17710	3016	17.0	1	-	-	1271	13390	7	7
Togo	1455	764	52.5	24	21	87.5	112	196	44	35
Uganda	3473	2411	69.4	152	104	68.4	173	313	186	201
United Rep. of Tanzania	7442	2855	39.4	174	114	65.5	548	2472	108	91
Vietnam	25115	512	2.0	300	13	4.3	2456	9494	88	291
Yemen	5959	1207	20.3	145	61	42.1	360	2550	13	53
Zaire	12336	2804	22.7	66	7	10.6	1294	5539	-201	-5
Zambia	6573	2794	42.5	369	223	60.4	602	1984	-120	2

Source: UNCTAD secretariat calculations, based on World Debt Tables 1996 (Washington D.C., 1996), Vol. 2.

BOX 1

THE UGANDA MULTILATERAL DEBT FUND

Even after a commercial debt buy-back and a stock-of-debt operation on Naples terms, Uganda's debt situation remained unsustainable because of the heavy burden of multilateral debt, which accounted for almost 70 per cent of its total debt and debt service in 1994. With the financial support of a group of donors (Austria, Denmark, Netherlands, Sweden and Switzerland), the Uganda Multilateral Debt Fund (UMDF) was established in July 1995. The creation of UMDF involved a comprehensive assessment of debt sustainability in which the Government of Uganda played a leading role, in consultation with the donors and the Bretton Woods institutions. It was made possible by Uganda's good policy track record, and donor contributions are contingent on continued adjustment efforts. To further safeguard against moral hazard, there are specific commitments on fiscal and reserves management, as well as limits on new borrowings.

It needed only pledges in principle from three major donors of around $30 million to launch the Fund. This had a catalytic effect in generating pledges from other donors. However, the request for contributions from IMF and the World Bank was not successful. The UMDF will pay a portion of the debt service as it falls due, with donors providing an up-front contribution, to the extent possible, at the beginning of each financial year. Allowance has been made to provide donors flexibility with regard to payment methods and timing. The Fund is managed by the Government of Uganda. Such responsibility has encouraged improvements in debt management as well as in fiscal and reserves management. Coordination is achieved through the annual Consultative Group meeting and local quarterly meetings called by the Government, with the participation of donors and the Bretton Woods institutions.

The UMDF is the first country fund which focuses on multilateral debt relief. Its efficient payments method has avoided even transitory arrears. As for the possible applicability of this approach to other LDCs or to other poor countries, it would require the existence of a global coordination mechanism to establish clear criteria of need and adjustment track records and, of course, willing donors. In some donor countries, such as those that have launched this fund, there is strong political support for debt relief based on the perception that the debt overhang is a key barrier to development in some poor countries, and that debt relief is more valuable than other forms of aid because removing the overhang would improve growth prospects for debtors and reimbursement prospects for creditors.

The IMF/World Bank proposed framework for action to resolve the debt problems of HIPCs includes as options the creation of a special (multi-country) trust fund and/or single-country trust funds to which multilateral development banks and bilateral donors could contribute. Thus, country funds similar to UMDF could very well fit into this scheme.

Source: M. Martin, "A Multilateral Debt Facility: Global and National", Report to the Group of 24, 31 March 1996, to be reproduced in UNCTAD, *International Monetary and Financial Issues for the 1990s*, Vol. VIII (forthcoming).

The Enhanced Structural Adjustment Facility (ESAF) is regarded by IMF as the centrepiece of its strategy to resolve the debt problems of HIPCs. For these countries as a whole, concessional debt to the Fund increased substantially over the past two years - by 24 per cent in 1994 and a further 41 per cent in 1995. This led to a largely enhanced share of concessional debt in total IMF debt in 1995, of 72 per cent, compared with 56 per cent in 1993. It also led to the reversal of the protracted negative net transfers from the Fund, which had lasted for a decade (1984-1993). These countries accounted for a large proportion of total IMF concessional lending, reaching 69 per cent in 1995. Current terms for ESAF loans are an interest rate of 0.5 per cent, a maturity of 10 years and a grace period of five-and-a-half years. The concessionality of ESAF loans is expected to be enhanced in the context of the proposed HIPC debt initiative, through extension of maturities and grace periods.

In the face of serious budgetary constraints in major donor countries, the replenishment of the soft windows of MFIs has been under threat. The process of negotiating IDA-11 replenishment, which covers fiscal years (FY) 1997-1999, proved lengthy and complex. The decision by the United States Congress to appropriate only $700 million for FY1996 instead of the $1.25 billion annual commitment for IDA-10 resulted in a conflict between the traditional burden-sharing formula and adequate replenishment. This led to agreement on the adoption of extraordinary measures in Tokyo in March 1996, including the creation of a one-year Emergency Trust Fund for FY1997 to which all donors, except the United States, are to contribute over SDR 2 billion while the United States clears its outstanding IDA-10 commitments. The United States will be excluded from decision making and from procurement contracts for activities financed by the Emergency Trust Fund. Subsequently, there will be a two-year replenishment of IDA's general resources, to which all donors will contribute a total of SDR 5 billion. Another SDR 7.5 billion will come from past donor contributions, reflows and IBRD transfers, resulting in a package totalling close to SDR 14.5 billion over FY1997-1999. While less than originally hoped for, this amount will nevertheless allow a continuation of IDA activities at currently planned levels, although estimated contingency requirements are largely unfunded. However the IDA-11 replenishment represents a significant decline from that of IDA-10 of SDR 16 billion which had been agreed to in December 1992. The drop in donors' contributions is substantial, from SDR 13 billion to SDR 7 billion. The latter amount is significantly less than what IDA is likely to require in the future, even after taking into account increasing reflows.

The Enhanced Structural Adjustment Facility, too, faces funding problems. At the October 1995 meeting of the Interim Committee, there was consensus on the establishment of a self-sustained ESAF. The Facility's existing resources are expected to last up to 1999 and it is projected that by 2005 there will be enough resources to finance lending of about SDR 0.8 billion a year on a self-sustaining basis. However, for the interim period 2000-2004, there is a need to secure financing for annual loan commitments of about SDR 1 billion and associated subsidy requirements totalling SDR 2.1 billion. Among the options proposed to finance the principal component are use of IMF's General Resources Account and further borrowing by the ESAF Trust from bilateral sources. As for the subsidy, the following possibilities, which could be combined, were mentioned: bilateral contributions; investment income on the profits from a modest sale of IMF gold; use of resources in the Second Special Contingent Account (SCA-2), with these resources first refunded to member countries and then rechannelled to the Fund; and limited early use of amounts accumulating in the ESAF Reserve Account, which would imply a lower level of self-sustained ESAF operations.[47]

The funding impasse over the seventh replenishment of the African Development Fund, the soft window of the African Development Bank (AfDB), finally ended in May 1996 with an agreed replenishment of around $2.6 billion, which is $400 million short of the amount requested. The impasse lasted for more than two years as donors wanted assurance of tighter credit policies and management controls. There has been no new loan approval from the African Development Fund since 1994. The payment of sums pledged was made conditional on the Bank's restructuring and continued implementation of recommended reforms. The Bank recently adopted a credit policy based on World Bank criteria, which would restrict lending to low-income countries to soft loans and have the effect that only 12 countries would be eligible for non-concessional loans. However, private sector projects assessed to have a commercial rate of return can be provided loans on non-concessional terms in any African country. The new credit policy should help reconcile the imbalance between the degree of concessionality of loans and income levels of borrowers.

(ii) Other measures

The Rights Accumulation Programme (RAP) was introduced by IMF in 1990 for countries with protracted arrears to the Fund at the end of 1989. In accordance with a phased schedule, a country can accumulate rights to future drawings of Fund resources up to the amount of arrears outstanding at the beginning of the programme, while establishing a track record on policy performance. Zambia was the third country to have successfully completed a RAP in December 1995, following Peru and Sierra Leone. Facilitated by bridging finance provided by several donors, Zambia cleared its $1.2 billion arrears with the Fund, thereby considerably reducing the total of outstanding arrears to the Fund, since Zambia had the second largest arrears. There remain, however, four LDCs (Liberia, Somalia, Sudan and Zaire) with substantial arrears totaling almost $2.8 billion in January 1996 and accounting for virtually all arrears to the Fund. Sudan's arrears amounted to $1.6 billion, representing 55 per cent of the total. The World Bank has a similar progamme, but arrears of the same four countries were much smaller, amounting to $415 million at the end of FY 1995 and comprising 17 per cent of total arrears to the Bank. Arrears with the African Development Bank, currently running at around $800 million, remain an acute problem. In May

1996, 24 countries were in default to the Bank,[48] of which 6 countries alone Zaire, Congo, Cameroon, Angola, Liberia and Somalia – accounted for 75 per cent of the total. In its effort to control arrears, AfDB recently approved the following measures: tightening the policy on sanctions; systematic application of directives on loan cancellation; and enhanced coordination with the Bretton Woods institutions.

It should be noted that the settlement of protracted multilateral arrears since 1990 has depended critically on bilateral financial support, through loans, grants, Paris Club reschedulings and bridge financing. This has been the case for countries with large financing requirements relative to quotas and those that have cleared arrears without recourse to the RAP. Support groups have typically been led by one or two creditor countries with particularly strong ties to the debtor. For example, a support group provided $65 million in grants to help Haiti clear its arrears to IMF and other multilateral institutions in December 1994.[49]

The Fifth Dimension facility of the World Bank, which is largely financed through IDA reflows, allocated supplemental IDA resources of $178 million in FY1995 to 12 adjusting HIPCs, in order to assist them in meeting interest payments on their outstanding IBRD debt.

(c) A comprehensive approach to the debt problems of HIPCs

At the start of the debt crisis in the early 1980s, the prevailing view among official creditors was that the problem was one of liquidity. The strategy adopted was continued financial flows in conjunction with adjustment programmes to restore growth and debt servicing capacity, together with refinancing and rescheduling provided by bilateral creditors. In time it became evident that the problem was one of solvency and that the debt overhang was hampering development efforts. The most direct means of eliminating the overhang was, of course, debt reduction. While originally resisted by bilateral creditors, eventually debt reduction became an accepted principle of debt negotiations in the context of the Brady Plan deals for commercial bank debt and reschedulings on Toronto terms since 1988 within the framework of the Paris Club for official bilateral debt. This strategy, combined with sustained adjustment efforts, proved effective in resolving the debt problems of middle-income countries, but the situation of the heavily indebted poor countries continued to deteriorate, even in several countries pursuing policies acknowledged as sound. The low level of development in most of these countries, characterized by structural rigidities, weak institutions and administration, poorly functioning markets, and deficiencies in skills and infrastructure, prevented a rapid and strong response to reform efforts. There were other impediments to growth, such as adverse terms of trade and climatic conditions and, in some countries, poor implementation of adjustment programmes and the crippling effects of civil strife. Concern over the continuing plight of poor countries led to substantial cancellation of ODA debts by some donors and the adoption by Paris Club creditors of London terms in December 1991 and of Naples terms in December 1994 (see subsection 2(a) below on the Paris Club terms). However, studies on the impact of the Naples terms, including the assessment provided in *TDR 1995*, indicate that for a significant number of countries, even with the full implementation of the Naples terms, the debt situation would remain unsustainable mainly on account of the sheer burden of their multilateral debt as well as of non-Paris Club bilateral debt.

There has been growing pressure for stronger action from MFIs. The implicit refinancing of non-concessional debts by loans on concessional terms, while leading to some reduction in the present value of the debt, offers no exit prospect and would not resolve the overhang problem. Moreover, pressure to lend to prevent the build-up of arrears could distort lending decisions. The strategy adopted also runs the risk of an allocation pattern favouring countries with large multilateral debt and detrimental to countries that have been able to manage their debt well. The existing schemes, which involve contributions to soft windows and debt relief facilities and also the creation of support groups, absorb a large volume of bilateral resources. These resources have lately been under increasing budgetary constraints, with a risk of diverting scarce development funds for debt relief. The focus on multilateral debt has also raised the issue of the preferred creditor status of MFIs. This status is widely acknowledged, but there are different interpretations of what it implies. For MFIs, it means exemption of multilateral debt from debt rescheduling and reduction. The application of this principle has resulted in growing arrears on bilateral debt, despite write-offs and the provision by many bilateral donors of new financing on a purely grant basis to poor countries, in order to avoid the consequences of being in arrears on multilateral debt, particularly that owed to the Bretton Woods institutions.[50]

It has become evident that the solution to the debt problems of HIPCs requires bolder measures, going beyond the existing framework. The fragmented approach used so far has clearly not worked satisfactorily. An effective debt strategy needs to be comprehensive, covering all components of debt, and should involve equitable burden sharing among all creditors, including MFIs. Such an approach would require coordination among all parties concerned.

(i) Debt sustainability analysis

At their meetings in October 1995, the Interim Committee and the Development Committee requested IMF and the World Bank to continue their work on how to address the debt problems of HIPCs, including country-specific analysis of debt sustainability. In response to the request, the two institutions have recently undertaken a detailed and comprehensive analysis of debt sustainability for a number of countries. Debt sustainability implies the ability to meet fully current and future debt obligations without unduly compromising growth. The methodology employed involves the choice of a time horizon, projections of principal macroeconomic variables and capital inflows, and focusing on the evolution of two key debt indicators. Threshold ranges of 20-25 per cent for the ratio of debt service to exports and 200-250 per cent for the ratio of the present value of debt to exports were used as indicators of sustainability. These conventional thresholds served as a starting point but other risk indicators[51] were also considered, especially in borderline cases. The fiscal burden of external debt service is particularly relevant for HIPCs, as their debt is primarily public debt and past experience with debt crises indicates that, in a number of countries, the principal problem has been the fiscal burden rather than balance-of-payments difficulties. Recent debt burden indicators for HIPCs are presented in table 20. During 1992-1994, only 5 of the 41 countries had, on average, a ratio of present value of debt to exports of less than 200 per cent, and only 6 had ratios of debt service to exports lower than the threshold range. For the fiscal indicators, 1994 scheduled debt service was greater than 50 per cent of government current expenditure in 22 countries and represented over 50 per cent of government revenue in 25 countries. In 13 countries, it even exceeded total government revenue. Current debt burdens are clearly unsustainable for most HIPCs. However, debt sustainability prospects are likely to evolve, and the question is whether with the full use of existing mechanisms the debt burden will reach sustainable levels within a reasonable period.

The preliminary results of the debt sustainability analysis indicate that the situation of eight countries has been classified as "unsustainable". These are the counties with debt indicators remaining above threshold ranges for more than 10 years despite adherence to sound policies and full use of existing debt relief mechanisms. Twelve other countries face a heavy debt and debt service burden in the medium term; for them judgment on sustainability would depend on country-specific risk factors.[52]

(ii) A framework for action

The IMF and the World Bank proposed a framework for action to resolve the debt problems of HIPCs for discussion at the April 1996 meetings of the Interim and Development Committees. The two Committees welcomed the proposed framework and endorsed the following six principles to guide such action: (1) the objective should be to target overall debt sustainability on a case-by-case basis; (2) action should be envisaged only when the debtor has shown, through a track record, the ability to put to good use whatever exceptional support is provided; (3) new measures should build, as much as possible, on existing mechanisms; (4) additional action should be coordinated among all creditors involved, with broad and equitable participation; (5) actions by multilateral creditors should preserve their financial integrity and preferred creditor status; and (6) new external finance for the countries concerned should be on appropriately concessional terms.

TABLE 20 **DEBT BURDEN INDICATORS FOR HEAVILY INDEBTED POOR COUNTRIES, 1992-1994**
(percentage)

| | 1992–1994[a] | | | | | 1994 | |
| | Debt to exports | | Debt to GNP | | | Scheduled debt service to | |
	Nominal value	*Present value*	*Nominal value*	*Present value*[b]	*Debt service to exports*	*current expenditure*	*Government revenue*
Angola	302	278	204	188	32	63	98
Benin	272	142	82	43	11	45	46
Bolivia	457	332	85	62	46	35	31
Burkina Faso	201	104	38	20	12	24	28
Burundi	891	388	111	48	40	31	33
Cameroon	303	250	79	65	36	68	111
Central African Republic	464	243	79	41	22	39	68
Chad	400	195	70	34	13	23	48
Congo	434	370	292	249	52	47	63
Côte d'Ivoire	557	486	263	228	64	79	91
Equatorial Guinea	435	308	177	126	14	105	111
Ethiopia	608	383	77	49	38	30	31
Ghana	392	242	84	52	27	37	29
Guinea	402	255	94	59	31	82	74
Guinea-Bissau	1934	1280	328	217	106	123	144
Guyana	479	345	563	405	31	102	92
Honduras	347	271	134	104	41	65	54
Kenya	307	225	114	84	39	36	29
Lao People's Democratic Rep.	791	214	149	41	7	6	6
Liberia	374	339	142	128	8	-	-
Madagascar	694	495	160	114	71	100	165
Mali	523	280	115	63	31	65	75
Mauritania	469	327	226	158	60	113	87
Mozambique	1367	1030	444	337	95	141	183
Myanmar	600	442	38	28	32	6	7
Nicaragua	2879	2579	604	720	172	409	415
Niger	544	322	82	48	45	52	110
Nigeria	277	250	109	99	38	75	105
Rwanda	1142	533	93	44	47	22	80
Sao Tome and Principe	2082	1101	788	418	97	78	183
Senegal	253	166	77	50	23	48	50
Sierra Leone	835	637	203	156	93	99	111
Somalia	4711	3745	321	254	150	-	-
Sudan	3384	3057	188	169	87	196	189
Togo	367	226	112	69	25	54	99
Uganda	1285	733	99	56	89	33	31
United Republic of Tanzania	1005	719	317	228	79	62	74
Vietnam	638	524	198	162	44	17	15
Yemen	239	188	176	139	30	12	24
Zaire	706	594	136	114	46	624	608
Zambia	592	465	217	170	49	152	186

Source: World Bank, *World Debt Tables, 1996* (Washington D.C., 1996), Vol.1; IMF, *Official Financing for Developing Countries,* Washington D.C. December 1995.
Note: Exports include goods and services.
a Average of three annual ratios.
b The present value of debt takes account of different borrowing terms and is calculated by discounting future debt service, defined as the sum of interest payments and principal repayments over the next 40 years. The discount rates used are the interest rates charged by the OECD countries for officially supported export credits (Commercial Interest Reference Rates), except for IBRD loans and IDA credits, which are discounted using the latest IBRD lending rates, and obligations to IMF, which are discounted at the SDR lending rate.

The Committees also agreed that further action beyond existing mechanisms was needed, including contributions by MFIs from their own resources, contributions by bilateral donors and appropriate action by the Paris Club and by other creditors. They requested IMF and the Bank, in close collaboration with other concerned parties, to put forward specific proposals as soon as possible, with the aim of reaching a decision by the next IMF/World Bank Annual Meetings, to be held in October 1996.[53] At the Lyons Summit in June 1996, the G-7 also acknowledged the need for additional action, in particular to reduce debts owed to multilateral institutions and non-Paris Club bilateral creditors. Paris Club creditors were urged to go beyond the Naples terms, where they deemed appropriate. The G-7 looked forward to a concrete solution being agreed to by next autumn at the latest.[54]

The proposed framework for action offers eligible countries a commitment by the international community to ease their debt burden in order to bring about debt sustainability, on the basis of an extended period of proven policy performance. It involves two stages. The first stage would build on the existing three-year track record needed to qualify for a stock-of-debt operation from the Paris Club and would involve the use of existing mechanisms for concessional financing and debt relief. At the end of the first stage, a comprehensive assessment would be made of a country's debt situation and prospects for sustainability. If the analysis suggested that the stock-of-debt operation would not produce a sustainable situation, an additional three-year track record would be needed to qualify for comprehensive treatment of the stock of debt under the HIPC initiative. A consultative group meeting would be convened to agree on a financing plan and identify required additional relief. From the beginning of the second stage, bilateral and commercial creditors, multilateral institutions and also bilateral donors could provide enhanced assistance. At the end of the second stage, the Paris Club would agree on a stock-of-debt operation with increased concessionality and the MFIs would undertake to reduce the present value of their claims to a level consistent with overall debt sustainability.

At least 8, and as many as 20, countries could qualify for additional assistance on the basis of the debt sustainability analysis described above. Once an internationally approved programme, within the proposed framework, has been adopted, potential candidates will have two years in which to participate, after which there would be a review to determine whether the programme should be extended in time so as to include other eligible HIPC's.

An illustrative IMF/World Bank costing exercise shows that of the 19 potentially eligible countries (excluding Sudan), 13 would need additional debt relief (beyond current mechanisms) under the initiative to reduce their present value of debt-to-export ratios to below 200 per cent by their completion dates. A broad estimate of the cost of such relief is $5.6 billion in present value terms. Should official bilateral and commercial creditors provide up to 90 per cent reduction on eligible debt, the cost to multilateral creditors would be $2 billion.

If they granted up to 80 per cent debt reduction, the cost would be $3.2 billion. Estimated total costs would rise to $7.7 billion with nominal export growth two percentage points lower than the baseline growth. Costs would be much higher if Liberia, Sudan and Somalia were included.

This is the first concrete proposal for multilateral debt action agreed to by both IMF and the World Bank. It represents an important change in their official position, in that they now accept that the multilateral debt problem requires measures beyond current schemes. This is a most welcome initiative. However, close attention will need to be given to the following specific features of the framework for action to ensure a lasting and rapid solution to the debt crisis.

Debt sustainability: The assessment of debt sustainability is expected to play a key role in determining country eligibility and the amount of relief to be provided. A number of studies presented empirical evidence suggesting threshold levels for debt indicators lower than those used in the debt sustainability analysis of 20–25 per cent for the ratio of debt service to exports and 200–250 per cent for the ratio of the present value of the debt to exports.[55] In view of their importance in the proposed initiative, great care must be taken in establishing such thresholds so as to ensure that countries following sound policies will not revert to a crisis situation some time after the conclusion of the programme. The choice of the time horizon for reaching sustainability is also an important factor in determining eligibility. A 10-year period appears too long in view of the fact that many HIPCs have already been in an unsustainable situation for some considerable time.

The highly uncertain nature of projections of relevant economic variables and the wide margins of error to which such projections are normally subject call for great care to be exercised in the assumptions to be made on, for example export growth and capital flows, which have a bearing on future debt indicators.

• *Required track record and the timing of debt reduction:* A satisfactory policy track record by the debtor is clearly an essential ingredient in any new approach. However, some flexibility in the application of the requirement of a track record over a six-year period before the final debt settlement, as well as in the timing of enhanced debt relief, may be desirable as there will be gains to all from assisting eligible HIPCs in resuming growth and normal debtor/creditor relations as rapidly as possible.

• *Contributions of individual MFIs:*[56] Each multilateral institution is expected to contribute in broad proportion to the present value of its outstanding exposure to the countries involved, as of the start of the second stage. An approach indicated is for MFIs to choose from a menu of options to reduce the burden of their claims. This menu could include the provision of grants to pay a portion of the multilateral debt service as it falls due or pre-pay part of the outstanding stock at the completion date; and/or the provision of concessional funding in greater amounts and with enhanced concessionality. While there appears to be logic and equity in this proportionality, as it implies that each institution would be assuming responsibility for past lending decisions, the capacity to offer relief varies among MFIs. Some may be in a comparatively weak position and may, therefore, need support should difficulties arise in meeting their expected contributions.

(d) Financing multilateral debt relief

In order to avoid introducing distortions in the country allocation of development assistance it is essential that the resources underpinning any scheme within the framework described above be additional. Additionality implies the release of funds which are not already intended to be used for development purposes. Additionality could also be achieved by creating new resources such as through a special issue of SDRs. Alternatively part of a general allocation of SDRs could be set aside for multilateral debt relief. However, there is little political support for the SDR options. A special issue would require amending the IMF Articles of Agreement. Moreover, the use of SDRs carries market-related interest rates, so that there would still be a problem of financing interest subsidies.

Concerns have been raised with regard to the heavy burden imposed on bilateral donors by existing debt relief schemes especially in the light of the fiscal constraints they confront. These restraints have led to growing demands for greater contributions from MFIs through the use of their own resources. The HIPC initiative is likely to strengthen these demands, since it calls for substantial additional efforts from bilateral creditors with respect to bilateral debt. However, any proposal concerning the use of MFIs' resources must ensure that the financial integrity of the institutions is preserved and that no prejudice to their credit rating would result. Among the various measures proposed which would meet the additionality criterion and are unlikely to affect the financial integrity of the institutions are:

• *Sale of a portion of IMF gold reserves:* IMF's contribution to reducing the debt burden of HIPCs is expected to involve ESAF, and it is therefore important that ESAF be placed on a sound financial footing. The financing of the continuation of ESAF had been under discussion even before the HIPC initiative was put forward. For this purpose, the Managing Director of IMF has proposed the sale of a minor portion (around 5 per cent) of the IMF gold stock and investing the profits from the sale. The Fund holds more than 103 million fine ounces of gold, which are valued in its accounts at around SDR 35 per ounce. The current market price for gold is about $380 –$390 per ounce. The investment income from the proposed gold sale would enable it to finance half of the required resources for the subsidy account needed to sustain a volume of operations of SDR 1 billion per year for the period 2000-2004. To avoid disruptions in the gold market, the sale could be phased, as was done during the previous gold sales to finance the Trust Fund.[57] To allay fears that such a gold sale might set a precedent for future sales for less legitimate purposes and in order to reach a solution, it has been proposed to formally limit the amount of gold reserves that IMF can sell by amending the Articles of Agreement. At the Lyons Summit, the G-7 called on the Fund to consider optimizing its reserves management in order to facilitate the financing of ESAF.

As for IMF's direct contributions to the HIPC initiative, various options involving ESAF are being considered to reduce the present value of its claims. This is expected to be achieved largely through greater concessionality in ESAF lending to eligible countries by extending maturities and grace periods. The proposed gold sales would provide some margin to accommodate part of the costs of the Fund's contribution to the initiative, assuming that bilateral donors provide one half of the subsidy requirement for the interim period. While in the past the subsidy account was largely financed by donors, some of them have expressed reservations in connection with financing the interim ESAF.

• *The use of net income, surplus and reserves of multilateral development banks (MDBs):* The principal mechanism for MDBs' participation in the HIPC initiative is through the creation of trust funds (multi-country and/or single-country funds), to which both MDBs and bilateral donors can contribute. The World Bank is considering the provision of grants to the trust fund from allocations of IBRD net income and/or surplus. In that event additionality would not be clear-cut. The net income of IBRD for FY1990-1995 averaged over $1.2 billion per year. The net income for a particular year is subsequently allocated to maintaining a target reserves-to-loans ratio; making transfers to IDA and the Debt Reduction Facility[58] and transfers for similar purposes; and to surplus. The surplus consists of earnings from prior years, which are retained until a decision is made on their disposition or conditions for specified uses have been met. In FY1995, the surplus amounted to $226 million. To ensure additionality, allocation for the HIPC trust fund needs to be associated with changes in reserves allocation or with raising net income through, for example, cutting costs. Reserves have increased significantly since 1990, particularly in the last two years, both in absolute and in relative terms. The reserves-to-loans ratio, which was 10.8 per cent in FY1990, rose to 14.3 per cent in FY1995. Reserves amounted to over $17 billion on 30 June 1995. A number of financial analysts consider the Bank's reserve policies as excessively conservative, especially as, in addition to reserves, it has loan-loss provisions equal to 3 per cent of total loans outstanding plus the present value of guarantees. These provisions amounted to more than $3.7 billion at the end of FY1995. There is, therefore, considerable room for the use of reserves to finance multilateral debt relief, although such use could affect the Bank's earnings, as they are also a source of income. Among the other measures proposed by the World Bank to contribute to the HIPC initiative at the second stage are: supplemental IDA allocations over and above basic IDA allocations to ensure positive net transfers; and the selective use of IDA grants to prevent an increase in the present value of the debt due to the Bank as a percentage of exports. These measures involving the use of IDA resources would not be additional, but would certainly provide relief and programme support to beneficiaries. The management of the Bank has proposed the allocation of $500 million in 1996 to the debt relief initiative and substantial amounts in subsequent years. It is expected that the overall contribution of the World Bank will be of the order of $2 billion.

(e) Conclusion

A lasting solution to the debt problems of poor countries must address both long-term and immediate needs. For the long term, it is important to provide sufficient development finance on terms and levels consistent with the recipient's capacity to pay. This can be achieved through the adequate replenishment of the soft windows of MFIs, which would benefit all low-income countries. The difficulties encountered recently in connection with the replenishment of the soft windows raise concerns about the longer-term prospects of multilateral development assistance.

For a significant number of heavily indebted poor countries with an unsustainable debt burden, a special mechanism would be needed to address their debt overhang problems immediately and to ensure debt sustainability for the future, as existing schemes are clearly inadequate to deal with their critical situation. The framework for action proposed by IMF and the World Bank provides a comprehensive and coordinated approach to resolve their debt problems and is guided by sound principles. However, some flexibility in the application of certain conditions determining country eligibility, as well as in the timing of enhanced multilateral action, may be justified to ensure a lasting and rapid solution to the debt crisis. The differences that have arisen concerning contributions of various creditors also need to be ironed out, so as to arrive at an equitable burden-sharing arrangement that is acceptable to all. Financing such contributions should be based on additionality of resources to prevent further diversion of scarce development funds for debt relief. Furthermore, it is important to define clearly the modalities of the various contributions and how coordination among all the parties concerned could best take place. The problems of some MFIs in meeting expected financial contributions must also be addressed. It is urgent to formulate a workable plan of action for decision at the Annual Meetings of IMF and the World Bank in October 1996.

The severity of the situation faced by a number of heavily indebted poor countries calls for additional efforts from all parties concerned. For eligible debtors continued strong commitment to reform would be required not only to safeguard against moral hazard, but also, and above all, to enable them to create the right conditions for sustained growth, thus ensuring the successful resolution of the debt crisis.

BOX 2 **MEASURING CONCESSIONALITY**

In the past few years the Paris Club has adopted new terms for developing debtor countries, involving debt reductions that may be as large as 67 per cent. Since such reductions can be applied only to non-ODA debt, the definition of ODA debt is of crucial importance.

The definition of concessionality used over the years by the Paris Club has been that of OECD's Development Assistance Committee (DAC). The IMF, which had in the past also used this definition, has introduced a new one which reflects the recent evolution of interest rates.

Under the DAC definition, which was originally established in 1969, ODA loans are those (of more than one year) provided by Governments or official agencies which meet two criteria; first, they must be administered with the promotion of economic development and welfare of the developing counties as their main objective; second, they must be concessional in character, with a grant element of at least 25 per cent using a discount rate of 10 per cent.

The continued use of a fixed discount rate of 10 per cent has posed problems in recent years, due to the marked decline of interest rates in virtually all countries as compared with the early 1980s. Indeed, a loan can meet the DAC definition even if, compared with the market rate of the currency concerned, it is clearly a commercial loan. For instance with a 10 per cent discount rate, a fixed-rate loan with a 10-year maturity and a 5-year grace period would qualify for the DAC definition of a concessional loan if its rate of interest were less than 5.2 per cent (a rate which has been above market rates in some developed countries in the past 18 months). The difference in market rates at any point in time among major developed countries also raises issues of the comparability of concessionality among major countries.

Recognizing these problems, OECD has used since 1987, in the framework of its Arrangement on Guidelines for Officially Supported Export Credits (often referred to as "the OECD Consensus"), a formula based on individual OECD countries' market interest rates, known as Commercial Interest Reference Rates (CIRR), to assess the discount rates for calculation of the grant element.[1] Using this discount rate, a loan must have at least a 35 per cent grant element to be considered concessional; for LDCs the threshold is 50 per cent. In 1994, it was decided that for loans contracted after 31 August 1996 the discount rate used would be CIRR plus a margin reflecting the maturity of the loan. It is interesting to note that these two definitions of concessionality (that of DAC and that of the Consensus) coexist within OECD. Consequently, today a 10-year loan in yen, with five years of grace and a 4 per cent interest rate, for example, would confer to the DAC definition of concessionality but not to that of the OECD Consensus.

The IMF has moved in the direction of the OECD Consensus definition, and has applied a CIRR-based discount rate and a 35 per cent grant element from October 1995 in assessing the concessionality of loans in the context of limits on foreign borrowing in IMF arrangements.

Under the Naples terms, ODA debt - defined according to the DAC criteria - is rescheduled over 40 years, with a grace period of 16 years and at an interest rate at least as concessional as the original one. The implied reduction in net present value (NPV) terms for ODA debt - over and above its original grant element - is likely to be less than the 67 per cent applied to non-ODA debt.

Under the Naples terms, the discount rate used to calculate NPV is the "appropriate market rate", i.e. the interest rate determined bilaterally between the debtor and each individual creditor country. The appropriate market rate is usually very close to the CIRR. If the interest rate on rescheduled ODA debt equals the original rate but is not lower than the appropriate market rate, no NPV reduction can be obtained - a situation which might arise, for example, in the case of OPA loans in low-interest currencies, such as the yen. Even if the ODA debt rescheduling rate, as well as the original one, were, say, 2 per cent, as compared with a 7 per cent appropriate market rate, the effective NPV debt reduction could be as low as 30 per cent, under reasonable assumptions on the residual maturity of the original ODA debt.

The adoption by the Paris Club of a new definition of ODA loans, along the lines of that used in the OECD Consensus, would better reflect the reality facing debtors and creditors. In that event, a significant portion of currently defined ODA debt, especially that denominated in low-interest currencies, would be classified as non-concessional and could thus benefit from NPV reduction of 67 per cent under the Naples terms.

1   For the definition of CIRR and movements in the rates in 1995 and early 1996, see table 14 above

Bilateral debt

Following the adoption of the Naples terms in December 1994, the number of countries which went to the Paris Club in the first half of 1995 increased substantially: during that period 13 agreements were signed. Thereafter, however, activity at the Paris Club declined markedly, with 10 agreements during the ensuing 12 months, thereby resuming a downward trend which could already be noticed in the early 1990s. A large number of countries still remain in need of debt rescheduling; as of June 1996, about half of the 36 countries which had not graduated from the Paris Club had no current agreements in effect. For more than half of them, the Paris Club agreement had expired more than one year earlier and substantial arrears were accumulating. One of the main obstacles to their achieving a new rescheduling was the difficulty encountered in reaching a new agreement with IMF.

The debt situation of many developing countries, especially the HIPCs, remains extremely difficult despite the efforts made to alleviate their debt burden through increasingly concessional rescheduling at the Paris Club and additional bilateral debt relief, as noted in the preceding sub-section. The Naples terms, while alleviating the bilateral debt burden, have at the same time revealed the extent of the multilateral debt burden for a number of developing countries, as well as of the burden of non-OECD official bilateral debt. While the international community is actively considering the multilateral debt problem, progress towards a solution of debt to non-OECD creditors is advancing very slowly and lacks a coherent framework. This is illustrated by the treatment of the debt due by countries in sub-Saharan Africa to the Russian Federation and to Arab countries, which is reviewed in the annex to this chapter.

(a) Recent developments concerning implementation of the Naples terms

Since the late 1980s, Paris Club creditors have applied increasingly concessional terms to the debt rescheduling of the heavily indebted poor countries. These terms have evolved from a reduction of debt service payments by a third under Toronto terms agreed in 1988 to a 50 per cent reduction under the London terms (also referred to as enhanced Toronto terms) adopted in 1991. The Naples terms of December 1994 further increased the level of concessionality, to 67 per cent, in response to the enduring debt distress of HIPCs. Such a reduction can be applied either to debt service payments (flow rescheduling) falling due during a relatively short consolidation period (up to three years) or to the stock of eligible Paris Club debt (stock-of-debt operation). The possibility of applying the reduction to the stock of debt, one of the major innovations of the Naples terms, was designed to provide eligible debtor countries with an exit from the debt rescheduling process as the beneficiary would no longer need to go to the Paris Club for further rescheduling.[59] The Naples terms have also added a new feature by allowing debt that has already been reduced through previous rescheduling on either Toronto or London terms to be further diminished so as to achieve a percentage reduction on the original claims of either 50 per cent or 67 per cent. This is referred to as the "topping up" principle. In the past, such claims could not be further reduced, but could, at best, be rescheduled on non-concessional terms. Only non-OPA debt is eligible for reduction under Naples terms, which raises the question of the definition of ODA debt (see box 2).

Since adoption of the Naples terms in December 1994, 19 HIPCs (roughly half of this group of countries) have rescheduled their Paris Club debt on those terms (as of 30 June 1996). Most of them received the maximum reduction, namely 67 per cent. Only three countries, (Cameroon, Guinea and Honduras), obtained the smaller reduction, of 50 per cent. Stock-of-debt treatment was granted to only five countries: Bolivia, Burkina Faso, Guyana, Mali and Uganda, the remaining 14 countries being accorded flow rescheduling.

The extent of Paris Club debt relief has continued to be determined by the balance of payments financing requirements as assessed during negotiations on IMF-supported programmes. In virtually all cases, all pre-cutoff-date debt that was never rescheduled or that was rescheduled on non-concessional terms was reduced. In flow reschedulings, the topping up principle was not always applied. Some countries benefited from it in respect of their claims restructured under Toronto terms; very few did so in the case of the debt restructured more recently under London terms.

The pace of stock-of-debt agreements, though accelerating in the first half of 1996, remained modest, largely due to the fact that only a few countries had completed the three-year probationary period required by Paris Club creditors before considering a stock-of-debt reduction under Naples terms.[60] Two such reduction agreements were signed in 1995 and three in the first half of 1996, and all involved the 67 per cent option.[61] With the exception of Uganda,[62] all of them covered not only the stock of debt that was never rescheduled, or that was already rescheduled but never reduced, but also debt restructured on Toronto and London terms; to the latter category of debt, the topping up principle was fully applied. However, none of the stock-of-debt agreements concluded to date has covered moratorium interest[63]: such a possibility nevertheless exists under the Naples terms, whereby moratorium interest can be rescheduled or reduced, depending on the debtor country's specific circumstances. This exceptional feature was included to take account of the fact that in the early years following a stock-of-debt operation moratorium interest tends to be higher than under a flow rescheduling.

In the case of Uganda, the reduction agreement implies a reduction (in net present value terms) of 17 per cent in its total Paris Club debt, and of 3.2 per cent in its total outstanding debt. For Bolivia, the impact is greater (partly as a result of the more extensive coverage of the agreement): the reductions will amount to about 31 per cent of its total Paris Club debt and 11 per cent of its overall external debt. For Mali, Guyana and Burkina Faso the impact will be much smaller, mainly because of the level of Paris Club debt (before any debt reduction) in relation to their total external debt. It should be noted that, even after the 67 per cent stock-of-debt reduction under Naples terms, debt indicators for Bolivia, Guyana and Uganda are such that these countries are still considered as having potential debt sustainability problems, which may necessitate additional debt relief measures under the proposed HIPC debt initiative described in the preceding sub-section.

Finally, in a very few cases, the Paris Club has continued to agree to exceptional deferral of payments on arrears on post-cutoff-date debt.[64] In the past two-and-a-half years, four countries benefited from this exceptional treatment. The period of deferral (over which the arrears have to be paid) has varied from two to three years.[65]

BOX 3
GRADUATION FROM THE PARIS CLUB: THE CASE OF THE RUSSIAN FEDERATION

In April 1996, a five-day Paris Club meeting took place to restructure the debt contracted or guaranteed by the former Soviet Union and for which the Russian Federation had assumed responsibility. The Paris Club creditors agreed to a comprehensive rescheduling of the debt with a view to supporting Russian stabilization efforts and avoiding the need for further rescheduling. The agreement involves restructuring in two stages: a flow rescheduling, followed by a stock-of-debt operation. It is hoped that this will provide an exit strategy for the country.

The flow rescheduling covers 100 per cent of the principal and interest payments due from January 1996 to 31 March 1999 on debt that was never rescheduled, as well as on that resulting from the three previous Paris Club agreements (of 1993, 1994 and 1995)[1] This debt is rescheduled over an unusually long period of 21½ years, including 3 years of grace. As in the three previous agreements, part of the debt contracted after the cutoff date (determined to be 1 January 1991) was also rescheduled; payments on such debt due over the period 1996-1998 were rescheduled, though with a somewhat shorter maturity, of about 17 years. Furthermore, the moratorium interest and short-term debt that were rescheduled in the previous agreements were also rescheduled, on the same terms as those granted on post-cutoff-date debt.

In the second stage, principal payments falling due on or after 1 April 1999 are to be rescheduled, also with a maturity of 21½ years, including 3 years of grace. This restructuring covers only the debt resulting from the three previous agreements and excludes all post-cutoff-date debt. For this stock-of-debt operation to be implemented, a number of conditions have to be met, including, for instance, the approval by IMF of the review of the 1997 and 1998 progammes, as well as of the final quarterly review scheduled under the Fund's extended arrangement, and the fulfilment of financial obligations due up to 31 March 1999.

The agreement with the Russian Federation is exceptional for two reasons. The first is the substantial amount involved (about $40 billion), the largest in the Paris Club's history. The second is that it is a stock-of-debt operation on non-concessional terms, the first of its kind in the Club's 40 years of existence. This agreement is along the lines of London Club restructuring of commercial bank debt outside the Brady Plan framework. The other stock-of-debt restructurings which took place within the Paris Club, either on Naples terms or those agreed to in 1991 for Poland and Egypt, included a reduction in the present value of debt.[2]

1   For the last three months of the consolidation period, the percentage of debt rescheduled falls to 40 per cent for debt that was never rescheduled.
2   For the terms accorded Poland and Egypt see TDR 1992, box 2.

(b) Middle-income countries

Over the past 18 months, only 6 of the 23 rescheduling countries belonged to the middle-income category, among which were Croatia and The Former Yugoslav Republic of Macedonia, which signed their first agreements with the Paris Club in 1995. One of the most notable features of the treatment applied to the debt of this group of countries has been the increasing use of graduated repayment schedules whereby, following a short grace period, payments take place with a progressively increasing amortization schedule.[66] The most interesting new development was the treatment granted to the Russian Federation for its debt restructuring in April 1996. The Paris Club had hitherto retained the flow approach to deal with the debt of middle-income countries. In contrast, the agreement with Russia allows for the rescheduling of the stock of debt as of 1 April 1999 (see box 3). Some other middle-income debtor countries would also like to benefit from a comprehensive rescheduling through a stock-of-debt operation. It remains to be seen, however, whether the Russian agreement signals a change in the Paris Club practices regarding middle-income countries, or whether it is truly and "exceptional" rescheduling, as were those for Poland and Egypt five years ago. If it does indeed signal a change, other middle- income countries (not eligible for Paris Club debt reduction) might be able to benefit from a comprehensive debt approach similar to that applied to the Russian Federation.

Notes

43 The group comprises 41 countries: the 32 countries classified as severely indebted low income countries (SILICs) in *World Debt Tables 1994-95, External Finance for Developing Countries* (Washington, D.C.: The World Bank, 1994); an additional 7 countries that have received concessional treatment from the Paris Club; and 2 lower middle-income countries that have recently become IDA-only countries.

44 See *TDR 1995*, Part One, chap. II, sect E.2, for a discussion of the debt problems of these countries since the emergence of the debt crisis.

45 International Monetary Fund, *Official Financing For Developing Countries*, Washington D.C., December 1995, table 21.

46 For a detailed discussion of schemes adopted by MFIs to alleviate the debt burden of poor countries, see *TDR 1995*, Part One, chap. 1, sect. E.

47 See the excerpts from the press conference held jointly by the Chairman of the Interim Committee and the Managing Director of IMF, on 23 April 1996 (*IMF Survey*, Vol. No. 25, 6 May 1996). Resources held in the ESAF Reserve Account are meant to be used to make payments of principal and interest for the Loan Account, should actual debt service payments (including interest subsidy) by the debtor be insufficient to cover the amount due. SCA-2 was created in 1990 to safeguard against potential losses arising from purchases made under a successor arrangement after the successful completion of a Rights Accumulation Programme, and to provide additional liquidity to finance such purchases. As of 1 January 1996, holdings in the ESAF Reserve Account amounted to SDR 1364 million and in SCA-2 to SDR 898 million.

48 *Financial Times*, 23 May 1996 (reporting a statement by the President of the Bank).

49 IMF, *Annual Report 1995* (Washington D.C. 1995), p.147.

50 See T. Killick, "Solving the Multilateral Debt Problem: Reconciling Relief with Acceptability" (London: Commonwealth Secretariat, forthcoming).

51 Among the risk indicators considered were the fiscal burden, reserve coverage, aid dependence, export diversity, sensitivity to export shortfalls, resource gap and policy track record.

52 The eight "unsustainable" cases are Burundi, Guinea-Bissau, Mozambique, Nicaragua, Sao Tome and Principe, Sudan, Zaire and Zambia. The 12 other countries with potential debt sustainability problems are: Bolivia, Cameroon, Congo, Cote d'Ivoire, Ethiopia, Guyana, Madagascar, Myanmar, Niger, Rwanda, United Republic of Tanzania and Uganda.

53 See the Communiqués of the Interim Committee (22 April 1996), Development Committee (23 April 1996), and the Group of 24 (21 April 1996), reproduced in *IMF Survey*, 6 May 1996.

54 G-7 Lyons Summit, Economic Communiqué, 28 June 1996.

55 A number of studies, which used different approaches, arrived at consistent results, indicating a critical level of 200 per cent for the ratio of the present value of debt to exports. According to *World Debt Tables 1994-1995*, Vol.1 (p. 40), debt profiles and track records of selected SILICs suggested that debt service ratios that consistently exceeded 15 per cent were high and that debt-to-export ratios greater than 200 per cent had generally proven unsustainable over the medium term. In *TDR 1995* (Part One, chap. II, sect. E.1) a benchmark debt service ratio of 20 per cent was used because, over the period 1983-1994, countries in the sample were actually able to make debt service payments equivalent on average to 22 per cent, but only after debt reschedulings and accumulation of large arrears. It must be emphasized that debt sustainability implies the ability to meet debt obligations without resorting to debt relief, rescheduling or accumulating arrears.

56 In addition to the World Bank, IMF and regional development banks, MFIs include other multilateral intergovernmental agencies, such as the International Fund for Agricultural Development (IFAD), a number of Arab funds and the multilateral institutions of the European Union.

57 The sales, involving a much larger volume than that currently proposed (50 million ounces), were carried out over a four-year period (1976-1980) and had little discernible depressing effect on the market price.

58 This facility, which is co-financed by donors, provides grants to IDA-only countries for commercial debt buy-backs at a sharp discount.

59 To be eligible for a stock-of-debt operation, a country must fulfil three main conditions: (1) it must establish a good track record with IMF-supported programmes; (2) it must comply with Paris Club bilateral agreements; and (3) Paris Club creditors must be confident that the country will be able to fulfil its obligations under the stock reduction agreement. For details of the Naples terms, see *TDR 1995*, box 3.

60 Debtor countries restructuring their Paris Club debt for the first time under the Naples terms initially receive a flow rescheduling. The agreement signed includes a clause whereby a three-year or, in some cases, a four-year probationary period is required during which a good track record of relations with IMF and with Paris Club creditors has to be established before a stock-of-debt operation can be considered.

61 As noted above, the reduction applies only to non-concessional debt.

62 The Uganda agreement signed in February 1995 reduces only previously rescheduled debt (as there was hardly any eligible debt which had not been rescheduled). It excludes debt restructured in 1992 on London terms.

63 Moratorium interest refers to interest payments on amounts deferred or rescheduled under the rescheduling agreement.

64 The cutoff date is the date prior to which loans must be contracted in order for their debt service to be eligible for rescheduling. Loans contracted after the cutoff date are expected to be serviced in full. The cutoff date is determined at the first Paris Club rescheduling and typically remains fixed in all subsequent reschedulings.

65 Guinea-Bissau obtained particularly generous treatment in 1995, with the rescheduling over 10 years of arrears on post-cutoff-date debt.

66 Graduated payment schedules enable debtor countries to avoid the bunching of debt service obligations which takes place at the end of the grace period in conventional reschedulings.

II

The Impact of the Market Economy on the Poor

Keynote address given at the Oxford III Conference on Christian Faith and Economics, Agra 1995

Raja Chelliah

INTRODUCTION:
GLOBALIZATION AND LIBERALIZATION
OF NATIONAL FINANCIAL MARKETS

I speak from the perspective of a practising economist: a committed democratic socialist who has been transformed into a believer in the market economy. This market economy cannot be allowed to be uncontrolled but must be regulated and guided on the basis of social concerns and social priorities.

This Third International Conference on Christian Faith and Economics is being held at a very important stage in the revolution of world economy. The whole world is hurtling towards a globalized market economy. The process which started with the collapse of the socialist economies, and in particular the Soviet Union, has now gathered considerable momentum, partly due to the revolution in information technology. A development of recent years is the globalization and liberalization of the financial markets of the world which have led to enormous rapid and unpredictable capital flows moving across continents. Further more, with the successful completion of the Uruguay Round, the Peru negotiations on international trade practices, with the GATT agreement signed, production of many commodities is being relocated in different countries causing misgivings and perhaps temporary unemployment in several countries, because exports from one country tend to flood the markets of other countries.

All of this of course, can be shown to raise productivity, output and incomes in general but there are certain basic problems and new ones are arising.

At present a large part of the world is globalizing and trying to cope with globalization. Therefore, in most countries, even in the universities renowned for the teaching of economics, there is no recognition of the difficulties and deficiencies of the market economy. There is no time to deal with these because we are dealing with the market that is overwhelming us. We are coping with globalization, we are not yet in a position to analyse the long-term effects of globalization.

Now, it is proper that we as Christians take stock of the situation. We must consider not only the immediate short-term impact of the spread of the market economy across the world, but also the long-term consequences of letting the world be swamped unintentionally by totally uncontrolled market economies. The market has almost come to stay. In India, reluctantly we have had to accept the fact that there was no alternative to a fairly free market economy. We adopted a mixed economy after we gained independence, which implied the co-existence of the public and private sector, but with the under-pinning of political democracy. We thought therefore we could fashion a new type of structure neither totally capitalist nor communist and at the same time preserve the values of freedom and democracy. Although the system enabled us to achieve notable results, we have to confess that it has not delivered the basic economic goods. Poverty has not been abolished in this country. At least 30 per cent of the people live below the poverty line, which is at a fairly low level compared with the standards of living in some of the developed countries.

THE DEFINING ESSENTIAL CHARACTERISTIC OF A MARKET ECONOMY

Though we said that we were going to have a mixed economy, we gradually let the state, that is the Government, dominate, control and stifle private effort and enterprise. This led to inefficiency in the use of resources, their misallocation and protection of entrance groups. These then became the hallmarks of the system.

Lack of competition within India and between India and the rest of the world has caused inefficiency because protectionist policy led to low productivity and loss of competitiveness. The low level of competitiveness in the international market gave us a constant balance of payments problem. The result was that we gained neither self-reliance nor prosperity. We had to recognize these serious defects and introduce elements of a market economy. The market economy as we understand it has three essential characteristics:

    1   Competition in order to ensure improvement in quality and productivity.

    2   Incentives, that is rewards in relation to effort, and

    3   Correct pricing and allocation of resources based on an undistorted pricing system.

Of course, it is difficult to define an undistorted pricing system, but we can derive the broad characteristics of a system although there may be disagreements on particular details. This allocation of resources according to proper pricing and valuation of scarce resources is extremely important to ensure efficient utilization of scarce resources. That in fact is the essence of the economic problem.

These essential characteristics of the market economy are being adopted in every sector of the economy. We are, therefore, abolishing many controls which stifle competition such as regulations which unsuccessfully attempt to suppress markets which cannot be suppressed. We are trying to take economic decisions out of political considerations as far as possible. We have, and I am sure many other countries in the developing world have also, realized that poverty can be abolished only by the creation of wealth; it can only be abolished by fast rate of growth. We cannot, therefore, do without the market economy which can enable us to accelerate the rate of growth of the economy. A lesson that all poor nations have to learn is that we can build an independent, humane and free society on a firm economic foundation only. The adjective 'independent' is extremely important because many of us in the developing world have lost our independence. We will continue to be servile and overpowered by the rich countries unless we increase our economic strength. Just as the poor in a country can improve their position only by becoming non-poor, the poor countries can increase or improve their relative position only by building their economic strength. This is again an important lesson the countries of the Third World have to realize.

REFORM: ITS EFFECT ON THE POOR

Just as we have many other developing countries have committed errors. They constantly complain about exploitation by the richer nations, but do exactly those things which will keep them subservient. The policies of many of the developing countries, including those of India, were such that they were designed to keep them poor and weak in the comity of nations. So one of the reasons that we in India have resolved to build our economic strength is that only by building the economic strength of the nation can we safeguard our security and our independence. This is true particularly in the context of many countries in our neighbourhood growing extremely fast and increasing their economic and military muscle. But, it is not just to gain a prestigious position in the comity of nations that we want to change our policies. It is mainly because we have realized that poverty in India can be abolished only if the rate of economic growth is much higher than the rate of growth of population. Part of this extra growth can then be used for education and health of the masses of the population, so that the rate of growth of population will come down.

Another mistake we made in the early years was to invest a lot of money in steel mills, aluminum production and copper factories, and not enough in education and health, particularly primary education and rural health. This then led to a higher rate of growth of population because education, particularly education of women, has an important impact on the fertility rate, as has been proved in some other states in India and also in the East Asian countries.

We are aware that a market economy, in terms of the three criteria that I laid down, is needed. We know that if society does not control the market economy, the market economy tends to control society. The market economy does not contain within itself any elements or motives to protect the common interest of the community. We also realize that the market economy often leads to unequal distribution of income and wealth which in turn leads to unequal distribution of power and hence to the exploitation of those with economic power over those who lack sufficient economic power. Therefore it becomes necessary to impose on the market economy from the outside rules and restraints that make the economy serve not the fortunate few or the rich, but the totality of the population. This means that we use economy to fulfil the requirements of an humane and just society.

In summary, then, the following are essentials for a market economy: competition, incentives, correct pricing. In addition, the element of individual choice must pertain. On the other hand, the following are the defects of a market economy: inequality of wealth distribution, allocation in favour of the wealthy and strong and potentially damaging divergence between the private and social cause. At its worst, this divergence can lead to the over-exploitation of natural resources, damage to the environment, pollution and many other evils. The challenge is how is it possible to use the economy to meet the requirements of a humane and just society without violating the basic characteristics essential to a successful market economy.

Some would say that this is to put too much faith in government. They would say that in the same way that there are market failures, so there are government failures: a system cannot keep switching from running the government for the market to running the market for the economy.

A TWO-FOLD ECONOMIC PROGRAMME: STABILIZATION AND ECONOMIC REFORM

Under a properly working democracy it should be possible to correct government failures from time to time. It is true that in many cases government intervention is ineffective. Therefore before a government decides to intervene there must be scientific study of the consequences of various types of intervention. Only intervention likely to succeed and yield beneficial results must be supported. But there is no doubt that the government has understood fully that the electorate, public opinion, the press and those who have been elected to office together will have to keep the market economy under control. It may not always be possible, but it is certainly necessary.

Does the economic reform process not only leave the poor out but positively worsen their situation?

POPULATION GROWTH AND POVERTY

So far I have not mentioned the word 'poor', although in the conference title the word 'poor' is written prominently. I do not believe that if the reform policies are wisely structured, formulated and implemented, there need be any significant adverse effect on the poor of this country, although I cannot speak for other countries.

However reform by itself will not directly benefit the poor. In the long-term everyone benefits because there is growth in the levels of employment, output and education. If compulsory primary education were introduced all children, from families of all incomes, would go to school and benefit immediately, but in most areas the poor are not benefited immediately. They will, though, benefit in the long-term and they are not adversely affected.

The poor were not created by the reforms which were introduced in 1991. The poor have been with us for a long time. There was probably not very much poverty in the ancient period, before 1000 AD. At that time India was a very rich country and, most importantly, had a very small population. Since that period there have always been poor people. The numbers increased greatly during the first forty-five years after Independence because there were very ill-judged policies on population growth control. In 1947, at the time of Independence, the population was 330 million people. This has grown to 880 million today. The rate of growth should have been reduced to 1 per cent by the 1970's, but even today it is 2 per cent. It is to the nation's credit that we have been able to increase agricultural production to feed this growing number of people. Much of this resource and effort could have gone to produce other goods and services which would have made the people more prosperous than they are today.

To summarize again, the poor have always existed and they remain. Although the reforms alone will not harm them, they will not for the most part help them immediately.

ECONOMIC INTERVENTION: A PRO-POOR POLICY

There is therefore no alternative to intervention in some form. This need not always be state intervention. Indeed it is the role of the states, voluntary organizations and academics everywhere, but especially in India itself. It can take the form of the pressure of public opinion, the work of activist groups or the spread of knowledge. In all these groups seeking to intervene in all these ways, Christians must be active participants.

The state itself naturally provides public good: it can change the structure of its public expenditure to benefit the poor. Much can be done in this country as in many other countries, provided we can bring our politicians under control and discipline. One of the great difficulties that we face here in India is that because we have periodic elections, the politicians tend to promise short-term gains to the people at the expense of their long-term interest. I believe this is the fault of the economists and planners of earlier years who have kept our people poor and ignorant rather than of politicians. Since the majority are poor and ignorant it is possible for our politicians to deceive and mislead them to get themselves elected on false promises.

It is imperative that we tackle this. We cannot be mere on-lookers: again, Christians with like-minded people have to explain to the population at large when they have been taken for a ride; the burden of social cost must be borne by the private agencies which produce goods. For instance, now it is widely accepted that the polluter must pay the cost of pollution. I have suggested that there is a large role for the State to supplement the market economy to make it more pro-community, pro-poor and to mitigate the possible damage it can do to the fabric of society as well as to natural resources.

As I said I am not quite familiar with what has happened in other parts of the world, but from my experience of Asia, I would say that structural reform itself does not affect the poor adversely. But in the programmes that we have undertaken, sometimes under the supervision of the International Monetary Fund, there are two components; one is stabilization and the other is structural reform. Stabilization refers to bringing back macro-economic stability to the country. Measures needed to bring back macro- economic stability could impose hardship on the nation.

This is the price to be paid for a programme to implement a macro-economic policy and for the government to gain efficiency quickly.

For example, in all the states in India, electricity is generated, transmitted and distributed by state electricity boards. They are totally inefficient. They are in the red. They cannot invest more. The maintenance of equipment is so poor that we have a powercut every few hours.

Now, if we privatize electricity generation some people will say the poor are affected. How? The poor are affected because the electricity boards are so inefficient. They allow electricity to be stolen. The staffs of the electricity boards sell power to people without metering. All that money could have gone to help the poor to fund education.

If I maintain that it is necessary to privatize the electricity boards leftists object saying that I am anti-poor. They have a dogmatic belief that whenever the public sector is touched the poor are harmed. On the contrary, I believe that India will be unable to progress if the electricity boards are not reformed and the only successful reform is privatization.

THE POLICY IN PRACTICE: DIFFICULTIES AND GAINS

Stabilization is essential as a programme for reducing the budget deficit. India's rapid accumulation of public debt has repercussions that erode international confidence. To deal with a difficult balance of payments situation it is necessary to squeeze government expenditure which can often at first disadvantage the poor: if food subsidies are reduced, it is the poor who suffer; if government investments are reduced then employment in the construction industry is reduced, and it is workers who suffer. All this is true, but these are necessary costs to pay for the unsound policies of the past. Just as in a family in which large debts have been incurred, consumption must be cut to repay the debt. In this way our country had to contract its socio-cultural programme and reduce employment in the construction and other industries in the short-term for about two years, but now that phase is over and the economy is picking up.

On the other hand structural reform does not directly affect the poor in an adverse or any other way. Earlier I gave the example of the state electricity boards. I might equally cite the way I allowed our exchange rate to be determined by the market rather than maintain it at an over-valued level. Import duty was also reduced to improve our competitiveness. The labour force of the few industries affected by this have to be cared for, but on the whole poor people in the industrial sector are not affected. To sum up, the general perception that the economic reform programme has worsened the situation of the poor significantly is not warranted, while the stabilization part of the programme has led to necessary short-term difficulties for the poor, in this and every country which has introduced such measures.

Some countries have suffered in implementing reform, but that is because they have implemented the programmes without due care, caution or in proper sequence. Some, especially the smaller countries, may have been pressured to act rashly by junior IMF officials. There should be no fear of disruption of the economy if such policies are followed judiciously. For example, since 1991 our GDP has never failed to increase. Of course per capita GDP fell in the first year because growth was less than 2 per cent. However in the next years it increased to 3 then 4 per cent. This year growth is expected to be 5.5–6.0 per cent. From now onwards it should be possible for the government to obtain much larger revenues from the growing economy, in particular from the tax reforms we have initiated. These revenues can be used to provide social benefits such as more employment opportunities and to promote a lower rate of population growth by such means as improved education for women. This is imperative for our nation's future prosperity. In Kerala the rate of growth of population is down to 1.2 per cent, compared with a national average of 2.1 per cent. Slowly this demographic change is taking place elsewhere, but there has been no encouragement for this trend and we must provide such in the future.

THE DEFICIENCIES OF THE MARKET ECONOMY

We have accepted the market economy because we see other systems as worse. Churchill used to say that democracy was the worst form of government, but all the others are worse. We cannot improve upon it immediately, but must accept it of necessity. In the long-term thinkers and particularly Christian thinkers must study the deficiencies of the market economy.

THE IMPOSSIBILITY OF FULL EMPLOYMENT

I want now to mention one of the major defects of the market economy about which western economists are silent and which they tend to push under the carpet. Despite the implementation of Keynesian policies and much thinking and practical work done on western capitalist economies, the achievement of full employment has remained a dream. To quote from an American economist in the presidential address at the American Economic Association in January 1993, taking the definition of 'full employment' as being a situation in which there are at least as many unfilled job openings as there are individuals seeking work, the United States has not had anything approaching full employment since the Korean War, or, during peace time, since 1925.

There are two ways in which I see that the market economy is inherently unable to provide governments with a means to achieve full employment:

INFLATION

Economists have developed a new concept of the state of unemployment: the non-inflation rate accelerating the rate of unemployment. Currently in the United States this appears to be around 4-6 per cent. This means that if unemployment falls below 5 per cent there will be inflation. The government dare not let unemployment fall below 5 per cent because the middle classes who do not suffer when there is unemployment, will not tolerate inflation, because this does affect them.

The prevailing condition of political democracy will not allow inflation to grow, so the government cannot try to limit unemployment. Further, the unemployment of 5 per cent which exists is not evenly distributed. If it were evenly distributed a government could ask all workers to take a few weeks unpaid holiday and the problem would be eliminated. In the USA and Western Europe the level of unemployment is much higher amongst minority and disadvantaged groups, up to 40 per cent in some cases. Neither should it be assumed that a very high unemployment level exists only amongst blacks in America: London economists state that in Holland it stands at 3 per cent amongst Turks rising to 42 per cent amongst Moroccans compared with only 7 per cent for ethnic Dutch. Thus the market economy does not result in the achievement of full employment and indeed can often be the cause of unjust inequitable distribution of the burden of unemployment.

INVESTMENT AND GROWTH

The second disadvantage of the western capitalist system in reducing unemployment is that a relatively high level of investment is needed to keep the level down. In turn this implies that the economy should keep growing indefinitely. When the world economy is growing the World Bank, the IMF and the United Nations are all happy: the American economy grows, the European economy grows, the Japanese economy grows. Everyone is happy because that used to be the impulse to the momentum of growth in other countries too. According to the European Keynesian interpretation without economic growth there is unemployment. What therefore is the consequence for the world when in the last two or three years there has been low investment and high unemployment? It is that the rich countries will keep growing simply with the aim of reducing their unemployment level.

It is a matter for the whole world to consider whether this is the kind of economic system we want to see sustained. To sum up, although we may have accepted the major essential characteristics of the market economy we are aware that it has fundamental defects which in the long-term the world will have to address.

12

Business and Corruption

*An edited version of a paper presented at the
Consultation on Integrity in Business
in the Central European Context held on
11-16 March 1994 at Kastiel Kocovce, Slovakia.*

Vinay Samuel

Corruption is the distortion of a system of human transactions which makes room for and even promotes bribery. Bribery is a gift of inducement offered or received.

This is an important distinction. Corruption is the distortion of a system to create a corrupt system. A corrupt official represents a corrupt system. I believe corruption is far more systemic than this: it has to do with the climate; the culture which makes it possible to offer and receive bribes. This is one way to distinguish corruption. On the other hand, bribes are individual offers of gifts of inducement to influence decision-making: to gain unfair advantage: to escape with supplying substandard services or products: to receive "out of turn favours" to facilitate faster delivery of services.

The person offering the bribe expects to receive those benefits. The person taking the bribe expects to acquit the guilty or to expedite service. In doing this he overlooks faults, weakness and even guilt.

The Bible acknowledges this aspect of receiving bribes. The person in receipt of the bribe is expected to close his eyes. Like this, he can simply let things be. To me this symbolic gesture means much more. To me it signifies allowing things to happen, not just to remain the same. The recipient allows people to do what they want; to contravene rules; to set aside accepted standards and norms so that they can set their own standards to suit themselves. I find this an important aspect of the expectations of the parties in such a transaction, which again distinguishes it from gift-giving. I shall develop the distinction later in this discussion.

THE CULTURE OF CORRUPTION: ITS ORIGINS

We are looking at a culture of extortion and bribery whose origins I think we need to examine a little more deeply. The culture has its historical roots in rulers who developed taxes. For example, in the Old Testament, after Solomon there was with Reheboam the development of a ruling class and nobility and taxes were imposed. The problem began because it was not the same as taking wealth to pay for things by raiding or robbing neighbouring tribes, towns and countries. It was taxation of one's own people. The extortion of money from one's own people was a historical development, as were the means of enforcing the extortion: violence and a legal system. The system was to take care of a bureaucracy and nobility who were expected to protect their people from enemies and marauders in return. This was the context of the origins of early corruption.

In the contemporary world such systems have institutionalized extortion using the weapons of complex rulebooks and the fact that the institutions are the gatekeepers of licences and permissions which people must have.

CORRUPTION IN THE FINANCIAL SYSTEM AND BUSINESS: THE ROOTS OF ITS VALUES

Financial systems by nature create corruption of the financial system. They facilitate extortion. For example, they create artificial shortages. In an artificial shortage of capital, necessary products and services it is possible to insist on an "extra value" for these goods. One may ask who it is who suffers from this corruption: the business person who is tempted to sacrifice quality or the consumer who is manipulated by the business person to accept whatever he provides.

Consideration of the position of the business person and some of the aspects of corruption which his case raises illuminates some of the values of the culture of corruption. In the context of a corrupt business system the business person is often survival-oriented and therefore willing to compromise. Often he is quite frankly oriented towards profit at any cost or towards quick profit so he works out a means to gain unfair advantage, provide substandard services and gain favour for himself. These descriptions of types of corrupt business exist in a culture with values which find their origins in an emphasis on something which is entirely laudable: relationships and their supremacy over rules. In the Indian context greater importance is given to duty than to law. Duty is interpreted as duty to family, oneself and one's own community. Law is then interpreted as subordinate to duty and relationships as more important than rules. Therefore in communities in which there exist strong relationships, rules will always be secondary. As their function is to serve relationships, so they may be bent to serve relationships. In this frame of reference legalism may be resisted because a legal system sometimes seems to undermine relationships. Since there is this great emphasis on relationships and duty I intend to come back in this discussion to what I believe is a vital question:

Can communities provide the climate for business to be run without this oppressive culture of corruption, without building legal systems based on an entirely different set of relationships?

THE BIBLICAL VIEW ON BRIBERY
AND CORRUPTION

The Old Testament

I must first establish the biblical view. There are many references to bribery in the Bible. It is interesting that in the book of the covenant from Exodus 20 onwards there are clear references to bribery. This tells us two things: that there was a legal system which was part of a legal code which was part of life for the people of God and that even in these primal cultures the presence of bribery was already recognized. The key passage to study is Exodus 23: 1-9. The section is about bribery in a sense of perversion of justice. It concerns relationship to one's neighbour, setting loving one's neighbour by judging one's neighbour fairly against bearing false witness against him. Bearing false witness takes many forms: helping a wicked man; following the crowd; not treating even one's enemies even-handedly; denying justice to the poor and finally accepting or offering a bribe. This has the effect of blinding the vision of the truth and twisting the words of the righteous. In this way one does injustice to one's neighbour. Thus the first aspect of bribery I wish to underline in this biblical summary is that bribery concerns one's neighbour.

Another passage which illustrates an important theme of bribery which I want to emphasize is Deuteronomy 10:17; "For the Lord your God is God of gods and Lord of lords, the great God, mighty and awesome, who shows no partiality and accepts no bribes." God accepts no bribes: it is not in His character.

Finally, it is also important to bear in mind another critical issue when considering bribery and corruption, particularly in the biblical context: the question of who is disadvantaged by rather than gains advantage from the effects of bribery. The advantage always lies with the powerful and the harm is always to the poor. Bribery is never an isolated act. It always has consequences for one's relationship to neighbours and undermines the poor, compounding their misery and increasing the advantage to those who are already powerful.

Old Testament teaching

There are three areas of biblical teaching about bribery: the first is the Old Testament law of the first five books, the second is the wisdom teaching in Proverbs, Psalms, Ecclesiastes and Job and the third is the prophetic teaching particularly in Isaiah, Amos and Micah.

The law books

The legal section of the Old Testament deals with the individuals involved in corruption. It deals with who is the beneficiary and who is the victim of bribery. There are references to the innocent suffering most; to sin being promoted because those who collude in bribery close their eyes to and do not act against sin, as is the tradition in the law of the Old Testament. In Deuteronomy 10:17-18 there is a fascinating causal relationship between God's incorruptibility and His defence of widows and the fatherless. However Deuteronomy 27:17 introduces the idea that the corrupt mover of the neighbour's boundary stone is accursed by God. Here we see the theme of the relationship with neighbours referred to and also the idea that the perpetrator of bribery is harmed by the action too.

The wisdom literature

The wisdom literature presents a culture in which bribes are a way of life rather than isolated acts. It is important that Job, as a businessman, says that "fire will consume the tents of those who offer bribes." His friends are very self-righteous in suggesting to him that he could be suffering because his wealth could be due to bribes and that he should not be tempted by large inducements (Job 36:18) which could turn him aside. To give in to bribes is seen as giving in to and being vulnerable to temptation. In Psalm 26:10 sinners have "right hands full of bribes" and in Psalms 15:5 one reads "Do not accept a bribe against the innocent, he will never be shaken." Bribery is also a secretive transaction in the wisdom literature which generates a secretive and corrupt culture and a secretive and corrupt inner person, as at Ecclesiastes 7:7; "Extortion turns a wise man into a fool, and a bribe corrupts the heart." Certainly, the payment of a bribe, even for a medical privilege to benefit one's health, leaves one feeling unhappy about it: one feels dirty; the corruption brings sin. Thus bribery is clearly seen as being wrong. However the wisdom literature presents against this background of understanding, a culture which accepts that corruption is a way of life. It depicts the use of bribery in creating favourable relationships, broadly speaking, "currying favour." For example, Proverbs 19:6 ; "Many curry favour with a ruler, and everyone is the friend of a man who gives gifts." The second half of the verse recognizes that this is a reality in human life which is not restricted to money. I think that using generosity, kindness and gratitude to build relationships is an entirely different issue, even if these qualities manifest themselves in a given situation as "gifts". Gifts can show either generosity or corruption; can be acts of kindness or acts of bribery. These two types of gifts are distinct, as I indicated at the beginning of my discussion. The final judgement is that one should "refuse bribes" and that the one who does will live.

The prophetic literature

The prophetic books contain many references to bribery. Those in power seek bribes. Isaiah 1:23 depicts rulers who love bribes and seek gifts with the consequence that they abandon the cause of the fatherless and widows and harden their hearts against the needy. Isaiah 5:23 and Amos 5:1 recount how bribes oppress the righteous and deprive the poor of justice. It is the terrible words in Micah 3:11 "her leaders judge for a bribe" which gives one of the most dramatic accounts of the perversion of the cause of justice in the prophetic literature. Power dictates what they desire. The judges have the power of justice. The powerful can dictate judgements through them by paying bribes, so the guilty can dictate judgements. The guiltless are afflicted because the judges who are at the heart of justice, or the system which is supposed to bring justice, are corrupt.

Justice is especially important for the vulnerable. The courts are supposed to protect the poor and harassed but they tend to be used by the powerful. The system of law in fact thus oppresses, destroys and undermines the vulnerable and supports those from whom it was devised to protect the weak. There is no doubt that the Bible regards bribery in a very serious light.

New Testament teaching

The New Testament orientation is quite different. Surprisingly there is little said by Jesus himself about corruption. Luke addresses issues of money and it is he who deals with extortion. In Luke 19:1-9 theft and cheating are discussed. There is also the story of the shrewd manager who was able to use his gifts to achieve his own ends in Luke 16:1-18.

"Loving your neighbour"

The fundamental New Testament issue which I want to look at is that of relationship to one's neighbour: "loving one's neighbour" is a New Testament principle. What does this principle do to my relationship to my neighbour? This neighbour is the person to whom I am giving my bribe.

Addressing bribery and corruption in business

Bearing in mind some of the biblical principles I have highlighted, how should corruption and bribery be met? I will consider several ethical stances which can be adopted in the face of demand for bribery.

The "lesser of two evils"

First, the "lesser of two evils" theory, which has often been propounded. I myself have used that as justification for an action, but when one does adopt that view I have also always said that one has to be very careful to think about who are the real beneficiaries and victims. The "just war" theory arises from the lesser of two evils theory. In a just war one likes to believe the innocent are not hurt and one believes that one should aim not to hurt the innocent.

Uncompromising rejection

Secondly, uncompromising rejection. This means being willing to pay the price of not giving into the pressure to comply with the system. Of course it does little in itself to change the system, even though it is courageous.

Transforming the system

Thirdly, transforming the system. I suggest that this is attacking the roots of the problem. One protects the vulnerable and develops alternatives. The solution is developing resistance to corrupt practice.

I am going to put forward six areas for consideration which I hope will provide help to our resistance of bribery and corruption.

Six keys to resisting corruption

1. The culture of corruption

It is essential to be aware of how pervasive and ancient the culture is. Individuals cannot change it by resistance. I dread reading the British newspapers because my teenage children constantly attack me with the evidence of the corruption widespread in society. They are searching for some absolute values and believe that people are basically selfish and self- interested and nothing more. They tell me how wrong I was to tell them that British society was not corrupt. In the face of this I feel that it is so widespread and endemic that individuals standing out against the system will not be enough to change it.

2. *The cost of resistance*

In the short-term the cost of resistance is always greater economically than giving in. However, the cost of giving in is spiritually, economically and in terms of community change greater in the long-term.

3. *Communities of resistance*

a. *Working as a group*

Since individuals cannot resist successfully, we must form communities of resistance. The battle of resistance must be shared. The tendency is because bribery confronts one in one's own daily experience for it to be seen as a personal matter. One reacts by doing what is necessary to remove the immediate obstacle and then continues as if the event had not happened. In fact it should be a shared issue which a group of people work on together. I have tried this approach with evangelical Christian groups in India.

b. *Finding alternative means*

Once a group has formed to resist it is essential to find alternative means to operate. We must go to our leaders as a group. We must look for and exploit signs of integrity in our leaders and amongst people in power. There are always some people with a witness and integrity at the seat of power: it is not true that God has not left some honest people in these positions. I have found many times that in the midst of, for example, a whole property department of a development office of some 2,000 employees there will be some individual who is willing to stand out against the rest in an honest way for me. It may have been necessary to trawl for a long time, but I have found this one person. A very important relationship is then established. Often this person will turn out to have some Christian connection, even if he or she is not a Christian. Sometimes he or she will be a Christian who wants to resist the corrupt culture. While I have been looking for them, they have been looking for a chance to act righteously rather than just give in. There is indeed integrity in many places so that I believe we can build a community of resistance.

c. *Openness*

A third factor towards creating this community is insisting on openness. Secrecy in resistance continues to cover up practices and is no fight at all.

4. *Prayer*

The fight against corruption is a fight against principalities, powers and systems shaped by evil. I have sensed almost palpable evil in these places. Therefore all our resistance should be bathed in prayer.

5. Perseverance

The fight will require unremitting perseverance. This is a Christian quality which must be employed because the struggle will be a long one.

6. Continuous taking of stock

In any campaign it is essential to monitor progress and to weigh up the disadvantages and advantages in a given situation in order not to lose sight of the goal.

THE THEOLOGICAL VIEW OF COVENANT COMMUNITIES

Transforming the system by strengthening resistance and developing alternatives is critically important. The problem posed for any society is how it should combine law with relationships. It is difficult to build a legal code which has enough sensitivity and flexibility towards relationships. Further, the law in all societies, including western societies, has become so discredited that no one respects it. Even relationships themselves have broken down. It seems that nothing remains of either, and yet law and relationships are vital components of any society.

To me the biblical vision of "covenant communities" is the answer. In a covenant law is combined with relationships. The law is not just a set of rules but rules with commitments. Malachi is the book of the covenant community. It shows the application of the Law of the Covenant in all areas of life. Last spring I gained much enjoyment and personal satisfaction from teaching Malachi to *Spring Harvest*. Hundreds of people attended four bible studies which looked at the nature of the covenant community: covenant in relation to marriage; business; and within the church, between priests and congregations. Covenant provides an improved model for democracy because simple democracy has no inherent commitment or convictions. Democracy is based on an equality which does not really exist since equality cannot exist without mutual commitment. I believe that instead of democratic institutions "covenant democracy" is needed desperately all over the world.

CONCLUDING THOUGHTS

To conclude, I believe that the church should be covenanting with people and encouraging business to work on a basis of covenant. This is a daring thought, but is it possible that rightminded business people could propose that they work on a covenant basis with officials and agree on a set of mutual and shared expectations of certain standards of behaviour and obligations? It must be possible for business people to build covenant relationships with bureaucrats with interdependent rules and commitments. I believe that this is the only practical way forward in making progress against the corruption culture in business.

CUSTOMER ORIENTATION IS A NEW CONCEPT
FOR CENTRAL AND EASTERN EUROPE

Another group at the Consultation thought about the customer relationship in the context of the changing business ethos of Central and Eastern Europe. Their discussion highlighted the following points:

Case study

In Bulgaria ten per cent of the paper transported to a press plant mysteriously disappears. There are several internal checkpoints but no losses are reported. Investigation shows that a sophisticated system of lies has built up to cover a scheme in which the printers were able to increase their low wages by selling the missing ten percent of paper for their own profit. Suppliers, production workers and managers and quality control officers all fill in, sign and file carefully forms, tables and invoices. Everyone knows about it. Even customers who also know react merely by accepting that they are a part of this game. They accept disappointment and helplessness as the norm.

What are the reasons for customer deception?

Economic

On the supply side: Lack of competition, shortages and monopolies. On the consumer side: No sense of ownership or a stake in the economy.

Ethical

At a more profound level the problem is rooted in human relationships: an inhuman value system creates alienating structures which become self-perpetuating. Suppliers lose their sense of accountability towards their customers.

Why is the customer important to business?

Customer service is the business itself.

It affects:

market and product research, product design, quality, the point of sale, after-sale services, sales tactics, advertising promises, even packaging.
The customer should be master of the process.

The past and the future in Europe

Forty to fifty years of socialist collective society have created economies in which the five-year plan and a national economy have been the focus rather than the needs of the individual.
Privatization and competition should create a business world with more opportunities for consideration of the individual.
A warning: increasingly in the West outsize packaging conceals undersize contents, cheaper materials are used in manufacture, people complain about dishonest advertising.

The Christian attitude to the customer: "My customer is my neighbour".

Consumer orientation should be people orientation.
"Love thy neighbour as thyself".
There are examples of prosperous Puritan or Quaker communities which were founded on commitment to such eternal values. These are evidence that honesty is rewarded. Ethics pays dividends.
Christians living in the presence of Christ should take courage and think long-term rather than seek instant gains. Christians know that in the end the eternal world of the Kingdom of God is more certain than dealing in the corrupt business environment which cheats customers and neighbours.

WHAT IS BRIBERY?

In his paper Vinay Samuel mentioned sharing some of the issues he raises. At the Consultation groups met to discuss the questions "Bribery – what is it?" and "Bribery – ethical responses". A summary of their conclusions follows:

Definition

A bribe is a payment which may be money, favours or gifts, to influence a decision.

Results

Bribery can:

a create an unjust advantage and distort justice

b create expectations and bind the receiver to the giver's agenda

c pervert normal power structures and maintain the perverted structure of extortion

d benefit the rich and disadvantage the vulnerable

e provide a short-term solution to a personal need

Expectations of what bribery will bring

a survival

b unfair advantage

c corruption

d motivating someone to do either what he normally might or might not do and motivating someone to do what he should do anyway

Distinction should be made between:

a Bribery: the giver initiates the corruption

b Extortion: the receiver initiates the corruption

c Gift giving: a legal and healthy cultural norm for building personal relationships and expressing gratitude

d Tipping: an expected reward above normal wages for a job well done

WHY DOES BRIBERY EXIST?

There are social and historical reasons:

First, human nature is fallen. It is naturally greedy and has a "selfish attitude of 'me first'".There exist entrenched historical and cultural traditions. There are, in such a climate of acceptance, low levels of law enforcement and social payments to the poor.

There are economic reasons:

Economic principles create a climate for bribery: the principles of exchange means that people are paid for work they do. If wages are low people will be ready to earn extra money dishonestly to survive. Limited resources and practical shortages force people to pay bribes to obtain things. Lack of an open market means that a few in power can demand payment for necessary commodities.

Responses to bribery

a Evaluation of motives - are we guilty of initiating corruption to gain unfair advantage?

b Evaluation of the results - who benefits and who suffers?

c Understand the character of God and his desire for justice.

d   Seek and use illegal methods of problem solving - even in difficult circumstances.
e   Speak out and campaign actively:
   • never say paying bribes is necessary in business
   • begin by developing and then sustain a reputation for not participating in bribery.
   Neither pay nor accept bribes, ever.
f.   Be prepared to pay the cost.

CASE STUDIES
THREE PRACTICAL APPLICATIONS OF FACING CORRUPTION IN THE BUSINESS WORLD

This principle has important practical implications. I want to mention briefly some applications of it which I have in mind. These cases were shared previously with my discussion group.

1   When I first went back into a pastorate in 1975 after having studied at Cambridge I became involved with twelve younger people who were employed by other people. I encouraged them to go into business for themselves and since I have useful links through my work with banks I helped provide start-up capital. They did very well and all except one are still prospering. One was in business selling fire-fighting equipment. He achieved success and was making a good living by honest practice. However, once he had reached a certain level he found that to go any further and get into the big league he was going to have to pay bribes to secure orders. He knew that if he did not make an agreement to pay regularly a percentage of his commission to the officials he would not be able to realize his ambitions to make it to the top; to buy the car he wanted; to build the house he wanted. He came to share his problem with us and we prayed at length with him about it. Together we decided that at twenty-two he was still very young and had plenty of time to become affluent. He had no family dependent upon him and as president of the youth fellowship he had a duty to give a leadership example to younger people of what ethical standards should be. It was a difficult decision but we supported him in his action. Needless to say he lost the contract and it took him many years of struggle to achieve what he wanted. Wonderfully, God removed the man who was director of fire services and he, as a Christian, was able to change the whole ethos of the organization by opting from his position of power for an open-tender system so that contracts were won on their merit. Since then he has gone from strength to strength. He has also been a great supporter of the church and evangelism.

2   Another interesting example is that of obtaining permission for a piece of land. In my own Indian context I believe that males are more open-minded about such matters of necessary bribery. I am a business-oriented person and knowing the problems which can arise for anything from six months to a year when trying to acquire land it seems simpler to pay and forget about it. The other route Christians have taken in India is to ask a "consultant" to take care of all the hassles of such transactions. He pays the necessary sums over and returns to his client an official receipt. I remember a representative of an evangelical organization telling me that his organization did not pay bribes. They had bought some land without paying a single bribe for the necessary permissions. I pressed him to tell me how much he had paid for consultancy fees on the particular property we were discussing. When he told me it had amounted to 25,000 Rupees I pointed out that he had better not let the official who had received the bribe know how much they had paid because he had received only 10,000 Rupees. Once he knew the organization had given over 25,000 Rupees he would ask

ANGLICAN LIFE AND WITNESS

the consultant to produce 10,000 Rupees more from them. The use of a consultant may keep one's own hands clean but it is perpetuating the system, and working the system.

3 I myself am faced with the problem of how to respond to the pressure to be involved in a corrupt culture in order to survive in my four small businesses. These are community businesses, contributing to the local community and also through our exports, though at about $225,000 worth of garments and leather goods per year in a very small way, to the supply of hard currency which our country so desperately needs. Despite the advantage our business creates for the community we are harassed by perpetual obstacles in obtaining even export permissions, not to mention problems to do with sales tax, income tax, awkward tax officials and the many other types of permissions which are demanded. As well as paying we are also forced to use influential friends who can protect us. I am aware that it is only a temporary defence because it does nothing to alter the system.

126

13

Media and Modernity

Quentin Schultze

Around the world today the same social processes are taking place that have already engulfed the industrialized West. The break-up of the Soviet Union, for instance, has unleashed democratic impulses while promoting nationalistic tendencies in the face of a wave of worldwide capitalism. Both the scholarly pundits and the popular press are now speaking of the world economy and of the cultural conflicts brought on by new communications technologies, from cable TV to satellites and fax machines.

What is the role of media technologies in society? Is technology driving culture and society? Or are new technologies the result of political and economic interests? In short, are the mass media the cause of modernization or its product? Should evangelicals care?

Consider two fairly recent events: CNN's global coverage in 1991 of the Gulf War in the Middle East, and international syndication of the television series "Dallas". One was a relatively short-term news coverage, the other a decade-long process of economic expansion. Yet they say the same things about the role of media technologies in worldwide modernization. After establishing a biblical base for thinking about the media, we will examine these two examples of the relationship between technology and culture in the modern world.

COMMUNICATION AND CULTURE

Most of us underestimate the significance of the media in culture and society. We fail to see the *fundamental* character of communication in all human action. Adam's initial "task" was to name the creatures. This basic act of symbolization was the initial mandate of God to Adam as the first steward of culture. Our foreparents inherited this task as part of the responsibility to take care of and to develop the Creation. This "cultural mandate" was predicated on humankind's ability to use symbols (communication) responsibly.[1]

No area of human activity, from the arts to education, business and politics, could occur without our ability as symbol-using creatures. It makes all human relationships possible. It enables us to act collectively. It "mediates" between us and the Creator, whether through the scriptures (words), liturgy (words and images) or the Creation itself.

In other words, humankind is inherently a communicative species. It depends on its use of symbols to shape its experience and to establish meaningful frames of reference, often called "culture". Remember that the word "communication" is from the same Latin root as communism, communion and community. Through the gift of symbolization, God has granted all human beings a special power to "make common" with each other and with the Creator. This is the very process of communication, in and through which we make "common" actions, artifacts and meanings.

Communication is the process of creating, changing and maintaining culture, if we define "culture" broadly enough to include everything on this earth that would not be here except for the work (and play) of humankind.[2]

THE LENS OF MODERNITY

In this theological context, communication is a two-edged sword with respect to modernity. On the one hand, the mass media, as communications technologies, have contributed enormously to worldwide modernization. Television and radio, along with the printed word, have disseminated "modern" culture around the globe. Of course modern culture is always someone's culture, as I will explain shortly.

On the other hand, modernity itself is interpreted through the cultural lens established by the media. As some of the Marxist social critics were so quick to point out, the media can foster "false consciousness" - a "misperception" about an audience's real economic or political situation.[3] Advertising, for instance, may promote an image of the ideal woman without ever questioning the real value of such beauty to the individual's mental health and personal happiness. We cannot analyze modernity totally apart from the existing cultural milieu. Because of our inability to communicate perfectly with God, first, and each other, second, we will always feel alienated and we will always be alienated - even in the church.

MODERN CULTURE

In a very significant way, then, the media shape both modern society and humankind's ability to understand modernity. Media create and reflect culture, back and forth, in a rapid process that fuels modernity. Here are some of the major ways that the media promote modernization:

Commodification of culture: The media are among the most influential social institutions that transform cultural artifacts into commodities. By helping to infuse artifacts with meaning and significance, the media can turn everyday products into desirable brands and attractive styles. Some products are sought virtually worldwide. "Dallas" contributed greatly to the global popularity of western American clothing.

Preoccupation with the immediate: It is fairly easy to grasp the importance of the media as sources of immediate audience gratification. The electronic media are especially preoccupied with attracting and holding fickle audiences. This is partly what made CNN's coverage of the Gulf War so attractive; viewers felt like they were getting the "news" as it happened, with a nearly steady stream of updates and live reports.

It is more difficult to see how the media's emphasis of the "here and now" fosters cultures that are disinterested in the past and the future. By and large, tradition is not as attractive as the newest, latest and most novel media commodities. Similarly, modern people's concept of the future is nearly always short-term, so concerns over such things as ecological threats, if addressed at all in drama or news, are limited to definable "crises". The lack of historical insight in Gulf War coverage on CNN was utterly inexcusable but thoroughly understandable. "Dallas" portrays many characters who have nearly no sense of tradition and certainly no concerns with their long-range futures. They are quintessentially modern.

PROFESSIONALIZATION

Each of these media-supported trends is part of the globalization of modernity. They are more or less true, depending both on the extent of technological development and the social uses of the media technologies. Every society has to make decisions, explicitly or implicitly, about which technologies to develop and how they should be used. These decisions are, in Raymond Williams' words, part of the "long revolution" that has shaped modern culture in the West and increasingly the rest of the world. In his view, the "whole theory of mass-communication depends, essentially, on a minority in some way exploiting a majority." Mass media put the professionals in charge of culture.[4]

Probably the most significant trend in media organizations has been the professionalization of work. Modern media are not mere vehicles of personal artistic expression, individual religious conviction or any other personal insight or belief. Instead, the media are increasingly complicated organizations with institutionally defined norms for their members. Work in them is not so much a matter of personal will and intellectual freedom as much as it is an organizational mandate. There are defined ways of reporting news (actually, defining or creating news), established standards of writing and directing television drama, formulaic lists of musical recordings for radio air play, and so forth.

Even though these organizationally defined rules are created by workers, none of them is individually in charge of the process. Every one of them is assumed to be replaceable - a cog in the present machine. Their work is valued in terms of what is contributed to the overall goals of the organization, not in terms of its ultimate truth or transcendent value. Media professionals are taught not to express what they truly believe, but to be "professional", whether it is defined ideologically, as in the former Soviet Union, or economically, as in most privately operated media systems. For this reason, Jacques Ellul's critique of "technological society" was cross-cultural and cross-ideological. He recognized that the real threat was not technology per se, but a technological-mindedness that placed values like "efficiency" and "control" over all others.[5] That kind of managerial revolution is one of the major factors in determining cultural content in modern media.

Responding to the worldwide trend toward media privatization, media professionals are increasingly defining their work in commercial terms. And this is as true in religious media as it is in so-called "secular" media (which I would prefer to call "mainstream" media). Modernity has tended to move media in the direction of audience support, whether through direct subscription fees or indirectly through advertising sales. The days of individual patrons and government subsidies are rapidly disappearing. Media professionals today tune their products to the audience, thereby minimizing their own intellectual work and routinizing communication. The newspaper or TV programme is pretty much like another, except for recurring variations on established formulas - variations that usually help media moguls fine-tune their product for a particular demographically-defined market.

THE LOSS OF A PROPHETIC VOICE

These important historical processes have largely eliminated the prophetic role of the media in society. Very few media offer any sense of the significance of religious faith and transcendent values in modern life. Instead the audiences receive mounds of repetitive information. Years of imitative drama, millions of commercial appeals. Where are the public voices for justice? For love? For truth? Facts and entertainment are sorry replacements for truth, justice and compassion.

In the case of news, the only prophetic voice is evident dimly in the rhetoric of commentators and columnists. However, these forms of mass communication lose their truly prophetic edge when they are contextualized by media professionals. The result is right-wing *vs.* left-wing voices that are mere reflections of existing social dichotomies. It appears that the work of such "prophets" is really pandering – pandering to the needs of audience for publicly legitimized voices that confirm what right and left, liberal and conservative, pro-choice and pro-life already believe. This is generally true of news reporting in religious publications, too. As Ellul argued, the most effective propaganda tells people what they *want* to believe.[6]

Drama is similarly infected in the modern world. Entertaining narratives cannot ask serious questions and maintain their popularity. Audiences seek closure and confirmation. In Robert Altman's latest film, *The Player*, audiences are treated to a "traditional" Hollywood ending in which "everything works out for good". Actually, Altman offers a satire on the Hollywood system; the movie producer gets the Hollywood ending by causing all kinds of grief to others and by promoting some of the most despicably selfish goals. It turns out that the main character's selfishness matches the institutional interests of the movie company. By giving the audiences the happy endings they want, Hollywood is able to equate selfishness with altruism. Modernity's symbolic deceit is expressed metamorphically through a sardonic look at the movie industry. Needless to say, Altman's film was hailed by the critics and largely ignored by movie-goers, who seek a secular version of Romans 8:28, not the prophetic reality.

MODERN MYTHOPOETICS

Technological, economic and political forces have conspired to give the media special standing in cultures all over the world. To put it briefly, the media are not essentially in the information or entertainment businesses. They are in the business of mythopoetics, linking audiences together for shared values and beliefs. Narratives are the principal form of communication, and market-driven confirmation is the essential cultural function. Perhaps the best metaphor is the media as modern society's central nervous system, responding to people's need for culturally defined homeostasis. The media attempt to control and manipulate, but nearly al- ways in the context of some pre-established cultural end. Modern media professionals willingly exploit eager audiences.

The postmodern crisis, when looked at from the vantage point of media institutions, is nothing less than a loss of faith in the "old" mythopoetics. When traditional, confirmatory narratives lose their power to capture the "faith" of audiences, modern media face a difficult task. Non-narrative forms of entertainment, especially many contemporary commercials and rock videos, are attempts to hang on to audiences through the raw emotional power of stimulating images, moving soundtracks and rapid visual changes. This new style of mass communication appears to attract primarily younger audiences, and it is too early to tell if such audiences will still desire such postmodern messages when they reach middle age.

Probably the safest conclusion for now is that modern mythopoetics will continue to dominate the media. There will be more popular series like "Dallas", and certainly more "hypernews" such as CNN's coverage of the Gulf War. Modern culture seems to have an insatiable appetite for narratives, especially stories about the "real world". Clearly this is a long way from Adam's naming of the creatures, but it might not be all bad. Mass media have opened up the Creation by expanding the scope of humankind's symbolic universe. Unfortunately, the media have simultaneously filled the symbolic universe with commodities, celebrities, and non-prophetic mythopoetics. They have also fostered culture as a source of immediate personal gratification, elevated media professionals' mythopoetic role in society, and greatly confused people's sense of public and private life.

The church must be much more critically reflective about the media in modern society. After all, the media are contributing significantly to the cultural context in which the church exists. We need a prophetic response to the non-prophetic media - a response which challenges the very legitimacy of modern media culture while affirming the goodness of humankind's communicative ability.

The newer technologies, especially such things as fax machines, computer networks and cellular telephones, have the potential to improve life and to affirm prophetic responses to modernity. However, history shows how new media eventually become means for large, mainstream organizations to manipulate and control minority cultures, religious as well as non-religious. For this reason it is essential that Christians participate in public hearings about the regulation and ownership of media. In the selfish hands of modern organizations, the media will continue to promote modernity.

Notes

1   Among the books that have influenced me on this point are Henry R. Van Til, *The Calvinist Concept of Culture* (Philadelphia: Presbyterian and Reformed Publishing Co., 1959), and Albert M. Wolters, *Creation Regained* (Grand Rapids, MI: Eerdmans, 1985). For a critique of evangelicals' lack of cultural theory, see Clifford G. Christians, "Redemptive Media as the Evangelical's Cultural Task", in Quentin J. Schultze, ed., *American Evangelicals and the Mass Media* (Grand Rapids, MI: Zondervan/Academie, 1990), pp.331-356.

2   Probably the best treatment of this topic is in James W. Carey, *Communication as Culture* (Boston: Unwin Hyman, 1989). The major intellectual and theological issue is the relationship between symbols and "truth", especially ultimate, transcendent truth. One solution, argued by T.S. Eliot, was to posit that religion cannot be reduced to culture, but is at the root of all "real" cultures (Notes, *Towards the Definition of Culture* [NY: Harcourt, Brace, 1949]). Eliot's conservative view, which some critics saw as ethnocentric, contrasts with progressive or liberal views that culture is but an imperfect reflection of transcendent truths which cannot be completely grasped by any human beings in a cultural context. Closer to the latter view would be William F. Fore, *Television and Religion* (Minneapolis: Augsburg, 1987).

3   For a sampling of more or less Marxist critiques see Alvin W. Gouldner, *The Dialectic of Ideology and Technology* (NY: Seabury, 1976); James Curran, et.al., *Mass Communication and Society* (London: Edward Arnold, 1977).

4   Raymond Williams, *Culture and Society* (NY: Harper & Row, 1958), p.314.

5   Jacques Ellul, *The Technological Society* (NY: Vintage Books, 1964).

6   Jacques Ellul, *Propaganda* (NY: Alfred A. Knopf, 1971).

14

A Christian Response to Population Issues
An Oxford Statement Resource Document

THE NATURE OF POPULATION CHALLENGES AND RESPONSES

The focus of the consultation was on populations of the south. (The needs of declining and ageing populations in the north were not our theme.) Some perceive the problem to be that populations of the south are growing so much that they threaten the finite resources of the world. For others the issues relate primarily to the needs and rights of populations: identity, health care, the allocation of resources, and issues of justice since the populations of the north consume far more of the earth's resources per capita than the populations of the south. Our approach was to develop a global perspective; examine the effect of relationships between nations of the south and the north in respect to the challenges of population and speak to the whole church with a global Christian response.

Many countries of the south face challenges of rapid population growth and policies of population control. The roots of these policies go back to theoretical frameworks defined earlier in the north.

Population growth does not provide the drama of a financial crisis or political upheaval, but it has received more than its fair share of attention over the last fifty to sixty years from academics, policymakers and activists. Many people believe that what governments and their peoples do today to influence their demographic future will set the terms for a development strategy well into the next century.

There is a need to view the population issue from other perspectives than those formed from classical demographic transition theory which appears to be the dominant influence on responses to population issues. There is also a need to avoid perspectives which are premised on finite resources since statistics show that food supplies are increasing and may still increase further.

By the end of the nineteenth century it was common knowledge that the birth rates were falling in many if not all of the industrialized countries of the north. The classical demographic transition theory was born in 1945 when

Notestein offered a twofold explanation for why western fertility had begun to decline. Fertility was kept high in premodern societies through the maintenance of a whole series of support structures: "religious doctrines, moral codes, laws, education, community customs, marriage habits and family organizations ... all focused towards maintaining high fertility" (Notestein 1945). High fertility was necessary for the survival of families in the face of high infant mortality that would otherwise have led to population decline and extinction. Notestein (1945), Davis (1945) and Thompson (1929) put forward the view that the initial trigger of change was a decline in mortality, to which fertility responded by declining after some time-lag. Furthermore, fundamental to the understanding and application of the demographic transition theory was the idea that the development of industrialized and urban societies dissolved the largely corporate family- based traditional societies and replaced them with an individualism marked above all by the increasing secularization of urban societies. Therefore economic development and subsequent urbanization necessarily undermine traditional values that support high fertility in premodern societies. In 1953 the 'father of modern demography' Notestein pointed out the "urban industrial society" was the "crucible of the demographic transition theory".

These notions have been widely employed by policymakers and politicians and, until recently, largely accepted without significant modification. In 1972 Paul Demeny stated that the "... demographic transition theory has become the central preoccupation of modern demography because of the light it claims to shed on the rapid population growth in the developing countries." In the last twenty years, the improved availability of historical and contemporary data has revealed that there are considerable weaknesses in the classical formulation. More specifically, John Knodel and Eitteene van de Walle (1979) point out that there is no simple association between economic development and population growth. Furthermore, the French transition demonstrated a widespread decline in fertility whilst the country was still at a low level of industrial, urban and social development. Also, there was a simultaneous reduction in both mortality and fertility in the population as a whole. Demographers have begun to understand that within individual countries regional cultural factors, such as language and religion, seem to be more important sources of variation in fertility in many cases than economic variables.

Nevertheless, the central tradition of the demographic transition theory, that modernization is the route to lower population growth, is still an integral element in population policies in the two-thirds world. Proponents of radical action to reduce population growth see humans facing a new problem. Rapid and exponential population growth in this "closed system" will inevitably cause a systemic strain on resources. Poorer nations of the south will become "demographically entrapped" as the weight of current and projected numbers of people overcome the carrying capacity of the environment. Authors of this view (King, Elliot, Hellberg) argue that to avert a crisis, extreme measures are necessary. The provision of family planning methods is therefore a pragmatic response to an increasingly global environmental catastrophe. King *et al* have advocated the case for a "one child world". Despite the obvious ethical implications of the Chinese experiments, proponents of population control believe that since the tension between human demography and ecological limits is unprecedented so too must be the solution.

At the heart of the demographic transition theory and subsequent population policies is the need to do away with traditions, cultures, ideologies, ethics, gender sensitivities and religious implacabilities that are seen to promote and support high fertility in nations of the south. Radical proponents of control like King *et al* urge us to steel ourselves for a taboo-free discussion of radical solutions. However, it is the extent to which governments and individuals agree with this view of population growth that will determine the future action for population policies and programmes in the different cultures and contexts of the two-thirds world.

THEOLOGICAL THEMES RELEVANT TO POPULATION ISSUES

Whatever our perception of the population issue, in order to identify the appropriate contribution of Christian communities, in particular their role in shaping the policy of governments, we need a theology of populations. The understanding of populations must be understood in the light of God's purpose in creation as seen in the Genesis record and God's plans for the future as revealed in the images of the consummation of the kingdom of God.

Responsible stewardship of God's provision

God created the earth and its resources and proclaimed that they were good. He placed human beings as stewards on this good earth. Humanity is given dominion over the earth, and is to image and represent God the king. So humanity is to mirror God's kingly rule of the earth, which the Bible describes in such terms as the rule of a shepherd, a husband, a beneficent ruler, and a father (Ps. 23; Hos. 2:16; Ps. 10:16--18; Lk. 11:2; Hos. 11:1-4). God is actively involved in enabling us to fulfil that stewardship.

God enabled the creation to multiply and promised to provide for that fruitfulness. God's blessing of creation was to provide "every seed-bearing plant … every green plant for food" (Gen. 1:30). Humans are called to justice and love in stewarding God's provision. Our stewardship includes our relationships with God, one another and the environment. The Genesis material calls for development of God's resources through work, just distribution,caring relationships between men and women, and parenthood. All these are to be undertaken in accountability to the God who provides enough for all in justice. They therefore are to be exercised with responsibility since God's provision is not at the whim of human excess and irresponsibility. The transcendent dimension which requires responsible use of earth's resources is humanity's accountability to God, not necessarily to the transcendent notion of non-existent unborn generations in the future.

God created humanity in grace and freewill to be his image and representative. God's undeserved love for all humans he created and their calling to represent him in the task of developing the creation is the basis for the intrinsic value of persons, prior to their membership of a community or their economic role. It is the reason why people are ends and not means.

The Fall impacted both God's provision and humanity's stewardship. The task of securing food now from God's provision required real effort (Gen. 3:17-19). God's provision is no less. The failure is in the capacity of humans to steward God's resources so that they are able to feed themselves with abundance. The forces of unjust power, lust and greed frustrate relationships between men and women resulting in much of the suffering women experience. They also spoil the proper use and sharing of resources and create the poverty which puts pressure on human ability to support a rising population. In such situations stewardship has not been exercised responsibly or shaped by justice, and so some have consumed more at the expense of others.

The Fall has also affected women's role in being fruitful. The fruitfulness which characterizes women now has an extra cost in increased pain while bearing children. Men have the extra burden of providing for their families through harder toil, women experience extra pain in the bearing of children. To the woman God said: "I will greatly increase your pangs in childbearing; in pain you shall bring forth children, yet your desire shall be for your husband, and he shall rule over you." And to the man he said: "Because you have listened to the voice of your wife ... cursed is the ground because of you; in toil you shall eat of it ... by the sweat of your face you shall eat bread" (Gen. 3:16-18).

For men and women, excessive pain in work or lack of work both express the pain of the Fall and threaten their identity and self-esteem. The economic and emotional support of the family is to be shared by a male and female. In situations of unemployment, when men have no paid work, women can still bear children but men are further oppressed if they are denied a role in the support of the woman and her child.

In a Christian relationship, men and women are to support each other in bearing one another's pain whether that be the pain associated with childbearing, the pain of infertility, painful work or lack of work.

Shalom and responsible relationships

Humanity is still accountable to God after the Fall, and if we live responsibly in the light of that accountability we can still build shalom; just relationships in human communities. Shalom is experienced in justice, compassion and mercy, and needs to be expressed in law, covenant and regulated commitments (Jer. 32:38-41).

Children are not the product of the curse of the Fall, they are a blessing from the Lord. God's blessing to Abraham was the promise of many descendants, in particular through a barren wife, even when there was no human capacity to fulfil his promise. God also blessed Abraham's first son Ishmael and his mother,

Hagar. She was a single mother by the decision of others. While Hagar and Ishmael were a reminder to Abraham and his descendants of Abraham and Sarah's failure and unfaithfulness, God did not reject her but blessed her, promised her many descendants, and provided for her (Gen. 16).

The Hebrew slaves who had become numerous and were subjected to an enforced programme of population limitation (Ex. 1:8-22) became more populous. The Hebrew midwives who feared God and protected the babies were given families, and the Hebrews were promised a land flowing with milk and honey (Ex. 13:5). God's promise to Abraham was fulfilled even through conditions of slavery and oppression.

The future, freedom and choice

In the population debate projections about the future are important tools in understanding possible scenarios in our global future. They are often used to make decisions about the present. When they are used to portray an apocalyptic scenario, they create confusion and alarm. This is meant to motivate us into taking unprecedented action. More often people feel a sense of powerlessness and anxiety which can in turn produce the inertia which works against positive action.

While we listen as carefully as possible to the advocacy of demographers and historians, we ought to recognize that the final vision of the future that shapes our contemporary decision making is the vision of Kingdom of God in Christ and the right relationships, the shalom, it demands. Jesus was the one who brought the Kingdom of God, which is new relationships between people and God, between people, and between people and the whole of creation (Lk. 11:2-4, 20). His resurrection is the affirmation that the Kingdom of God has entered world history (Rev. 11:15; 21:14), and that Christ's return to consummate the Kingdom will bring a new heaven and a new earth to the climax and fulfilment world history (Rom. 8:23). As we await his return we live in the Kingdom in the power of God's Holy Spirit, which is the first fruits of the Kingdom.

The argument about accountability to future generations has in many debates tended to replace the transcendent accountability to God. The Kingdom of God is the only future reality to which we are finally accountable. Human projections must be related to God's revealed purposes of the consummation of the Kingdom and not force us into ethical pragmatism or ambiguity. We should therefore avoid panic, and making pragmatic and immoral decisions which do not respect human life and choice. The price we pay for God's moral choices will never undermine the future God has planned. Our goal is to build a community which practises and promotes Christian virtues of virginity and faithfulness (1 Cor. 6:16–20; Col. 3:12–17).

The Kingdom of God sets the context for our moral action and choices which express Christian virtues. The Kingdom of God is righteousness, peace and joy in the Holy Spirit (Rom. 14:17). In this Kingdom the Son of God makes us truly free (Jn 8:36). The freedom which is presupposed by the exercise of choice is not an anarchic freedom to choose any action we may please. Freedom means we are not hindered from fulfilling our calling to be the human beings God wills us to be, whatever the constraint. There are many obstacles to fulfilling this calling, many of which are expressions of human sin and selfishness. The activity of the Kingdom in the world em- powers society. Christians and others who accept this activity of Kingdom move society in the direction of the life of the final Kingdom of God, countering the moral disablement that evil brings in society, strengthening the good and restraining evil. The Holy Spirit, the gift of the Kingdom, works in society strengthening the wills of people who may not be Christians to turn God's way. Such empowerment does not guarantee that all will be able to live out the Christian ethic, but it enables them to see the possibilities and make their choices. Kingdom activity unmasks the activity of the evil one, convicts people and strengthens their wills to act (John 18:8-11). It conserves society and clarifies people's choice. This makes the invitation of the gospel of the Kingdom relevant in every situation.

We act therefore, not out of panic or pragmatism, but because we are convinced that God's future for the world will vindicate biblical obedience. New Testament Christians lived in the conviction that not history but Jesus would vindicate them when he came. We live in the same hope. In Colossians 3:1–4 and 12:15 Paul argues that the values and virtues that Jesus demonstrated are eternal. The resurrection vindicated these values and virtues which express the risen life hidden in Jesus until he comes: compassion, kindness, humility, gentleness, patience, tolerance and forgiveness. These virtues must direct our action, inform our choices, and support the choices that people make in the light of the life of the Kingdom.

In our commitment to enable people to exercise the choice which is fundamental to being human, we both recognize the "right to be wrong" and also the need to provide the context of the Kingdom which is necessary to enable people to make the choices which are "in the way" of the Kingdom and which express the life of virtue. This will require both information and support for individuals, and in the wider context of society, processes and structures which support and enable those choices to be sustained. It will also require teaching and sharing of the life of the Kingdom and the lifestyle that represents it. People do not make choices as isolated, independent, rational decisions, but in relation to a whole series of cultural, religious, traditional, and relational factors. In order to enable people to make informed and Christian choices in reproduction, we need Christian input to address all these areas.

The family

God is revealed in the New Testament as the Father. Parents not only receive children as a gift from God but see their parenting as being representative of God's care for his children. Marriage is at the heart of family life in that men and women together represent the image of God and in their permanent, faithful and public commitment to one another provide a stable and loving context in which children can flourish. Families provide a context in which mutual support, respect and love combine, and this can be the basis for including others who through bereavement, divorce, or exclusion of other kinds have become separated from the loving support of their original families. This inclusiveness means that families may have many members who may or may not be blood-related but who see themselves as belonging to a family group with whom they have made their home. Such inclusiveness provides the basis for a critique of the view of the nuclear family which is seen as complete when only parents and children are included. It also means that although marriage is at the heart of the family it is possible for people to become family together who share that mutual support, love and respect. The church is called the family of God and Christians see each other as brothers and sisters in Christ.

Christians are called to reflect biblical realism about the family. In a fallen world the family is threatened and becomes a place where there is pain. The work and employment which provide for the family's needs may be scarce or if available may be arduous toil. Unemployment becomes not only associated with low personal self-worth but also becomes a threat to the sustainability of the family. Reproduction and child-rearing, which should reflect fruitfulness and blessing, become intermingled with pain and frustration. Maternal morbidity, infant mortality, adolescent waywardness or other tragedy provide a context in which men and women are to share in each other's pain.

Sadly many families' relationships are not loving and respectful. Life becomes a tragedy for people when the life of the family becomes the very place where they are most abused. Children are particularly vulnerable to abuse not only through physical and sexual violence and emotional abuse, but also through under-age employment and in war. The church as the people of God the Father is the primary definition of the family (Mk. 3:35 and par.) and thus the Christian community is called to be the larger family in which people suffering the pains and hurts of human families can be supported and in which their healing can begin.

Christians must not idolize the family. Families are to be in the service of the Kingdom, not in the service of nurturing individual consciences. On the one hand, the Kingdom paradigm provides a warning to families where family life has become an idol. Families live for their security, welfare and fulfilment. Family life becomes an end. Jesus' teaching on the conflict of interest between family obligation and Kingdom service is clear. "No one," said Jesus, "who puts his hand to the plough and looks back is fit for service in the Kingdom of God" (Lk. 10:62). The service of the Kingdom is to be the goal of family life. Self-fulfilment and family wholeness and happiness are to be fruits of such service. On the other hand, in the Protestant west, the responsibility of nurturing and teaching individual consciences was assigned primarily to the family with support from the local church. This model of family places the emphasis on individual responsibility which a family must nurture and support. The individual needs take priority over family needs. The social vitality of the family is neglected in the commitment to promote individual fulfilment and responsibility.

Marriage and singleness

While marriage is the norm for most people, the church in many places is too directed to those who are married and neglects the single. In some cultures, there is a tendency (even amongst Christians) to disparage those (especially women) who have never married or who have been widowed or divorced. Paul sees singleness as a desirable state for Christians (1 Cor. 7:8). There is a widespread need for the church and individual Christians to give full acceptance to those who are single for whatever reason. The church must not be allowed to marginalize or exclude the single (for example by activities directed solely to the married and their families), and positively must ensure that singles have an equal place in the church, that their gifts are identified and fully used in the church.

Sex and sexuality

Sex and sexuality is God's good gift to us, but can be misused. God' s will is that the exercise of our sexuality should be restricted to the marriage relationship. Scripture says little about the procreational purpose for sex. Sex in scripture is primarily relational. In Matthew 19:65 Jesus quotes from Genesis 1:27 and 2:24 that God made humanity as male and female, and that therefore a man leaves his father and mother to be joined to his wife and become one flesh with her. Here, sexuality has its role within the one flesh relationship of marriage. In 1 Corinthians 7:1-5, Paul responds to those Corinthians who proposed that it is better for a man not to "touch", i.e., have sexual intercourse with, his wife: "Because of temptations to immoralities, each man should have his own wife, and each wife her own husband." He shows that each partner has a responsibility towards the sexual needs of the spouse, and that the body of the husband belongs to the wife and that of the wife to the husband. They may not deprive each other of a sexual relationship except by agreement for a short time for prayer. In Paul's discussion, there is evenhandedness between the sexual needs and responsibilities of both husbands and wives, and there is no reference to procreation. For Paul, sex has an important role in marriage apart from procreation.

We note with great concern the growing incidence of sexual activity and childbearing outside a marriage against biblical norms. The church should teach biblical chastity and responsible parenthood and affirm that it is wrong to engage in sexual relations and childbearing outside a marriage. The story of Hagar and Ishmael indicates that single parents should not be stigmatized. God entered into a covenantal relationship with them (Gen. 16 and 21). So such people must also be welcomed into and experience God's blessings in the covenant as families.

Marriage and in vitro fertilization

We recognize the strength of the desire of couples to have a child and to use IVF if pregnancy is not possible by other means. There is no inherent Christian objection to IVF for married couples, but it is open to grave abuse, particularly where fertilized ova are frozen and later used for experimentation. But we also hold two views about the use of IVF. One view, based on the belief that life begins at fertilization, is that a fertilized ovum is a human being. This view objects to freezing ova, keeping them alive as ova, implanting them, and throwing them away if not needed. It would be preferable to take ova for their immediate fertilization and implantation without freezing them. The other view is that there is no Christian basis for rejecting the freezing of ova, or their implantation in the mother at a suitable later time, or to the destruction of fertilized ova that are not needed for implantation, so long as abuses are avoided. There is room for Christian discussion of what is and is not acceptable.

Marriage and polygamy

The Bible neither condemns nor prohibits polygamy, and sets forth monogamy as God's perfect will. The Old Testament has numerous instances of polygamous marriages. and though accompanied by problems of suffering, they are recognized as valid marriages. The scripture provides for the protection of second and other wives from exploitation. When missionaries brought the gospel to polygamous cultures, they usually made no attempt to explore the reasons for polygamy in that culture. Missionaries usually required converted husbands to have only one wife. In some areas the husband was required to put away all except his first wife; in other areas the husband was permitted to choose which wife to keep. Both policies were contrary to the Bible's teaching against separation and divorce and assumed, contrary to scripture, that polygamous marriages were invalid marriages. These policies caused great anguish through the break up of loving, caring polygamous families, and brought great deprivation to polygamous wives and their children through forcing them out of their marital homes.

Some churches accept polygamous families in their midst, but do not allow the husband or his wives to be the communicants or be baptized. Christians are to adhere to the biblical ideal of marriage as a union of one man and one woman, but equally
   a) the church must recognize polygamous marriages entered into prior to conversion as valid marriages, even if less than the Christian ideal.
   b) policies adopted by the church in relation to the parties of polygamous marriages must take account of the biblical teaching noted above.
   c) the church must seek to change or remove the cultural, economic and other factors that have led to the practice of polygamy in a society.

Mother and child health

Mother and child health is an important part of shalom. Maternal mortality is the leading cause of death among women of reproductive age (15-44 years). Half a million women die every year as a result of pregnancy complications. 99 per cent of those deaths are in the two-thirds world. The risk of a woman dying as a result of pregnancy is 200 times higher in the developing world than in the west. The vast majority of these deaths are entirely preventable through improved access to maternal and child health resources. Spacing children has dramatic impact on the health of mother and child. A child born within two years of a previous birth has twice the risk of dying than one born over two years later. Providing maternal healthcare means healthy mothers and healthy babies and also affirms the dignity and value of women. The emphasis on women's childbearing role has led to a concomitant emphasis on reproductive health. But other areas of their health have been neglected.

Women in society

The education of women is a task which is inherently significant and important. This is not because of its consequences but because women are equal with men before God and should have access to wisdom and knowledge about the world they live in and which God has placed them in. This educational provision does not refer to health education alone but to all sectors of general education including primary education for girl children. In terms of fertility it has been repeatedly shown that every year of female education has the impact of lowering fertility. When women are educated they start having children later, space them further apart and finish having them sooner which is good for both mother and child health.

Women may suffer domestic violence, have the decision to have children imposed on them, be regarded as sexual objects or only valued for procreation. Infertility may bring disgrace and rejection, and widowhood may bring loss of status and even home. In such a society the woman becomes powerful as the mother of a son through whom she can exert power. A woman's identity can be tied up with the number of sons she produces and in society where women are not part of the labour market can only add to the income of the family through producing sons. Daughters have to be paid for and are not themselves part of the income of the family but are seen as a drain on its resources. This has implications for the need to change inheritance laws and to promote access to education and employment for women so that they may provide for their families. Women need access to the opportunities which men enjoy not because the education and employment of women lowers fertility, but because they are human and intrinsically have equal worth in God's eyes. Children may be forced to work as child labour or thrown out of home and have to eke out an existence as a 'street kid'. In countries where there is a boy preference, girl children may be aborted, given names which express dismay, lack adequate nutrition, or have their humanity disregarded in other ways.

Family planning

Is it ethically desirable to limit the potential size of our families? There seems to be widespread agreement that where couples desire to limit the size of their families this is an appropriate stewardship of resources and callings. However Christians also often celebrate larger families and some feel that family size should be left to the providence of God. We recognize that Catholics reject modern contraceptive methods in favour of natural methods of fertility postponement; but we affirm that people should have the opportunity of access to and informed choice from the full range of available methods of contraception. A person's view as to whether human life begins at fertilization or at implantation is likely to affect their decision concerning which methods of contraception are ethically acceptable. We endorse the statement of the Cairo conference that abortion is not acceptable as a means of family planning.

Across the world family planning is overwhelmingly the responsibility of women. The proportion of couples who rely on male methods—the condom, withdrawal and vasectomy – is 1–12% in most countries. The debate on family planning therefore usually focuses on the needs and preferences of women. Family planning is important where couples want to have smaller families, or where they wish to space their children. Where they do not family planning will not be effective. We see a difference between family planning and the use of contraception in population control. All too often state programmes or those of international agencies have had as their objective the lowering of fertility levels rather than enabling couples to plan their own families. Such programmes have been accompanied by population targets through which the success of the programme can be monitored. From the standpoint of the needs of women all too often the quality of these programmes has been low. There has been inadequate information, counselling and follow-up associated with them.

AIDS care and prevention

HIV/AIDS is a pandemic problem which has serious consequences for people, their families and communities, the church and the nations. It causes intense suffering to those who contract it and always results in death. Christians as a healing community are called to respond to the HIV/AIDS tragedy with acts of compassion. However the church community is also a source of values which result in permanent personal and social transformation. Churches can help to prevent the further spread of HIV infection:

- through effective and appropriate HIV/AIDS awareness campaigns.
- by addressing the socio-economic, cultural and other behavioural factors that put people at the risk of infection. For example, the culture of premarital and extramarital sex, widow inheritance, unfair economic systems, HIV/AIDS orphans, inappropriate sex education proposals and gender disparities.
- by being involved in practical medical help, homecare and counselling.
- by building appropriate coping mechanisms in their communities to support the affected families.

In our world we have to live with the consequences of our behaviour and take responsibility for behaviour which may be intrinsically wrong whether it has negative consequences or not. The link between HIV/AIDS and sexual behaviour has led some to see HIV/AIDS as a personal curse of God on someone who is sexually immoral. We do not accept this. If this were so it would be easy to continue the behaviour but avoid the curse by using "safer sex" methods which are still sinful if outside the marriage context. Also many people contract HIV/AIDS who have not been in- volved in immoral sexual behaviour. Spouses may contract it through unpro- tected sexual contact with their partners, infants through breast milk and haemophiliacs through infected blood transfusions. However, when societies depart from God's norms for communities in socio-economic, political and spiritual relationships, then they have to take the consequences. This is not only true of immoral sexual behaviour but also of the poverty which drives so many women into prostitution as the only means of providing for themselves and their children. God suffers with people in their distress, so Christians should be compassionate and sensitive to the needs of people living with HIV/AIDS and aim to be a source of healing love to them.

HUMAN RIGHTS

Rapid population growth is either left for future generations to address or tackled with the blunt instrument of economic and social policies which ignore the humanitarian aspects of the problem. Public policies designed to reduce poverty, urban growth or unemployment may violate the basic right to life and liberty and so aggravate rather than alleviate the problem. "Human Rights"– the idea that individuals possess certain fundamental rights – have been enshrined in national law and international treaty. The legal instruments attempt to define human rights and to argue for their universality. This framework is used as a starting point for the development of public policy.

But there is a tension between the legal provisions and practical experience. Policy makers are sometimes unaware of the humanitarian implications of their actions. Rampant individualism (the western preoccupation with "self-determination" and "self-fulfilment") can ignore responsibility for the neighbour and respect for the world. Human beings must always be the subject and never the object. From this perspective we need to go behind the legal instruments to recognize that human rights derive from the essential nature of the human being. They reside in the answer to the question "What is the right for humans?"

It is therefore difficult to separate the question of rights from a discussion of the origin and destiny of humankind. Made in God's image, spoiled by sin and yet reconciled and set free by Christ, the human being is destined to conform to the image of God's Son (Rom. 8:29). Whatever else may be intended by this idea, the image of God (sometimes understood statically as the possession of some inherent characteristic) is changed into a dynamic concept (being transformed into the image of Christ). To be human is to be "on the way" to this identity. Human experience (including suffering and death) is a means to this end.

This suggests a positive, transforming Christian view of human rights. The present legal instruments are often inadequate in the numerous particularities of human life. Action is needed inside the claims of those who live in pain and desperation. The reality of human life must be grasped as concretely as possible. Only then can despair be transformed into hope.

Life is a gift, ("I have come to bring life in all its abundance" Jesus said), and is protected by God. Not even a sparrow falls to the ground without the Father's knowledge (Matt. 10:29). The right to life is in his hands (Gen. 9:5–6).

The most basic human right, after the right to life itself, is to speech: the freedom to process pain in words. Suffering people will not receive help if they remain silent. The biblical records shows how human suffering, when articulated, calls upon God to act, and releases his power into the human situation. Barthimaeus was insistent in his cry for help (Mk. 10:47). Moses knew that silence leads to brick quotas. Words of pain or protest begin the transformation.

So, too, do honest words of confession. "I am a man of unclean lips" set Isaiah on his path to fulfilment. Until pain or sin is articulated, the human lot is not a happy one. When it is, human life is transformed in accordance with its purpose and people begin to discover "what is right for humans".

Thus we affirm that:

- Human beings, both male and female, are created in the image of God and are loved unconditionally by him. From this they derive rights and responsibilities.
- God has granted freedom of choice, which does not mean unlimited freedom to encroach on the rights and freedoms of others.
- Life is a gift from God, and all couples have the right responsibly to choose the number, spacing and timing of their children.
- God-given life is sacred and no one has the right to terminate life from conception on until God decides to recall that life.
- God intended that every human being has a right to life in all its fullness (Jn. 10:10).

The implications of this for population issues are for us as follows:

- The compulsory use of sterilization and abortion (also a means of contraception) should be condemned and its unqualified prohibition as a serious violation of human rights.
- We disapprove of all forms of incentives and disincentives for pro-choice behaviours as these could be of disproportionate value to the poor; this is an infringement of their freedom of rights.
- We believe that institutions, be it the state, church or NGOs, should not formulate and implement policies that interfere with and impinge on the conjugal life and rights of couples.
- We affirm the right of the people and the church to participate in the formulation and implementation of state policies and programmes in relation to population and reproductive health.
- We affirm that people have a right of access to full information and also the means of planning the welfare of their families. We should strive to spread awareness of an increase in access to such information.
- We caution that experiments both in positive and negative eugenics should be monitored for human rights violation.

- We categorically condemn infanticide and use of medical technology for sex determination leading to foeticide, and see this as an infringement on the rights of unborn children.

Rights should go hand in hand with responsibility and should be discussed in the contexts of God's purposes for creation. Programmes on human rights should go hand in hand with empowerment.

ECONOMIC DEVELOPMENT, URBANIZATION AND EMPLOYMENT

Economic development

There is no simple relationship between growth and economic development. Economic development is essential when one is focusing on the wider issues associated with population needs. Healthcare, housing, education and employment are all components of economic development. Countries such as Sri Lanka and Taiwan have succeeded in lowering fertility without being seen as economically "developed" nations. Despite this, the world's majority especially in the two-thirds world are increasingly being trapped in the grim realities of poverty.

Out of the biblical mandate to pursue and promote justice in society, the church is called to take her prophetic role and critically analyze and challenge inappropriate and insensitive population and economic policies. World peace and development will depend more on individual and corporate repentance at all levels and on the willingness to act justly. Unconditional love for neighbour should permeate all levels of policy formulation and implementation.

Urbanization

When urbanization is handled appropriately, it is possible for it to be managed in such a way that it can result in the celebration of family life. But the way urbanization is taking place in the two-thirds world produces increasing pollution, displacement of people, the phenomenon of street children, prostitution, unemployment and the disintegration of families: aspects which we Christians cannot ignore.

Rural-urban migration often threatens the integrity of the family. Poverty in the rural areas forces people to leave their homes to seek employment in the city. Such poverty can be the result of government funding being focused on urban areas to the detriment of rural areas. The lack of employment can bring about a sense of desperation and insecurity. Removed from their traditional values people can succumb to alcohol and drug addictions, prositution and theft. Those who remain at home bear the burden of providing food and other resources for their children and extended family. This migration also places kinship structures, local management systems, extended families and traditional support structures under great strain. Furthermore it reinforces an individualistic approach to life, found in the city, which rests uneasily with indigenous and traditional values. Despite these problems the migration to the cities in search of a better life continues. Cities are expanding at an enormous rate. Lack of proper housing, sanitation and the basic amenities of life leads to the growth of slum dwellings which are often illegal and constantly threatened with removal. The conditions in the slums are so poor that children frequently die from diarrhoeal and respiratory infections.

This is not a dilemma of the 21st century. This is a harsh reality of the 20th century to which we are called urgently to respond in a ministry of bringing wholeness of life.

Secularization

Where population programmes idolize low fertility, secularization and modernization can be seen as essential tools to make this possible. Though modernization brings some comforts of life, in many instances it has not enriched the spiritual life of many urban dwellers. Where low fertility is made the highest virtue, religious belief and custom, moral codes, and traditional family values are frequently disregarded. Definitions of freedom of choice derived from market economics are imported into cultures which see voluntary moral restraint and the promotion of virtue as an essential component of freedom. Secularization has not served the industrialized societies well and the individualistic and hedonistic definitions of freedom combined with consumerism have led to the breakdown of public and private morality.

Therefore as we participate in improving people's welfare, we should constantly remind ourselves about the duty we have of bringing people to Christ. We also recommend that the church sets the example of tackling urbanization by decentralizing more her services by taking more part in developing the rural areas of the south.

Employment

Between 1995 and 2000 AD the UN estimates that 100 million additional people will be added to the global population. This presents a challenge to policy makers and planners to create opportunities for employment for 40% of them that will make up the labour force. Structural adjustment policies in the third world have resulted in a reduction in employment. The impact of these policies have been felt most by lower skilled men and women who are the easiest to remove from the labour force in times of resource constraint. International debt repayments also hamper the ability of governments to use resources for internal development.

As we proclaim "shalom" and wholeness of life to the world, we should remember that work is central to self-actualization and fulfilment. The lives of many people today are miserable because they cannot access meaningful and fulfilling work. We are particularly concerned that if the gospel is to be a fulfilling gospel, the churches should:

i) examine the level and nature of unemployment in their particular communities;

ii) identify the factors responsible for this problem, and

iii) design and implement appropriate measures for dealing with this problem as part of the gospel.

Also work has been taken by many people as a curse contrary to the original biblical value of stewardship. The church should reconstruct an appropriate theology of work and encourage people to value and appreciate every type of work available to them, mindful of the fact that there is a divine duty of maximizing the productivity of whatever resources that have been availed to each of us as the parable of the talents teaches us.

Environmental issues

Though some environmentalists worship the creation in place of the creator, we are concerned that creation is being plundered and polluted at a rate that will make human life impossible in the near future. God called us to be stewards of earth, to develop, use and protect it.

We therefore call upon governments, the churches and all people to:
i) review the present environmental situation in their country or communities;
ii) identify the factors that are causing degradation of the environment and the extinction of species;
iii) review the existing policies that protect the environment, and
iv) develop appropriate measures for addressing the problem of environmental destruction and degradation.

These measures should stand against irreversible choices and harm; favour sustainable rather than one-off benefits and pay special attention to those groups of people, plants and animal species that will be especially vulnerable to policy choices and decisions.

Interfaith co-operation

We approve and support the move to understanding other faiths in order to find a base for dialogue and for positive action on global issues that affect our practice of the religion we follow. We are conscious however that witnessing to our faith should not be lost on account of dialogue and tolerance and that witness should not only be in word but also in action.

Further resources

On issues of development see *Transformation: The Church in Response to Human Need* (EFICOR Training Unit, India, Grove Booklets on Ethics,1986). (Available from Ridley Hall, Cambridge.)

On wider aspects of economic policies see "The Oxford Declaration on Christian Faith and Economics", *Transformation Journal*, (April 1990), published as chapter 9 in this volume and "The Market Economy and the Poor", *Transformation Journal* (July 1995), published as chapter 11 in this volume (Available from OCMS, P.O. Box 70, Oxford OX2 6HB).

On issues of church and state see "Osijek Statement on Church and State", *Transformation Journal* (July 1995).

On wider aspects of the environment see "International Evangelical Christianity and the Environment", *Transformation Journal* (October 1993 and January 1994).

On issues of migrant populations see "Refugees and Ethnic Identity", *Transformation Journal* (April 1995).

On the Kingdom of God see *Word, Kingdom and Spirit* (available from OCMS, P.O. Box 70, Oxford OX2 6HB), and in "Kingdom Affirmations" in *Transformation Journal* (July 1994), published as chapter 16 in this volume.

References

John Knodel and Eittenne van de Walle "Lessons from the past: Policy implications of historical fertility studies," *Population and Development Review* 5 (1979, pp.217–45).

FW Notestein, "Population, the long view", in TW Shultz (ed.), *Food for the World* (Chicago: University of Chicago Press, 1945).

15

Christian Feminism and Feminist Perspectives on Population Control

Harriet A Harris

"Women whether at home or at work, are generally more easily hurt by difficult situations and angry words, and less able to cope with the cut and thrust of life. We are made as complementary individuals to men and we need their strength, their objectivity and their protection at difficult times.

But equally, our very sensitivity and vulnerability makes us more ready to recognize our need of God and of His daily power and protection. While a man is often too busy to acknowledge his need of a Saviour, a woman knows her need because it is an integral part of her own make-up".[1]

INTRODUCTION:
PASSIVITY, SELF-IDENTITY AND OPPRESSION

Western feminism is to a large extent reeling against the same cultural understanding of women that has influenced such socially and theologically impoverished statements as that cited by Ann Warren (above) with regard to how Christian men and women relate to one another. In the Christian west, especially in the last 200 years, women have been regarded as the more emotional, less rational sex, less able than men to cope with the competitive world of business and politics, and best suited to the home and the private or at least domestic domain. Our culture is still under the legacy of nineteenth century notions of womanhood, in which women are praised for such virtues as sensitivity, prayerfulness and spirituality, moral obedience, and selflessness. While these are virtues with which men sentimentalize women, they are not characteristics which many men covet or to which they aspire because men do not want to be thought of as weak or effeminate. The virtues for which women are praised enculture them into passivity.

One fundamental objection of many western feminists, including Christian feminists, is that women need to establish their own identity. Women have been praised for their selflessness. but until they have found themselves they cannot truly give of themselves. A fundamental problem for the Christian feminist is how to maintain the vision of self-sacrificial divine love and of Christian discipleship as a laying-down of one's life, without re-inviting oppression. Many western Christian feminists hold the position that women's sin is more aptly described not as pride but as self-denial: women have not lived as liberated selves but have allowed themselves to be oppressed. There are problems with this position culturally because it is not applicable in contexts where women are thoroughly disempowered and so have no power to claim.

Theologically other difficulties arise in describing sin in terms of self-denial. The example set by Christ which we as Christ's disciples should follow is one of service and of self-sacrificial love. It is therefore problematic for Christian women to think in terms of self-empowerment. Christian feminists agree that a woman is free to give herself to God and in service to her neighbours, but ask that woman to be able to discover herself so that she has a self to give. Her self has been constructed for her by a patriarchal society. Liberation in Christ brings freedom from the bondage of sin. It is a freedom to serve God and not the devil. It is a freedom to serve, but this freedom is undermined by oppressive notions of female service. We find our life by losing it, but Christendom has not been able to contain this paradox. It has attempted to control the paradox by dividing society into the servers and the served, those who are passive so that others can be active, those who deny themselves so that others can feed themselves. Such social organization is not paradoxical at all. It manifests the all-too-human structures which feminism resists.

FEMINIST TRADITIONS IN WESTERN SOCIETY

There are different schools of feminism in the west, all of which have influenced Christian feminists. It is therefore not possible to point to the feminist position on the nature of true liberation for women. However, feminists are agreed that liberation for women is a precondition of liberation for society as a whole. Feminists look beyond the female self to the problem of social injustice. Janet Radcliffe Richards wrote a book called *The Sceptical Feminist* in which she defined a feminist as one who accepts the proposition that *"women suffer from systematic social injustice because of their sex"* (Penguin, 1980, pp. 13-14). Feminism is a movement against injustice, but one that proposes that empowering women is good for the community as a whole. The truth in this proposal is acknowledged in recent population policy. For example, emphasis is placed upon women's involvement in familial decisions about when to have children; efforts are made to decrease the "medicalization" of family planning and to put service delivery into the hands of women; and the education of women is recognized to be beneficial for the health of the family and of the wider society. At the ICPD in Cairo (1994) and the UN Conference on Women in Beijing (1995) women's education was acknowledged as a crucial element in effective family planning. But more than that, if women learn to read, child mortality is decreased, child care, nutrition, literacy in succeeding generations and family income-generating activity are all improved, which suggests that empowering women is one of the keys to transforming the community.

Four broad traditions of feminism have developed in the west:

Liberal, egalitarian or reformist feminism: (e.g. Simone de Beauvoir, Betty Friedan.) This type of feminism pleads for full equality and for autonomy, and argues that given equal opportunities women can be the equals of men. This reflects an Enlightenment view of human nature as essentially sex-less. All human beings are essentially rational, autonomous individuals. Liberation therefore involves being given such equal opportunities, not being held back by gender stereotypes.

Radical feminism: (e.g. Germaine Greer, Kate Millett, Shulamith Firestone.) Radical feminists view culture and society as so intrinsically patriarchal that for women to be equal in such society would be to go against women's own nature. The emphasis is upon women finding their own identity. Liberation must involve separation of women and an assertion of their biological superiority. The dividing line between oppressor and oppressed is located biologically: sex is a form of oppression, and however much the social structure is altered there will still be sexist men. It is among radical feminists that the strongest anti-male attitudes are found, in reaction against the self-devaluation it is said that women have been taught to experience through men's hatred of them. Some radical feminists, who find the cause of exploitation in the sexual differences between men and women, reject pregnancy and motherhood as the fulcrum of women's oppression.[2]

Socialist feminism: (e.g. Juliet Mitchell, Sheila Rowbotham, L. Vogel, M. Dalla Costa.) Socialist feminism (Marxist in some of its forms) replaces the Enlightenment emphasis on the individual as evident in liberal feminism with a belief in community. The oppression of women is said to result from the same factors as the oppression of men: the class struggle and the concentration of power in the hands of the few. The modern, nuclear family is rejected as propagating individualist competition and self-interest, and as revealing the wrong sort of social dependence, for example, mothers who seek satisfaction in their children and thus put them under unhealthy pressure. Liberation is thought to involve the abolition of all power relationships, and more corporate, societal responsibility for the next generation's upbringing. The ideology that keeps women in the home is repudiated as serving the capitalist enterprise by keeping labour costs low. Earlier Marxist feminists argued that women should enter the paid workforce; a demand which was then countered by a "Wages for Housework" campaign. Debate has arisen as to whether payment for housework would make visible its importance, or whether it would perpetuate the association of women with the home.

French, post-modern feminism (e.g. Julia Kristeva, Luce Trigaray, Helene Cixous.) Post-modernist feminists do not represent a unified body of thought. They reject in principle the search for a single, all-encompassing theory, and regard the positing of theories about sexual identity and difference as totalitarian. They do not think in terms of binary distinctions but of multiple, fragmented identities. Their emphasis is upon rediscovering that which has been repressed. Freedom from oppressive thought is their primary goal, and they attempt to break what they see as the male control over language. Much research focuses on patterns of infant care which in- form the development of the adult psyche. They disagree over whether there is an essential femininity based in biology, and whether only women can express themselves in 'feminine' ways.[3]

POPULATION POLICY:
CONTRACEPTION AND ABORTION

Having outlined these 4 basic types, we can now consider population policy. I shall focus on debates over artificial contraception. It is often assumed these days that feminists applaud artificial contraceptive methods because they are thought to increase women's control over their bodies. However, many feminists have not themselves assumed that the development of contraceptive technology is good for women. In the nineteenth century it was feared that artificial contraception would weaken what ever control women had gained over their own bodies by undermining their ability to regulate sexual access on the grounds of unwanted pregnancy. Liberal feminists argued that women's control over child-bearing should be achieved primarily through their control over marital sexual relations. The issue was one of sexual autonomy. Advocates of artificial contraception seemed primarily to be men concerned with their own sexual pleasures. Socialist feminists were less ambivalent than their liberal sisters towards artificial contraception, viewing it as a revolutionary change that would transform society toward free sexual expression, reproductive determination and human rights.

In the 1960s feminists were alarmed at two new developments in contraceptive technology: the pill and the IUD, because these can be harmful to women. Particularly alarming was the advocacy of birth-control as an anti-poverty and pro-development measure. Feminists want reproductive control for women, but do not want to be at the whim of methods and motives of population controllers. Feminists object to the way in which demographers target women of childbearing age as "risk producers", with little understanding of their social and economic security and survival. Reduction in fertility, for example, would worsen women's position in societies where fertility is their main source of satisfaction and exclusive claim to consideration.[4] Medicalization of birth-control technology represents a loss of female control. At the same time, the fact that male scientists experiment with female birth-control techniques signifies that they do not want to interfere with male sexuality.

In 1960s the argument became one of abortion rights, and this was seen as necessary for equality with men. For liberal feminists this was primarily a matter of equality of opportunity; for socialist feminists a way of questioning familial norms, and for some radical feminists a rejection of childbearing itself. Other radical feminists, by contrast, celebrated motherhood as the embodiment of women's superior creativity and virtue, and emphasized women's rights to have children if they wish. Abortion became so important because it represents women's ultimate veto power over unwanted pregnancy. Without this option, women cannot genuinely control their own reproduction and their own lives. Ironically, the debate over abortion itself became something over which women had little control.

FAMILY PLANNING

All feminists object that the question of abortion, particularly in relation to population policies, is fought in an arena not of their choice and in terms which are not their own. Abortion is either asserted in support of the population policies imposed by the North or it is opposed by religious groups whose "strong opposition...against women's self-determination in matters of procreation and sexuality" is believed to stem "from deep seated woman-hatred", although disguised in arguments expressing concern about family values and foetal life, and rejecting the so-called imposition of libertarian western life styles.[5] Cairo made no mention of women's rights to abortion, and feminists have objected that this means that other people can decide whether or not a woman is to terminate her pregnancy. Cairo did say that abortion should not be promoted as a method of family planning, and that prevention of unwanted pregnancies should be given the highest priority.

The question of women's autonomy is particularly pertinent here. How much say do women have in spacing their children? Who is it who is involved in family planning: who has the power, the knowledge, the information? The emphasis in Cairo was on families planning together. The development of gender-sensitive approaches to medicine, so that medical advice is given in terms of how this relates to your family and social situation, should help to make this a reality. So should recent attempts to turn back the medicalization of birth-control technology and service delivery, which signify a loss of female control. The feminization of birth control – that female methods have been developed at the expense of male methods – has the potential to give women a more active choice, but in practice can mean that women bear greater responsibility than men for fertility regulation and also are more vulnerable than men to its health risks.

WOMEN'S HEALTH AND THE RIGHT TO CHOOSE

Women's health issues are central to population concerns but they cannot be addressed without considering equality within the community and within homes, and without taking socio-economic factors into account, such as whether boys' health is given priority within families and communities. Reproductive health is now viewed more comprehensively than before, and this is generally in the interests of females. If a girl has low birth weight and is not well-nourished she will have problems with childbirth and her difficulties will be passed on to the next generation. However, feminists object to the narrow focus of population planners on women's fertility, and attempt to raise questions about the pro-life, sexist systems within which women live. The mould has not been broken in which women are viewed primarily in terms of their reproductive function, which helps to account for the lack of attention paid by demographers to the health of post-menopausal women.

It should therefore not be assumed that feminists and population controllers are natural allies. A feminist perspective values a broad range of choice, including the choice to use a less effective method, to use a method only sporadically, to switch between methods, or to use no method at all. Feminists generally agree that population policies manifest a western bias and cultural and political imperialism. However, they are caught between these objections and antifeminist movements which oppose the dissemination of any family-planning information or services. They oppose the ideology of birth controllers, particularly as it is adopted in population policies, but they want to insist on a woman's right to control her own fertility. Any government programme aimed at limiting (or increasing) fertility through economic or social sanctions of coercive family planning is seen as constituting a denial of women's freedom. Insofar as birth control enables women to take more control over their own lives, it is championed. Wherever it is distorted into a means to control women it is viewed with suspicion.

CONCLUSION: A CHRISTIAN PERSPECTIVE

Christian feminists, who are as varied as their secular cousins, are rather left behind in the population debate, but I shall end with some thoughts on how a Christian feminist might helpfully contribute. It should be questioned whether true liberation for women can involve an act of abortion which is so contrary to woman's physical creation and reproductive capacity. To say this is not to sanction vetoes on abortion, which are potentially oppressive and damaging to vulnerable women. The majority of Christian feminists prefer a situation ethic. However, the question whether to abort is a question posed from an unwanted situation. The primary concern of all feminists as regards family planning should focus on what occurs before that situation is reached. Yet for non-Christian feminists the issues are encapsulated in the right to abort, without which women cannot be said to have control over their lives. Christian feminists should rather focus on the identity of the mother who in childbirth opens her life and risks her life for the life of another. All life comes from God, and God's time is not our time. To some extent neither women nor men are able to choose when a woman gives of herself in giving birth. Still, the Christian feminist should ask that women are not controlled by men in this act of self-giving – lest the giving become stealing and the self become obliterated – and that their choices are made as partners in relation with men.[6]

Notes

1   Ann Warren, *Today's Christian Woman* (Eastourne: Kingsway, 1984), pp. 17–18.
2   For example, see Shulamith Firestone in *The Dialectic of Sex* (Jonathan Cape, 1971).
3   See E. Marks and I. de Courtivron eds., *New French Feminisms* (New York: Schocken, 1981).
4   See Jane S. Jaquette and Kathleen A. Staudt, "Women as 'at risk' reproducers: biology, science and population in U.S. foreign policy", in Virginia Saprio ed., Women. *Biology, and Public Policy* (Beverly Hills: Sage, 1985); Sandra Schwartz Tangri, "A feminist perspective on some ethical issues in population programs," *Signs: Journal of Women in Culture and Society,* 1/4 (1976).
5   Loes Keysers, "Reflection on reproductive and sexual rights during the ICPD", in Women's Global Network for Reproductive Rights Newsletter 47, July-September 1994, p.5.
6   I am indebted to Ruth Dixon-Mueller's paper "Redefining Family Planning: Feminist Perspertive on Service Delivery", prepared for the annual meeting of the Population Association of America, New Orleans, April 21–22, 1988.

Part Two

—

Holding and Sharing
the Faith

16

Kingdom Affirmations and Commitments

**God our Father, Lord of heaven
and earth**
You have come to us in your Son
Jesus
in whom all things hold together
By your Spirit make us into a
people
who in words, works and
wonders
bears witness to the power and
presence of your Kingdom.

We confess that we have failed
to live the Word we preach
and in our brokenness
we have torn apart
the wholeness of your gospel.

Give us the grace, O Lord
to commit ourselves, as your
body,
to love our neighbour as a whole
person
in the costly woundedness of
the cross
and in the power of the
resurrection.

**Grant us wisdom to commit
ourselves**
to proclaim your good news to
all people,
to care for your world
and so to live that society is
transformed
by the daily renewal of the Spirit
in us
and by the power of the
Kingdom.

**Make us one at the foot of
the cross**
as we struggle to overcome the
hostility
that divides men and women,
rich and poor,
young and old, races and
nations.

**That the world may believe
that Jesus is the Christ**
so that we may be liberated
from the oppression of demonic
powers
and unjust social structures,
and receive abundant life for
the present
and hope for the age to come.

Amen

PREAMBLE

From March 1–5, 1994, 85 Christians from six continents gathered in Malaysia to seek the Spirit's guidance on how an understanding of the Kingdom could help integrate the three streams of world evangelisation, social action, and renewal in the Spirit. After prayer, dialogue, and searching of the Scriptures, we offer these Kingdom affirmations and commitments to the church worldwide because we believe that focussing on the Gospel Jesus himself announced can unite and empower the church today for costly obedience and wholistic mission.

After John was put into prison, Jesus went into Galilee, proclaiming the good news of God. "The time has come," he said. "The Kingdom of God is near. Repent and believe the good news."[1] Our Lord Jesus commanded His disciples to pray daily, Your Kingdom come, Your will be done on earth, [2] and to seek first the Kingdom of God [3] in the totality of their lives. By word and action, in Galilee, Golgotha and the empty tomb, Jesus powerfully and visibly demonstrated God's reign over all of life. That reign is now powerfully present among us and will reach its fulfilment at Christ's return.

Around the world, in many different places and traditions, the theme of the Kingdom has become central in a new way in our time. It has inspired charismatics, pentecostals, evangelical social activists, ecumenical leaders, and people devoted to world evangelisation. Unfortunately, many Christians have yet to discover the full importance of Jesus' Good News of the Kingdom. But we believe that developing our theology and mission with particular attention to the way Jesus himself defined his person and work will help to unite the church to offer God's healing to a lost and broken world.

We confess that all too often –

We have obscured our witness to the Kingdom by tearing apart the interrelated tasks of proclamation of the Word and social transformation, and tried to do both without total dependence on the power of the Holy Spirit.

We have ignored the centrality of the Good News of the Kingdom of God in the teaching of Jesus, failing to present the Gospel the way Jesus did.

We have distorted Jesus' Gospel by failing to preach and demonstrate that it always includes Good News for the poor.

We have failed to recognise that love is the definite mark of the Kingdom of God – neglecting to love the Lord with all our heart, soul, strength and mind, and our neighbours as ourselves.

We have diluted Jesus' Gospel by neglecting to proclaim and live its radical challenge to the evil in every culture, society and socio-economic system.

We have disgraced the Gospel by failing to live what Jesus taught.

We have mocked by our proud divisions Jesus' prayer that our visible love for each other would convince the world he came from the Father.

Some have one-sidedly emphasised the individual and personal aspects of the Kingdom of God to the neglect of the corporate and communal, and others have done the reverse.

We have failed to serve our neighbours and witness to the Kingdom in the affairs of government, education, business, economics, trade unions, science, welfare, medicine, the media and the arts.

We have prayed Your Kingdom come and ignored the command to seek it first in our personal and societal lifestyles.

Therefore we repent of our failure to let Christ be King in these areas. We will redress these failures with biblical teaching, small group accountability, robust theological debate and wholistic congregations and ministries that integrate proclamation, social transformation and renewal in the power of the Holy Spirit.

BIBLICAL FOUNDATIONS

The Lord is a great God and king above all gods.[4] As the Creator, Sustainer, Owner and Ruler of the whole universe God has never given up, nor will God ever give up, his rule over this universe.

God placed the world under the stewardship of women and men made in God's own image.[5] Tragically they rebelled against their Creator, bringing devastation, disorder and evil into the entire created order.[6] Yet God still desired to establish his authority and rule in the lives of persons and societies. Through Israel his chosen people, God began to reveal the plan of salvation and restoration of creation. The prophets promised that some day the Messiah would come to bring God's actual rule on earth in a new, powerful way. In that day, there would be salvation, justice, and peace - wholeness in all areas of life - for men, women and children.[7]

Jesus the carpenter, son of David and eternal Son of God, fulfilled the prophetic promise and inaugurated the Messianic age by proclaiming and demonstrating the Kingdom of God.[8] As he healed the sick, cast out demons and announced the Good News of the Kingdom, he demonstrated and taught that the reign of God had broken decisively into history in his person and work.[9]

The character of this dawning Kingdom became clear through Jesus' astonishing words and works which followed his anointing by the Holy Spirit. He taught that God freely welcomes all who repent of their sins and seek God's forgiveness. He identified the enemies of God's Kingdom as Satan with his evil forces and all people who join him in opposing God.

Jesus challenged the evils of his society and showed special concern for the poor, weak and marginalised. To those denied human power and dignity, Jesus offered full access to the love and power of God and a dignified place in the human community. He taught that his Kingdom was not a political kingdom of this world that one could install through military power.[10] But he also showed that his Kingdom was becoming visible in this world both in miraculous signs and wonders and in the new community of forgiven sinners - women and men, prostitutes and tax collectors, young and old, rich and poor, educated and uneducated – who were beginning to live the Kingdom principles he taught. In fact, Jesus insisted that the love and unity of his disciples would be so powerfully visible that it would demonstrate that he had come from the Father.

So sweeping was his challenge to the established social order and so unacceptable his claims to be Messiah and only begotten Son of the Father, that the authorities crucified him to prove that his claims were false. On the cross, Jesus atoned for our sins and reconciled us to God so that we could freely enter his new Kingdom as forgiven sinners. His resurrection on the third day confirmed that the Kingdom of God had broken decisively into history. It also showed that Jesus' example of suffering love, self-denial and suffering for righteousness' sake is normative for believers and a central way in which the Kingdom brings life in this world.

After his resurrection and return to the Father, Jesus sent the Holy Spirit to equip and empower men and women to live, proclaim and demonstrate the Good News of the Kingdom to the ends of the earth.[11] In different settings and contexts, the first Christians described the Gospel as the Good News of Christ,[12] of God,[13] of salvation,[14] of grace,[15] and of peace.[16] They were not preaching new, divergent Gospels but rather retelling with different words the one story about Jesus, the Galilean teacher who is the expected Messiah, risen Lord and only Saviour, who now offers salvation freely to all who repent, believe, and join his Messianic community. The Risen Lord called the members of that new community to submit their total lives to his Lordship.[17] As the early church did that, society's sinful walls dividing men and women, Jews and Greeks, rich and poor came crashing down. So different was this new community of the King that Paul dared to teach that the very existence of this multi-ethnic, multi-class body of men and women was a central part of the Gospel he proclaimed and a major demonstration of the power of the cross.[18]

The early church's failure and sin underlines the truth that the Kingdom will not be present in its fullness until Christ returns.[19] Meanwhile the battle with Satan and the kingdom of darkness continues to rage. But the resurrection demonstrates that the Risen One will ultimately prevail.[20] At His return, Christ will complete God's plan of restoring the entire created order to wholeness. That ultimate salvation includes not only the resurrection of persons, but the restoration of the groaning creation,[21] and the inauguration of the new Jerusalem filled with the honour and glory of the nations.[22] Then the kingdoms of this world will truly be the Kingdom of our Lord.

THE KING AND HIS KINGDOM

1. We believe that the Kingdom of God and Jesus Christ the King are inseparable.[23]

Therefore we make the Lord Jesus Christ our central focus. We refuse either to substitute human programmes for the King and his Kingdom or to divorce the naming of the King from the doing of his will.

2. We believe that the Kingdom of God becomes evident where people confess the King and do his will.

Therefore by word and deed we seek to share the Gospel with men, women and children everywhere, inviting them to accept Christ as Saviour and Lord, join his new community, and submit their total lives to his rule.[24]

3. We believe that wherever people do God's will, signs of the Kingdom emerge in human society. Therefore we will co-operate with all who do God's will in their searching for peace, justice, life and freedom. In so doing we will always witness that the foundation and fulfilment of God's will are found in Jesus the King of the Kingdom.

4. We believe that God, through the Spirit, enabled Jesus to proclaim and demonstrate the Kingdom of God while he was on earth.[25]

Therefore we encourage women and men to seek the gifts of the Holy Spirit and know the Holy Spirit's empowering as they seek first the Kingdom of God.

5. We believe churches are called to be the visible expressions of Christ's dawning Kingdom.

Therefore we seek to be transformed communities whose loving unity convinces the world that Jesus came from the Father; we seek to be caring communities that demonstrate to our confused world that the divisions of race, gender and class can be overcome in Christ; and we seek, like Jesus, to challenge all that is evil in society, showing special concern for the weak, poor and marginalised.

6. We believe the Bible is the basis for our understanding of God's Kingdom.[26]

Therefore we fully acknowledge the trustworthiness of the Scriptures of the Old and New Testament, confess that Christ is their centre, and seek to interpret all matters of faith and conduct in the light of its teaching under the guidance of the Holy Spirit.

SIGNS OF THE KINGDOM OF GOD

We believe that the following are significant signs of the presence of the Kingdom of God:

1. The presence of Jesus in the midst of his gathered people.[27]

Therefore we look to the Church to be both a sign of, and a signpost to, the Kingdom of God as we experience the joy, peace and sense of celebration which Christ's presence brings.

2. The proclamation of the Gospel.[28]

Therefore we will seek to communicate the Gospel as Jesus did by all means, in all places, at all times and encourage all followers of Jesus to do likewise.

3. Conversion and the new birth.[29]

Therefore we will expect to see the Holy Spirit bringing people out of the kingdom of darkness and into the Kingdom of God.

4. The existence of the church, Jesus' new Messianic community, which unites in love young and old, rich and poor and people from all ethnic groups.

Therefore we pray and expect the church to be a faithful, although imperfect picture of Christ's coming Kingdom - a strikingly different community where the world's brokenness and sinful dividing walls are being overcome.

5. Deliverance from the forces of evil.[30] We take seriously the power of evil in human affairs: in people's personal behaviour, in the godlessness, injustice and inhumanity seen in every culture, and in occult practices.

Therefore we will minister in the name of Jesus to all who are under the influence of the devil, challenging the faulty teachings, world views, unjust social structures, and cultural and cultic practices that oppress men, women and children today.

6. The Holy Spirit working in power.[31]

We expect to see God transforming people, performing miracles and healings today, and sustaining people in their suffering.

Therefore we will seek to be willing vessels through whom the Holy Spirit can demonstrate that the Kingdom of God is amongst us.

7. The fruit of the Holy Spirit in the lives of people.[32]

Therefore we pray earnestly that all who confess and follow Christ be transformed from day to day into his image and likeness from one degree of glory to another.[33]

8. A courageous, joyous bearing of suffering for righteousness' sake.[34]

Therefore, as Jesus suffered, we will not be surprised if suffering comes to us.

ENTERING THE KINGDOM OF GOD

1. We believe that persons enter the Kingdom of God not by works and human effort but by the unmerited grace of divine forgiveness as they repent of their sins, trust in God's forgiveness accomplished at the cross, believe in Jesus Christ the crucified and risen Lord, and are born again by the Spirit.[35]

Therefore we do all in our power to urge women and men of all races to accept Christ, join his new community and submit every part of their lives to his Lordship.

2. We believe that faithful communication of the Good News of the Kingdom requires costly, incarnational identification with people whatever their need.[36]

Therefore we commit ourselves to forms of Kingdom witness that minister to the whole person in his or her context and refuse to isolate proclamation from social involvement.

3. We believe that Jesus both joyfully welcomed all people into the Kingdom and also taught a particular concern for the poor, weak, and oppressed, even warning that it would be hard for the powerful, the wealthy or the influential of this world to enter it.[37]

Therefore we resolve to practise a costly incarnational witness that demonstrates to the poor as clearly as Jesus did that the Gospel is for them and makes clear to the rich and powerful that they cannot accept Jesus' full Gospel without identifying with the poor the way that Jesus did.

THE KINGDOM OF GOD AND THE CHURCH

1. We believe that the church is the community of the King, the Body of Christ, a visible evidence of his presence and God's chosen people to demonstrate the Kingdom in this world.[38]

Therefore we will resist the constant temptation to conform to the brokenness of surrounding society, seek to renew the church so that it is a convincing picture of Christ's dawning Kingdom, and mobilise all Christians to be salt and light in their local communities and around the world.

2. We believe that the local congregation has many interrelated tasks - worship, fellowship, nurture, education, proclamation and social engagement.[39]

Therefore we will seek to develop biblically balanced, Spirit-filled congregations whose inward communal life and outward mission in the world faithfully reflect all that our Lord summoned the church to be and do.

3. We believe the church transcends all denominational differences and is made up of women and men from all nations, cultures, ages and walks of life who are being transformed by the power of the Spirit of God.[40]

Therefore we will seek to demonstrate visibly love and unity in the worldwide body of Christ so that the world may believe that Jesus came from the Father.[41] Furthermore, the worship and life of each local congregation should affirm the heritage of each culture represented in its midst, allowing this diversity to enrich and enhance our service of God. In addition, since no local congregation can embrace all the diversity of the global body of Christ, we will express in our international relationships a partnership that demonstrates our equality in Christ.

4. We believe that church growth is a normal outcome of seeking first the Kingdom of God.[42]

Therefore where Christians do this, local congregations will grow and new congregations will be planted and established.

5. We believe that a loving, servant heart towards God and other people is the prime characteristic of being Kingdom people.[43]

Therefore we seek to demonstrate this in our congregations, communities and all other areas of life.

6. We believe that the church does not exist for itself but was established by Christ as a witness to the Kingdom of God.[44]

Therefore in every area of church life, we will make decisions not in terms of ecclesiastical self-preservation but rather in terms of what promotes the Kingdom.

7. We believe that God delegates authority to women and men in the church, raises up men and women as leaders at all levels and expects those in such positions to act responsibly and with humility.[45]

Therefore we encourage those in authority in the church to model servant leadership, act with integrity, seek accountability, encourage team work, and nurture the spiritual gifts of everyone.

OPPOSITION TO THE KINGDOM OF GOD

1. We believe that Satan is opposed to the Kingdom of God and that there is continual and hostile conflict between the Kingdom of God and the kingdom of darkness.[46]

Therefore, expecting opposition to the establishment of the Kingdom of God in our own lives, in our families, in our local communities and in our world, we will boldly engage in the kind of spiritual warfare taught in the Scriptures.

2. We believe that the apostle Paul's teaching on the fallen principalities and powers refers to supernatural rebellious beings and the distorted social systems and unjust structures of society.[47]

When Christians name the unrighteousness of social structures, they become a target of these powers which attack through human or demonic means.

Therefore we combat the fallen powers by prayer, spiritual warfare, careful socio-economic analysis and political engagement. We reject onesided views that claim that we must either pray or do social analysis, either engage in spiritual warfare or political action. We will do all this in the power of the Spirit.

3. We believe that in the cross, Jesus disarmed the principalities and powers and broke down the dividing walls between groups that they create and reinforce.[48]

Therefore we will seek to ensure that the church is a community which admits no division of race, class or gender thus becoming a central witness to the principalities and powers that their dominion is over.[49]

4. We believe that Satan regularly seeks to seduce God's people to substitute false gospels for the truth Jesus revealed.

Therefore we reject one-sided gospels of wealth, health, self-esteem and salvation through politics. We refuse to replace divine revelation with subjective experience, to substitute personal preferences for divine commandments, and to exchange management skills and marketing techniques for intercessory prayer and dependence on the Holy Spirit.

THE KINGDOM OF GOD AND SOCIETY

1. We believe that God now reigns, though often unacknowledged, over every area of life, that God restrains evil and promotes good in society, and that God desires his will to be done on earth as in heaven.

Therefore we seek not only to live as Jesus' new redeemed community in the church, but also to work as responsible citizens influencing social institutions and systems toward the wholeness God intends.

2. We believe that the Kingdom of God transcends, judges and seeks to transform all cultures. It is radically different from, and challenges the fallenness of the status quo in every society.[50]

Therefore, we will, using the standards of the Kingdom of God, affirm the unique strengths and continuing good of each culture, judge every society, and seek to transform distorted cultural values and evil social structures.

3. We believe that God wills human community to be based on stable family life and life-long fidelity between husband and wife. The Kingdom of God calls into being family-like relationships of brother and sister and mother and father and provides a model for church life which assists in building healthy families. The rule of Christ thus brings dignity and sanctity to both the single and married states.[51] Therefore we will model and support fidelity within a permanent marriage covenant between one man and one woman, and chastity outside of marriage.

4. We believe that God has ordained a variety of institutions in society and that God wills that political rulers recognise their significant but limited role.

Therefore as we pray for all in authority, we will emphasise the importance of non-governmental institutions including church and family and seek the good of the social order by examining carefully what things are best done by government and what things are best done by intermediate institutions. We reject the political fallacy that the government should or can solve all problems, remembering that divine grace and personal conversion are needed to produce the transformed persons and wholesome families that are so essential for a good society. We also reject the view that dismisses government's responsibility to promote the good and seek justice.

5. We believe that the Kingdom of God affects the whole of every person's being.[52]

Therefore we are concerned about physical, cultural, social, spiritual, intellectual and emotional wholeness in human lives.

6. We believe that God is the rightful owner and ruler of this universe, but he has given the care of the earth to men and women.[53]

Therefore we are committed to a wise and responsible stewardship of all creation and we are opposed to all forms of greed and abuse.

7. We believe that an understanding of the Kingdom of God will bring men and women to a deeper appreciation of the peace and justice of God.[54]

Therefore we determine to act justly, search diligently for non-violent approaches, and promote freedom, peace and justice in society.

8. We believe reconciliation is at the heart of the message of the Good News of the Kingdom and is God's ultimate intention for humanity.[55]

Therefore, while recognising that complete reconciliation among per- sons is impossible without reconciliation with God and thus that violence and hatred will continue until Christ returns, we nevertheless work for that partial reconciliation between hostile cultures, nations, races and ethnic groups that is possible now, knowing that God's will is peace on earth.

9. We believe the Kingdom of God encourages caring and sharing lifestyles as opposed to materialism and individualism.[56]

Therefore we urge cooperation rather than excessive competition, and oppose the consumerism and materialism of much of society. We are personally committed to living a sacrificial and simpler lifestyle.

THE KINGDOM OF GOD AND THE FUTURE

1. We believe that Jesus Christ will return and that it is God's intention to reconcile all things through Christ.[57]

Therefore we wait expectantly for the time when the full reign of the Kingdom of God will be seen and the whole creation will be healed and restored.

2. We believe that the Kingdom of God is both a present reality and a future expectation. It is both already and not yet fully. We live in the period between the inauguration and consummation of the Kingdom. At that consummation all the kingdoms of this world will come under the reign of Christ.[58]

Therefore we seek its demonstration here on earth while awaiting its full revelation in the future.

3. We believe that there is an important role for this earth in the future under the rule and reign of Jesus Christ the King.[59]

Therefore we will value not only the spiritual but also the material and care for the creation as a sign of Christ's coming restoration of all things.

COMMITMENT TO THE KINGDOM OF GOD

1. We believe that commitment to the cause of the Kingdom of God will mean costly discipleship for people in terms of time, possessions, money and abilities.[60]

Therefore we urge prayerful evaluation of priorities, mutual accountability, and sacrificial obedience and call Christians to evaluate everything they possess in relation to the Kingdom.

2. We believe that people were created to live within the Kingdom of God and that they thrive under its rule.[61]

Therefore, it is living by the principles of the Kingdom of God in the community of the King, that people reach their maximum potential and experience life in all its fullness. Thus the Kingdom of God is not a threat to humanity, but God's wonderful gift.

3. We believe that the Kingdom of God confers a new identity on everyone who enters it whatever their standing in life. It affirms their ability to contribute to their neighbours.

Therefore we will encourage all members of the Church to see their work as service to God and to discover and exercise the gifts with which God has endowed them.

4. We believe that the Kingdom of God calls people to devote their talents to the service of the hungry, the stranger, the naked, the sick, the prisoners whom Jesus identified as his brothers and sisters.

Therefore we encourage people to develop their God-given talents in order that they may risk them in the service of the poor, weak and marginalised.

FINAL SUMMATION

As Christians gathered together from six continents, we affirm that Jesus' Good News of the Kingdom requires that we observe his Kingly rule:

in all things.

Therefore there is no human activity, no region of human endeavour which is beyond God's reign.

at all times.

Therefore we repudiate any distinction between the sacred and the secular which obscures that biblical truth that God is King of all times and places.

in all situations.

Therefore we urge all Christians to seek first the Kingdom of God in the home, in the church, at work, in study, in their local community, during recreation and in all other activities of their lives as our highest priority in our lives.

as our highest priority in our lives.

Therefore we will not permit anything to distract or deter us from seeking first the Kingdom of God and His righteousness.

It is therefore our consensus and determined resolve, with prayer and the Holy Spirit's enabling, to commit ourselves to the outworking of these affirmations and commitments. It is also our prayer that all who read them will join us in this commitment.

References

1   Mark 1:14–15.
2   Matthew 6:10.
3   Luke 12:31; Matthew 6:33.
4   Psalm 95:3.
5   Genesis 1:27–28; Psalm 8:6–8;
6   Genesis 3.
7   Isaiah 9:6–7; Isaiah 65:17–25
8   Matthew 9:35; Matthew 4:17–24.
9   Matthew 12:27–28.
10 John 18:36.
11 John 14:16-18; Acts 1:8; 1 Corinthians 14:1–5.
12 Philippians 1:27.
13 Romans 1:1; Romans 15:16.
14 Ephesians 1:13;
15 Acts 20:24–25.
16 Acts 10:36; Ephesians 6:15.
17 Philippians 3:7–8.
18 Galatians 3:26–28; Ephesians 2:11–3:6.
19 Revelation 11:15; 1 Corinthians 15:20–28.
20 Hebrews 2:14–15; 1 Corinthians 15:20–28.
21 Romans 8:19–21.
22 Revelation 21:22–22:2.
23 John 3:3–18; Mark 10:17–21; Philippians 2:9–11.
24 Matthew 28:18–20.
25 Luke 4:18–19.
26 2 Timothy 3:16.
27 Matthew 18:28.
28 Mark 1:15.
29 John 3:3,5.
30 Matthew 12:28; Ephesians 6:10–18.
31 Luke 11:20; 1 Corinthians 12:4–11.
32 Galatians 5:19–26.
33 2 Corinthians 3:18.
34 Matthew 15:1–12; 1 Peter 4:12–16.
35 John 3:3,5; Acts 2:38; Romans 1:17.
36 Matthew 25:31–46.
37 Mark 10:25.
38 Ephesians 1:22–23; Ephesians 3:10.
39 Acts 2:42–4.; 1 Corinthians 12; Ephesians 4:7–11; Romans 12:4–8.
40 Galatians 3:28.
41 John 17:21.
42 Acts 2:42–47.
43 Luke 10:25–37; Matthew 20:25–28.
44 John 13:34–35; Ephesians 3:8–10.
45 Hebrews 13:17; 1 Timothy 3; Acts 18:24–26; Romans 16:1,7.
46 Matthew 12:28; Colossians 1:12–13.
47 Colossians 2:8; Ephesians 1:12–13.
48 Colossians 2:15.
49 Ephesians 3:8–10.
50 Galatians 3:28.
51 Matthew 19:4–6. 1 Corinthians 7.
52 1 Thessalonians 5:23; Matthew 25:31–40.
53 Psalm 24:1; Genesis 1:28, 2:15; Psalm 8:6–8.
54 Micah 6:8; Romans 14:17.
55 Colossians 1:20; 2 Corinthians 5:18–21.
56 Acts 4:32–35.
57 John 14:3; Colossians 1:19–20.
58 Luke 17:21, 19:11; Revelation 11:15.
59 Romans 8:19–22; Revelation 21:24, 22:2; Zechariah 14:9; Psalm 2:8; Colossians 1:18–20.
60 Mark 8:34–38; Luke 18:22–20; Luke 14:25–33; Philippians 3:7–11.
61 Matthew 6:25–34.

17

The Gospel and the Transformation of the non-Western World

Kwame Bediako

> Take my face and give me yours!
> Take my face, my unhappy face.
> Give me your face,
> With which you return
> When you have died,
> When you vanished from sight.
> You lie down and return –
> Let me resemble you, because you have joy,
> You return ever more alive,
> After you vanished from sight.
> Did you not promise me once
> That we too should return
> And be happy again after death?[1]

Thus runs a prayer text of primal religion from South Africa. This section on Christianity as a non-Western religion began in Chapter 6 with a discussion of the primal imagination and the opportunity it offers for new formulations of the apprehension of the transcendent in Christian experience. This prayer returns to this theme, serving as a fitting point of entry into a concluding discussion on the transforming impact of the Gospel upon the life-patterns, the value-systems and the ideas which have hitherto shaped human outlook and destiny in the non-Western world.

The non-Western world is a large and diverse world, but unified to a significant extent by the impact of the Western world, both through the economic, political and cultural expansion of the West and through the Western missionary transmission of the Gospel reaching back over four centuries. As has been shown, only a superficial reading of the missionary history of the Christian religion can lead to the conclusion that the Western missionary enterprise has done little more than transmit a 'Western religion'. An 'infinitely culturally translatable' reality, the Christian faith has, in the process of its assimilation in the non-Western world, overturned any Western cultural possessiveness of it. As this fact has become more apparent in the post-missionary setting of the non-Western churches, and as Christianity's centre of gravity has shifted to the non-Western world, so also has it been possible to recognise the Christian religion as a non-Western religion. To assess the prospects of the Christian religion it is therefore essential to study that part of the non-Western world that has become Christian, at least to the extent that it gives evidence of having significantly welcomed the Christian religion and seems poised to seek ways of making it incarnate in large areas of its life.

THE SIGNIFICANCE OF AFRICA
IN THE NON-WESTERN CHRISTIAN EXPERIENCE

Africa, perhaps, provides the most interesting context for such a study. Latin America, which like twentieth-century Africa is largely Christian, has been a Christian continent for much longer. Its present Christian ferment is as much a re-working of Christian substratum (for Roman Catholics) as it is the result of some radical evangelism (for Protestants, mainly Pentecostals). Asia so far does not demonstrate a similar uniform, massive Christian allegiance, except in a few regions, as in the Philippines and South Korea. Oceania is perhaps the closest to the African situation.

The comparison of Africa with Oceania is also interesting because Christian penetration has come into contact there with primal religious traditions in something approaching their primordial forms. This is also true for certain regions of India that have experienced mass movements to Christianity in the twentieth century. If, as Sri Lankan theologian, Aloysius Pieris, has suggested, the major Asian religions of 'Hinduism, Buddhism and to some extent Taoism' must be understood as 'metacosmic soteriologies' which rest on a 'domesticated' primal substratum which he calls 'cosmic religion',[2] then one cannot exclude the prospect that as Asian Christian theologians relate the Christian faith ever more deeply to Asian cultures, Asia also might yield evidence to confirm the historical connections between Christianity and primal religion.

By virtue of its scale, the African story is particularly interesting and almost a test case of the whole process. In the second decade of the twentieth century it was possible for a Western Christian scholar and missionary to write a book about the primal religions of Africa and call it *The Religion of the Lower Races*.[3] In the century's closing decades, when Africa appears to have tipped the balance and transformed Christianity, according to its best-known statistician, 'permanently into a primarily non-Western religion',[4] there is the opportunity to think of Christianity itself in new ways.

THE TRANSFORMATION THROUGH THE GOSPEL
IN NON-WESTERN TERMS

The significant transforming impact of the Gospel upon the non-Western world arises from non-Western responses to the Gospel in its own terms and not in terms of Western expectations. What needs to become explicit in the process of such an impact is the experience of Christ within the religious, social and cultural settings of African, Asian and Latin American Christians; they respond to their own, not to other people's experience of Christ.

'Take my face and give me yours.' In its primal religious setting, the prayer is addressed to the moon, and so exemplifies the widespread African phenomenon of sky symbolism in which the celestial bodies become symbolic, focal points for the experience of transcendent realities, very often of the Supreme God. The waxing and waning of the moon here symbolises immortality, thus the prayer is a plea for participation in immortality, a plea for transcendence. That much of the religious imagery as well as the expressed sentiments in such a prayer can pass with ease into Christian experience and spirituality, is perhaps the proof that in Africa, as Adrian Hastings wrote in 1976,

> it is in the experience of vernacular prayer, both public and private, both
> formal and informal, and in the spirituality which grows up from such
> experience, that the roots for an authentic African Christianity will most
> surely be found.[5]

It is important to note not only that African Christianity is overwhelmingly vernacular, but also that it is through the vernacular that the living forces of the primal imagination are perpetuated and carried forward into Christian usage. Even prayers derived from Western sources, in translation, take on resonances rooted in primal spirituality. When John Mbiti wrote in 1968 that in passing from primal religion into Christianity, 'the man of Africa will not have very far to go before he begins to walk on familiar ground',[6] what he had in mind was the 'wholeness of African life', which in its religiousness found an echo and an answer in the 'wholeness' of the Gospel of Christ. Because of the significance of the vernacular across the whole spectrum of African Christian experience (not least in the rise of independent churches) where it encountered the translated Scriptures, it is possible to restate John Mbiti's conclusion from different premises. The African evidence may perhaps confirm the dictum by Aloysius Pieris that 'language is the "experience" of reality, religion is its expression', which makes language, each language, a distinct way of apprehending and experiencing truth.[7] Thus, in Africa, it is not in African adoption of Western social and cultural mores, not even when these are specifically associated with Christian transmission, but in African languages and in their significance in the whole process of the local assimilation of Christianity, that one must look for the true proportions of the Gospel's impact in Afrian life. In 1982 Andrew Walls wrote:

> The notion that religions are not mutually exclusive entities which
> succeed one another in the process of conversion, but that the whole
> social life of a community must be taken together was perhaps more
> readily learned in Africa than elsewhere.[8]

There is a specific application that relates to the significance of language. The early and profoundly vernacular character of African Christianity has meant that not only has the primal imagination found a place, permanently, in the Christian mind, but also, through the persistence of the primal world-view carried by indigenous languages, Christ has, to quote Paul Jenkins, 'as it were, shouldered his way' into that world and altered the way people view it and seek spiritual help.[9] The requests that would have been addressed to spiritual powers and their human agents in a primal religious setting have come to be addressed to Christ too; the Christian minister in Africa is often called to the performance of duties ranging from prayer for fertility, the dedication of a baby at an 'outdooring', for success in an examination, the blessing of a newly built or occupied house, to the blessing of a newly purchased motor car to ensure safety for user and vehicle alike.

This leads to the recognition of perhaps the most important impact that the Gospel has had on African life, as seen in the African response to Christ. Far from obliterating the African primal view of things, in its essentially unified and 'spiritual' nature and replacing it with a two-tier modern Western view comprising sacred and secular dimensions, the Christian faith has in fact reinforced the African view. Even though African Christian communities were generally the earliest to be exposed to Western education through the missionary enterprise, African Christians have, on the whole, avoided any significant secularisation of their outlook. New knowledge in science and technology has been embraced, but it has not displaced the basic view that the whole universe in which human existence takes place is fundamentally spiritual. The African experience here points to the African insistence, as Aylward Shorter has rightly noted, that technology has to be 'without materialism. God is an inner necessity for humankind.'[10]

What the Gospel has done, therefore, is to affirm a spirituality that was there already, even if it has also pruned off some of its features and sharpened its focus, this time, upon Christ. It is hardly surprising that the Christologies that have emerged in African theology so far are predominantly 'pneumatic', presenting a Christ who is a living power in the realm of spirit. African Christological titles like 'Eldest Brother' (H. Sawyerr), 'Ancestor', 'Great Ancestor' (J.S. Pobee, C. Nyamiti, K.Bediako), are neither 'from below', nor strictly 'from above'; rather they are indicative of the way the primal imagination grasps the reality of Christ in terms in which all life is essentially conceived - as spiritual.[11] The 'intuitive' theology of the Prophet Harris is paradigmatic of an African experience that is likely to emerge as academic theologians probe into the actual lived experience of African Christians under the impact of the Gospel.

Perhaps the Gospel's affirmation of the essential spirituality of the African primal world-view explains why African theology has so far been predominantly a theology of inculturation. True, it seems to have been much less preoccupied, consciously that is, with the quest for an 'African spirituality' and much more with 'African theology'. And yet, the actual content of African theology may indicate that it is the affirmation of the primal spirituality which has provided its foundation. Since the 1960s it has been greatly concerned with the theological reinterpretation and rehabilitation of the pre-Christian primal tradition and can be said to have been quarrying amid the spiritual treasures of the African past. If the result of this theological investigation has been to show, in the words of Desmond Tutu, that 'the African religious experience and heritage were not illusory ...' and that 'many of Africa's religious insights had a real affinity with that of the Bible,[12] then African theology can also be said to be part of the vindication of the primal spirituality of the past. African theology as the theology of inculturation has thus involved a twofold process: on the one hand 'the evangelisation of African culture in such a way as to enable it to be integrated into the eternal Christian heritage and to continue to make this heritage more "Catholic"', and on the other hand, 'the Africanisation of Christianity to the point where it becomes a constituent of the spiritual and cultural inheritance of Africa'.[13] In that sense, African theology has been about the redemption of African culture. Earlier Western missionary theology had taken a negative view of African culture, underestimating it and even dismissing it as of scant significance. But it was the Gospel itself which, by declaring that God has never left Himself without witness in the life of humankind,[14] gave the impetus to African Christian scholars to embark on the study of the heritage of African peoples. After nearly two decades of investigations into the primal religions and spiritualities of numerous African societies, often with authors studying their own particular peoples, Africa's theologians came to a virtual consensus on a matter of prime concern: recognising 'the radical quality of God's self revelation in Jesus Christ' – they were nonetheless convinced that 'this knowledge of God was not totally discontinuous with African peoples' previous traditional knowledge of Him'.[15]

More informed Western interpretation of African tradition was to arrive at similar conclusions. However, it has been important for Africa's self-respect that African theologians should reach these positions through their own scholarship, since the redemption of African culture has, at a deeper level, been about the redemption of African humanity. It was vital that the melancholy history of Africa's contact with the Western world should be transcended through the discovery of Africa's role within redemptive history, so liberating Africa to work out her own unique contributions to the fullness of the apprehension of Christ in anticipation of the *eschaton*.

It is true that this positive appropriation of Christianity as belonging within the spiritual and cultural inheritance of Africa has not been unanimously welcomed. There are African intellectuals who, reacting to the historical entanglement of the Christian missionary endeavour with Western colonial dominance, have retained a suspicion of the Christian religion in Africa. On the other hand, there are secular-minded Westerners who are distrustful of any claim that a religious conviction can form the basis for developing a viable social and intellectual tradition for new and young nations seeking paths to modernisation. African Christians are not bound to accept either of these criticisms at face value.

To the one, it can be pointed out that the alleged close alliance between the missionary endeavour and colonial dominance is an overdrawn picture which conceals a historical *naïveté*. In many parts of the continent, Christian missionaries had established independent centres of influence far in advance of any European administrations, colonial or commercial. Yet more significant is the fact that in actual evangelisation and church planting, many of the pioneer missionaries were Africans. This is the case whether one considers the significant African missionary force which emerged out of the tiny settlement of Sierra Leone to serve the Anglican Church Missionary Society in West Africa, and even beyond, or the evidence uncovered by Louise Pirouet, regarding the work of Ganda evangelists often operating as 'foreign missionaries' in areas other than their home base.[16] And all this was before the continent-wide emergence of African independent prophets with the distinctive African initiatives that they have exemplified. 'There is something symbolic', as Andrew Walls has pointed out, 'in the fact that the first church in tropical Africa in modern times was not a missionary creation at all'. The 1100 so-called 'Nova Scotians', Christians of African birth or descent who arrived in Sierra Leone in 1792, brought their own preachers and leaders, and their churches had been functioning for twenty years when the first missionary arrived'.[17]

Equally, there is something intrinsically right about Lamin Sanneh's claim that the history of African Christianity must seriously recognise African Christian antecedents in antiquity, including Biblical history. On this view, the flight of Joseph, Mary and the infant Jesus to Egypt has to be reckoned to be 'the first tradition connecting the African continent with the Christian story'.[18] At least one prominent African theologian has written that 'Christianity in Africa can rightly be described as an indigenous, traditional and African religion'.[19] Thus, although in more recent history as Godwin Tasie and Richard Gray have pointed out, 'The alliance between Christian missionaries and European colonialism was intimate, it was never complete, the equation of missionaries and Christianity was never absolute. There was always a gap between [Western] missionaries and African Christianity.[20]

To the other criticism, it can be objected that Western secular categories need not be any more successful in interpreting African realities than some aspects of the Western missionary estimations of African culture and tradition were in the past. Indeed, it can be argued that the Western secular outlook on life and history may itself be the product of what Lamin Sanneh has called a 'cultural self-flattery',[21] which conceals an undue limitation of the range of human experience by jettisoning the dimensions of transcendence and spirituality. The secular outlook wedded to technology can give an illusion that humanity has effectively tamed and even dismissed the spiritual realities and cosmic forces which are presumed to operate within a primal frame of reference. In the words of Aloysius Pieris:

> Technology is as ambivalent as the cosmic forces it claims to domesticate. Its unwise use, far from making cosmic forces really submissive to humanity, has only provoked them to retaliate and enslave humans with pollution, consumerism, materialism and a host of evils that a technocratic society has produced in the First World [the West]. Besides, it has deprived the human mind of myth and ritual, two things by which humanity enacts its deep yearnings and keeps itself sane in mind and body. Can technology liberate the person? Certainly not in the form in which 'Christian' nations have offered it to us. It takes away cosmic religion from the masses and replaces it with neurosis. It takes away religious poverty only to give us mammon instead.[22]

And yet the full African Christian response (and indeed I would include, *mutatis mutandis*, also the Asian and Latin American), will be not merely that 'the Africanness which has its roots in the soil of our continent... is basically a religious phenomenon',[23] but rather, that in Christ, African Christians have found a principle of understanding and interpretation which is superior to anything that a secular world-view is able to offer.

CHRISTIANITY AND THE AFRICAN FUTURE

'No one can miss the vitality of the [Christian] religion in much of the [African] continent', Lamin Sanneh wrote in 1983.[24] The question now is to explore what possible promises this African religion holds for moulding and transforming African life in the future. This discussion will relate particularly to African political thought, and to the institution of polygamy.

One could write the history of post-independent African as the history of political instability. Ali Mazrui has described the spate of military overthrows of elected civilian administrations as the warrior tradition of Africa taking its revenge on its new educated class, that is, educated on Western models.[25] I should like to suggest that African religion too can give a clue to African politics, and that African Christianity may have an important role to play in the moulding of new political models and ideals.

Issues affecting church and state tend to be seen as relating essentially to the church and the political institutions that have come into place following decolonisation. Such an approach ignores the fact that in many parts of Africa, the church had a previous history of relating to the pre-colonial traditional state. Furthermore, in contemporary independent Africa, the coming of central government has not totally eclipsed the traditional state, and there are many Africans who are thoroughly 'modern' in the sense of being at home with the new centralised political organisation who also maintain a significant degree of loyalty to traditional rule associated with kinship and its attendant obligations. In fact, it would be no exaggeration to say that in places where traditional rule and its rituals and symbols still exert some influence on people's lives, the church, because of its own closeness to grassroots, possesses a deeper and richer experience in relating to traditional rulers than to central government. Whilst traditional rulers have been known to willingly dissociate themselves from some actions and duties of their office that Christian conscience finds offensive, in order to retain their link with the church, Christian leaders seem, on the whole, to have had less impact on the policies of the presidents and heads of state of the new republics. In John Pobee's study of the relationship between the socialist government of Kwame Nkrumah and the churches in Ghana between 1949 and 1966, it is the churches which come out worse, for their ineptitude and 'lack of theology' in their numerous clashes with the late Osagyefo.[26]

That adopted title of Nkrumah is itself a pointer to the political mission that may belong to the church in the future. When Nkrumah took the honorific title which eventually became something of a personal name, Osagyefo (Redeemer, Saviour, or else Messiah), he was adopting a title reserved for traditional sacral rulers. He must have known what he was doing, for Nkrumah was not royal, nor was he concerned to promote the interests of traditional rulers. In the religious cosmology that undergirds the traditional social organisation, the traditional ruler was regarded as the channel through whom cosmic forces operate for the well-being of the community while his power was derived from his position as 'one who sits on the stool (throne) of the ancestors'. The power of the ruler among the living members of the community, being sacral power, is therefore, strictly speaking, the power of the ancestors. Even the royal title, Nana, properly applies to the ancestors.

It is a fact that throughout history, Biblical faith has been a desacralising force in the world. That Christianity has had a similar impact in Africa is evident from the history of the relationship of traditional rulers to the churches. Indeed, in several areas this can be written as a process of desacralisation. If, in the field of politics, a sufficient level of desacralisation was achieved in people's attitudes, it may well explain, at least in part, the fact that in the new independent republics, there was no overt return to the 'ontocratic' pattern of the traditional state.[27] It has not, however, been impossible for resacralisation to occur. Harold Turner – who wrote on this subject several years ago and gave part of the credit for the desacralisation process to the independent churches in their role as modernisers – recognised that Nkrumah and other heads of state of his generation (Azikiwe, Banda, Kenyatta, Houphouët-Boigny, Lumumba) who were founders of independence, were 'given a messianic and sometimes almost divine status'. Turner, however, dismissed the trend as 'more superficial than substantial' which did not belie the radical secularisation and modernisation that have occurred.[28]

It is my view that the terms in which Turner discussed the subject obscured a fundamental issue that the desacralisation with which he credited the independent churches failed to resolve, and which perhaps explains why it was quite often these independent churches which were most effusive in the ascription of 'messianic status' to Osagyefo. Turner was more interested in tracing a development 'from an ontocratic to a modern society'. That, in actual fact, is an institutional problem. The deeper problem is the sacralisation of power; the political history of African countries since independence shows that the sacralisation of power is not the prerogative of the 'founders of independence', nor, for that matter, of the old 'ontocratic' order.

What African societies seem to stand in need of is a new conception of power that will eliminate from politics its present sacral overtones. But desacralisation need not mean secularisation, while the 'spiritual' character of the African view of life should remain. The real problem here is that though the traditional sacral state had its own mechanism for restraining autocratic rule through the institution of royal counsellors, nevertheless, by locating the source of power in the realm of ancestors, it effectively placed power within the range of human capriciousness. It is this conception of power that modern presidents and heads of state have inherited. What is needed is an understanding of power that secures its source beyond the reach of human manipulation, at least conceptually, and so transforms the exercise of power in human community from rule into service. African Christianity may have no greater political mission in African societies than to assist in this transformation of outlook, a subject to which I will return later.

The other issue in African social life to which African Christianity should make a contribution from the standpoint of its full participation in the history of redemption is that of polygamy. It is not inconceivable that a really serious African wrestling with the problem from the standpoint indicated above may well be led to deeper insights into the subject for the simple reason that the West has from time to time had misgivings about marriage. That this is so can be seen in the fact that not only has the Western church produced the Christian ascetic ideal and, for a period at least, promoted it as the highest form of the spiritual life, but there is also the modern problem of homosexuality within the Western church and how to deal with it. Africa, on the other hand, has been overwhelmingly committed to marriage, heterosexual marriage. What will the understanding of Christian marriage be in a continent which appears to believe so deeply that to be unmarried is to remain in a state of permanent adolescence?

The discussion of polygamy has so often started from an assumption that it is the African form of marriage, so that the essential universal challenge of the Gospel concerning marriage has sometimes been obscured. Writing in 1960, the Ghanaian philosopher William Abraham claimed that African marriage was 'polygamous in definition' and so found himself having to defend it as 'not immoral'. And yet, when he weighed the merits of polygamy against those of monogamy, he could conclude that within the self-same Africa,

> It must nevertheless be admitted that the preference, certainly the longing of women, is for monogamy. Monogamy implies the acquisition of new sensibilities, a readiness to attain an integrated discipline, an offering of the self in service and sacrifice, a closed communion. One might even say it is a delightful prejudice. It is always an ideal.[29]

In other words, there is more than one strand within the African tradition. The failure to recognise that 'there is nothing inherently African about the institution of plural marriages' and hence the tendency in some circles in Africa to treat monogamy as merely a Western institution being forced upon Africans, leads to a misunderstanding both of monogamy itself and of 'the West's painful inconsistency on the subject'.[30] Western society's coupling of legal monogamy with ease of divorce and remarriage, as well as the various other forms of cohabitation, in effect amounts to the practice and legitimisation of plural marriage. What significance should be given in discussing polygamy, to the insight that 'the other African tradition' relates to the views and sensibilities of women? Is this not equally important, if not more so? Is it of any significance, for instance, that the 'modern proponents' of polygamy are 'mostly men'?[31]

African Christian reflection on the subject, availing itself of its 'feminine' insights – which means men and women listening and reflecting together – may come up with some interesting conclusions.

Within the constraints of this chapter, I can only give some indicators of possible directions of such reflection. If African Christianity were to take seriously its own background in the primal unity of humanity as man/woman, I have little doubt that it will grasp that insight in the well-known apostolic commentary[32] on the primary text of Genesis 2:24, 'the hidden truth', 'the mystery' of the Genesis text relates to the marriage relationship itself, that there is such a thing as the mystery of marriage, a positive mystery which affirms marriage and does not give it a spiritually secondary status.

If the way the apostle passes the Genesis text first through the prism of Christ and the church before letting its light refract upon the man–woman relationship is the norm of interpretation, then Paul implies that the Genesis statement contains a mystery that has existed from the very origins of the institution of marriage, but which is made known only with the coming of Christ. The meaning of the mystery is revealed in the understanding of the spiritual relationship between Christ and the church. This also means that the unity of man and woman in Genesis 2, dramatised by the formation of woman from man (and continually reaffirmed also in the birth of man from woman),[33] is to be seen as a kind of parable which is ultimately made plain in the spiritual union between Christ and the church as His Bride. Accordingly, the man–woman relationship in marriage is meant to serve as a reflection of the all-embracing and eternal spiritual union between Christ and the church. Although the Christ–church relationship appears to follow the man–woman union, in actual fact the former anticipates the latter and is its paradigm. All true marriage therefore is intended to approximate this model of spiritual union as much as possible.

If this is the theology of marriage, then marriage itself becomes a fruit of the Kingdom of God which comes with the coming of Christ, and is a context for discipleship. But polygamy is incapable of fostering the kind of discipleship in exclusive and sacrificial loving which Ephesians 5:21-33 requires, and so cannot abide. As Lamin Sanneh writes: 'We need to avoid the danger of describing it in such a way that it is made to embody all the ideals of the African past. There was much abuse in the system and its benefits were not always the unmitigated boon claimed.'[34] Therefore, not through prompting and prodding from the West, but by assuming its firm and self-assured place within the history of redemption, African Christianity must courageously recognise polygamy as *not* a peculiarly African form of marriage, but as a *theologically* false way, a merely *human* contrivance and one which is ultimately incapable of fostering the righteousness of the Gospel of the Kingdom of God. And yet the fact of its incidence within *redeemed* African humanity means that it has been taken into the divine call to conversion and is to be brought into the same relation to the mind of Christ as everything else in African sosiety. It forms part of the fabric of the nations to be discipled.[35] Christ must become visible in African marriage as in every other facet which constitutes Africanness – a costly, demanding and intensely theological process.

It is reasonable to anticipate that African Christianity will make significant contributions towards the transformation of African societies, particularly in relation to the two areas of African thought and practice discussed above. This may be expected because Christianity in the non-Western world has introduced, as has been noted earlier, genuinely novel ways of thinking of the Christian religion as being relevant to a vast range of issues and problems in daily life. Curiously, this cannot be understood in isolation from the nature of the faith's transmission. Thanks to the modern missionary movement, Christianity in the non-Western world is both a scriptural and a vernacular religion lived through hearing the Word of God 'in our own language'. It has, therefore, provided the conditions in which the ordinary people's experience of faith can become more significant and important for theological articulation than has happened in the development of the theological tradition of the West.[36] This, in turn, can have far-reaching implications for understanding the nature of theology. Essentially, theological activity in non-Western Christianity is also being seen increasingly as involving the participation of people who are not academic and professional theologians. In the words of Samual Rayan (of India),

> It is likely that the greater the part played by the poor in insighting and articulating the meaning of the faith for today, the lesser will be the use of sophisticated scientific mediations and erudite language. Should not theology be expressed more and more in art forms – in dance and drama, in pictures and lines, in carving and sculptures? It should become embodied above all in new and beautiful relationships, in deeds of love, and finally in the new social order itself, in the beauty and shape of the just and free and equal fellowship of God's children and Christ's friends.[37]

Surely here Samuel Rayan speaks for us all, and so perhaps provides the clearest testimony that Christianity, in becoming a non-Western religion, has become in actual experience the most universal of all religions.

Notes

1   Quoted in Aylward Shorter, *Prayer in the Religious Traditions of Africa*, Nairobi: Oxford University Press, 1975, p.116.
2   Aloysius Pieris, *An Asian Theology of Liberation*, Edinburgh: T. and T. Clark and New York: Orbis, 1988.
3   E. W. Smith, *The Religion of the Lower Races*, New York: Macmillan, 1923
4   David B. Barret, 'AD 2000: 350 million Christians in Africa', *International Review of Mission*, vol. 59, no. 233, January 1970, pp.39-54.
5   Adrian Hastings, *African Christianity - An Essay in Interpretation*, London: Geoffrey Chapman, 1976, p.49.
6   Johil Mbiti, 'Christianity and East African culture and religion', *Dini na Mila*, vol. 3, no. 1, May 1968, p.4.
7   Aloysius Pieris, *An Asian Theology of Liberation*, p.70.
8   Andrew F. Walls, 'A bag of needments for the road: Geoffrey Parrinder and the study of religion in Britain', *Religion*, vol.10 pt 2, Autumn 1980, p.145.
9   Paul Jenkins, 'The roots of African Church history: some polemical thoughts', *International Bulletin of Missionary Research*, vol. 10, no. 2, April 1986, p.68.
10 Aylward Shorter, *African Christian Spirituality*, London: Geoffrey Chapman, 1978, p.114.

11 Harry Sawyerr, Creative Evangelism - *Towards a New Christian Encounter with Africa*, London: Lutterworth Press, 1968; J. S. Pobee, *Toward an African Theology*, Nashville, Tenn.: Abingdon Press, 1979; C. Nyamiti, *Christ as our Ancestor - Christology from an African Perspective*, Gweru: Mambo Press, 1984; K. Bediako, 'Biblical Christologies in the context of African Traditional Religions', in Vinay Samuel and Chris Sugden (eds), *Sharing Jesus in the Two-Thirds World*, Bangalore: Partnership in Mission-Asia, 1983, and reissued by Grand Rapids: Eerdmans, 1984; subsequently see *Jesus in African Culture - A Ghanaian Perspective*, Accra: Asempa Publishers, 1990.

12 Desmond Tutu, 'Whither African Theology?', in Fasholé-Luke et al. (eds), *Christianity in Independent Africa*, London: Rex Collings, 1978, p.366.

13 E. Mveng, 'African Liberation Theology', in Leonado Boff and Vergilio Elizondo (eds), *Theologies of the Third World - Convergences and Differences*, Edinburgh: T. and T. Clark, 1988, p.18. Acts 14:17.

15 See K. Dickson and P. Ellingworth (eds), *Biblical Revelation and African Beliefs*, London: Lutterworth Press, 1969, p.16.

16 Louise Pirouet, *Black Evangelists: The Spread of Christianity in Uganda*, 1891–1914, London: Rex Collings, 1978.

17 Andrew F. Walls, *The Significance of Christianity in Africa*, Edinburgh: Church of Scotland/St Colm's Education Centre and College, 1989.

18 Lamin Sanneh, *West African Christianity - The Religious Impact*, London: C. Hurst, 1983, p.1.

19 John Mbiti, *African Religions and Philosophy*, London: Heinemann, 1969, p.229.

20 Godwin Tasie and Richard Gray, in Fasholé-Luke et al. (eds), *Christianity in Independent Africa*, pp.3 and 4.

21 Lamin Sanneh, in a review of Salman Rushdie's *The Satanic Verses* in *The Christian Century*, 21-28 June 1989, pp.622-6.

22 Aloysius Pieris, *An Asian Theology of Liberation*, p.79.

23 See Aylward Shorter, *African Christian Spirituality*, p.45

24 Lamin Sanneh, *West African Christianity*, p.250.

25 Ali Mazrui, *Political Values and the Educated Class in Africa*, London: Heinemann, 1978.

26 See J. S. Pobee, *Kwame Nkrumah and the Church in Ghana 1949–1966*, Accra: Asempa Publishers, 1988.

27 For the word, denoting the effectual union of throne and altar, see Arend van Leeuwen, *Christianity in World History: The Meeting of the Faiths of East and West* (English translation by H. H. Hoskins), London: Edinburgh House Press, 1964.

28 H. W. Turner, 'The place of independent religious movements in the modernisation of Africa', *Journal of Religion in Africa*, vol. 2, no. 1, 1969, pp.43-63, see pp.50f.; reprinted in Turner, *Religious Innovation in Africa (Collected Essays on New Religious Movements)*, Boston, Mass.: G. K. Hall and Co., 1979.

29 William E. Abraham, *The Mind of Africa*, London: Weidenfeld and Nicholson, 1962, pp.82 and 189–90.

30 Lamin Sanneh, *West African Christianity*, pp.248–9.

31 Ibid., p.249.

32 Ephesians 5:31–33.

33 1 Corinthians 11:12.

18

Adolescence, Youth Ministry and World Mission

Oxford Centre for Mission Studies and Oxford Youth Works

60 youth workers, theologians and mission practitioners from 20 nations gathered in the UK in January 1994 at a conference sponsored by the Oxford Centre for Mission Studies and Oxford Youth Works. The impetus for the gathering came from the sense that Popular Youth Culture, broadcast through the media, has had a major impact on young people. Churches in almost all countries have found this culture alien and difficult to understand or address. Youth leaders within the church are exploring innovative patterns for youth ministry as they wrestle with a wholistic gospel response to young people's situations.

The conference produced a 25 page report of which the following is a summary.

FAMILY, SOCIETY AND YOUTH CULTURE

Youth ministry could make a positive difference in the following areas:

Political: Corrupt governments in certain countries have led to gross mismanagement of funds resulting in inadequate provision of social welfare benefits. Young people are manipulated by political parties into social activism and terrorism. On the other hand in Central Europe new exciting opportunities exist for political involvement.

Social: Family disintegration has been a common problem worldwide. The instability of homes robs children of parental role models and the absence of parents from the home leaves the children to the influence of the media and other external forces such as peers, maids etc. The impact of the media as the channel for modern values has caused a tension with traditional values.

Poverty, disillusionment and the struggle to survive have made young people increasingly resort to violence.

Youth are searching for an identity which they usually find in their peers. Cults and gurus seem able to touch young people in a way that the church does not.

STRATEGIES

Young people are part of complex social systems and need to be seen in the context of their families and societies. The soteria of the young person may well involve the soteria of their entire family. Local churches should act as a role model of family and community, and operate as a family for young people who have come from dysfunctional and broken homes. This requires a wholistic theology of ministry based on the salvation of the whole person and the whole creation.

We should expect to meet evidence of God's preparatory activity in the lives of those we meet. This requires respect for and serious study of young people's creative expression in youth culture.

Young people need to grow as disciples of Jesus Christ by active involvement in service projects. In developing countries young people themselves are in need of basic care.

Youth ministry demands new models of reconciliation which are wholistic and address pervasive problems of ethnic violence, drugs, AIDS. One model would be a camp which intentionally brings together groups which are mixed in regard to class and ethnic division and whose leadership reflects the diversity of the Body of Christ.

Because youth culture changes rapidly, and where government, schools and social services are out of touch with the needs of youth, leaders need to become advocates for youth to promote understanding between generations.

The living out and proclamation of the Gospel, the need for personal acceptance of Christ as Lord and Saviour, and the power of the Holy Spirit along with prayer must be kept central.

REGIONAL STRATEGIES

The growth of Christianity in *South East Asia* has provided its churches with a strong platform of believing young people. Issues of strategy reflect the need to train young people to be involved in mission to family and peers and to meet social needs locally, for example young people going for short periods of work in villages in construction or medical work.

Youth ministry must be in partnership with effective children's ministries as a preventative approach to the problems of youth.

In *Latin America* the preaching of the gospel must be connected with helping youth in their social environment with their basic needs. Wholistic attention requires programmes which emphasize the family relationship through parenting courses, marriage retreats etc. To help families in their basic needs requires for example co-operatives, and hostels for homeless children.

In *Central Europe,* under Communism, Christian youth work was illegal and there has been no tradition of voluntary welfare provision. Churches need to be made aware of the possibilities of working with young people.

In *Western Europe and Australia* strategies which focus exclusively on Christian young people will not effectively stem the decline of youth attendance in churches. The first step in sharing Jesus' love is for accepting friendships with young people and an attempt to encourage personal growth. The activity of young people in social and political arenas would open the church's heart to young people.

MEDIA AND YOUTH CULTURE

The report highlights the need to equip young people to move beyond passive receptivity of the media and analyse the messages they receive and the effect those messages are having on them. Youth ministries should create Christian arts and encourage Christians to be involved in the national media.

The church and the family provide the evaluative filters through which young people could analyse the influences of media, peers and school.

THE CHURCH AND YOUTH CULTURE

In the *United Kingdom* Christian youth workers rarely receive non-managerial supervision and support from within the church. Secular supervisors would have difficulty in relating to their agenda. Pastors, vicars and church leaders with no training in youth work or line management in the social field usually set the agenda for youth workers. The awareness of the church needs to be raised about the professional standards for Christian youth workers.

In *Asia*, Christian schools established to teach biblical values and evangelise unchurched children sooner or later become victims of secularisation. This must be addressed.

In *Latin America*, the authoritarian style of many pastors makes change, accountability and confrontation difficult. Many young people leave the church hurt and disappointed. There is a great lack of training institutions for Christian workers among youth.

In *Eastern Europe*, the nineties began with sincere curiosity from young people in the church. But churches were ill-equipped to embrace and minister to this interest. Many western organisations are trying to help the church respond to this. But they frequently fail to distinguish the cultural appropriateness of their theology or its application.

In *Western Europe* young people are looking for lifestyles that work, not philosophies or principles to be agreed with. If something is true for me, it might not be true for you. This cuts across rational presentations of the Gospel. Freedom of choice is an idol with youth. Meanwhile the churches still present one option, the church-based youth group.

The primary strategy for change is to develop culturally appropriate training programmes; secondly, to develop wholistic models of mission which offer life- and world-changing opportunities for community and service as a witness to young people; thirdly to develop programmes which integrate youth into participation and leadership opportunities.

In *Africa* the need is for new approaches which seek basic structural change in a society which hurts young people; and for training of volunteer youth workers who are able to support themselves.

In *Asia* youth training centres are needed to produce indigenous materials and prepare workers to minister in various languages. Continuing education is needed for both pastors and youth workers.

In *Eastern Europe*, young people and families need to understand forgiveness, trust and personal integrity in the light of the oppression from which they come.

In Western Europe, young people are testing the sincerity of people's care for them. If we are willing to enter into real relationships with them, they will see we are serious about what we say.

THEOLOGICAL CONCERNS

There is a need for study and discussion on 1. the family and community, 2. the theology of culture ("is youth culture one of the cultures mentioned in Rev. 5:9, 7:9, 21:24–26?"), 3. biblical anthropology, especially the personal responsibility of youth as vulnerable and sinned against, 4. the impact of liberation theologies and charismatic movements on youth ministry.

Two-thirds world participants suggest the theological theme of youth as vulnerable: despised (1 Tim. 4:12); tested and tempted (Daniel, Joseph, 2 Tim. 2:22); developing with a sense of insecurity; marginalised and manipulated.

The good news for young people is that they can have a relationship with God and be empowered and equipped to be what God created them to be (Luke 2:52). They can be called to take responsibility (Jeremiah, Mary, Joel 2); victorious (Joseph, Daniel, 1 John 2:13); growing wholistically (Luke 2:52); healed, restored and liberated to develop to their fullest potential to do God's will in the world.

Case Study – Kenya

In the wake of decades of political struggle and recent multiparty unrest, many African young people find themselves alienated ethnically, socially and economically from other groups of young people within their own nations. In Kenya, since mid-1992, tribal divisions have been inflamed by manipulative leaders, and young people been used as the vanguard for politically provoked "ethnic clashes". Youth ministry which seeks to play a positive nation-building role must therefore confront issues of reconciliation.

In December 1993, a fellowship of youth leaders led two outreach work camps at the foot of the Ngong Hills, an hour's drive from Nairobi. Young people of a variety of tribes, including urban Kikuyu, rural Maasai, Luo, Kalenjin and Kamba attended the camps.

During the first week reports reached camp that a group of Kikuyu men had attacked two Maasai shepherd boys about 35 miles away. One boy barely survived, the other died. The Maasai men of the area began meeting to discuss their community's response. Five hundred armed men from other Maasai areas arrived to share in the expected retaliation. The government despatched troops to control the escalating potential for violence.

Faced with growing community tension, the camp leadership agreed that their role in the situation was to incarnate the reconciling love of Christ. Teams and groups in the camp mixed young people of various tribal and social backgrounds. Situations which enabled leaders to minister across ethnic and economic lines opened new doors of understanding.

- A Kikuyu held the safety line for a Maasai climbing a rock cliff.
- A Luo guided a frightened Kamba in repelling down the long stone cliff.
- A Kikuyu woman filled in to present the Gospel while the Maasai pastor travelled to conduct the murdered boy's funeral.
- The Kalenjin, Ugandan, American, Kamba singing team led the camp in worship.

In a tense and potentially dangerous time, young people in the camp found unexpected peace and security, centred in the love of God, expressed through leaders who cared for them.

19

Dialogue in an Age of Conflict

Michael Nazir Ali

We have seen that dialogue is an aspect of the human condition and, in fact, all human societies presuppose a certain amount of encounter and of dialogue as the basis for their existence; 'as iron sharpeneth iron so the countenance of man his fellow', as the Bible says (Prov. 27:17). We should not forget that today there are different ways in which communities and people continue to have dialogue with one another. There is, for example, dialogue which is internal to a society; how laws should be made, how a society is to be defended against its enemies, what will ensure a society's prosperity. At the same time there is dialogue between communities; how to promote trade, for example, or keep the peace, or plan together for scientific research.

THE SCOPE OF DIALOGUE

The Church too is engaged in dialogue on a number of fronts, and its dialogue is not limited to that with people of other faiths. For example, the Church is and should be involved in dialogue with the scientific community about religious beliefs and the ever-changing perceptions of science, and how the one relates to the other. The Church needs to be in dialogue with the arts and the ways in which perceptions of transcendence are appreciated by artists. A very significant book on this by George Steiner called *Real Presences* shows us the importance of dialogue with those in the arts; Steiner believes that all art raises profound issues regarding religion.[1] If this is true, it provides an important basis for dialogue between the Church and the arts. So as we talk about dialogue with people of other faiths, this has to be put in the context of the Church's call to dialogue with the world in its several manifestations.

On what is the Church's dialogue based? It is based first of all on the recognition that men and women everywhere are created in the image of God (Gen. 1:27). It is true that this image has to some extent been affected by human sin, both communal and personal, but nevertheless the image survives, it has not been destroyed and we have dialogue with people who are not Christians, because we believe this image is there and that this image has something of God, both in communities and within individuals. Second, we recognize that the Eternal Word, the Logos, incarnate in Jesus Christ, has illuminated all human beings everywhere, as St John tells us clearly at the beginning of his

Gospel (John 1:4, 9). We saw that this recognition of the universal illumination of the Eternal Word was present in some of the early Fathers of the Church, in Justin Martyr and Clement of Alexandria, for example, who believed that some of the greatest achievements of their particular civilization, Stoic and Platonist philosophy, for example, were possible because of the presence of the divine Word in them. At the same time, we need to note that Justin and Clement were much more reserved about the presence of the Eternal Word in certain, contemporary religious expressions of the time. Now the presence and illumination of the divine Word in human societies and individuals is obscured by human sin, and although we recognize its presence we also recognize the obscuring and distorting effects of human sin. Then third, we base our dialogue on the presence and work of God's Holy Spirit in the world and not merely in the Church. Once again in the Johannine writings, we find teaching about the Holy Spirit as present in the world, bringing the world to a knowledge of righteousness and sin and judgement (John 16.8). In the Pauline writings, we find a recognition that the prior work of the Holy Spirit is indeed necessary for conversion itself (1 Cor. 2:14–16; 12:3; 2 Cor. 3:4–4:6; Eph. 1:17–20; 3:14–19). In other words, if the Holy Spirit were not working in the world, not working among men and women everywhere of all cultures, of all kinds, the recognition of the truth of the gospel would not at all be possible. So we base the possibility of dialogue with people of all kinds on these principles, which we believe have been derived from the Bible.

THE WITNESS OF THE BIBLE

More generally, we need urgently, I believe, to recognize that the Bible is a complex collection of documents written in a variety of situations and contexts and cultures, and that, although there is an underlying unity about the Bible, there is also a great variety in the Bible's responses to many matters, including the question of people of other faiths. Let us explore some of these approaches. There is first of all an approach, or a response, that is wholly negative. Let us put within such an approach the ways in which the Israelites treated the Canaanite city states when they arrived in Canaan. (I won't at this time examine whether they arrived by conquest or infiltration; perhaps it was a bit of both.) At any rate when they arrived their commitment to a theocratic egalitarianism made them destroy these city states. Those who are working on the sociology of the Old Testament see the egalitarianism of early Israel as a leading characteristic of this emerging people at the time. The Canaanite city states were very hierarchical, and so one can see why Israel responded in this negative way. Then you have Elijah and the prophets of Baal: once again a negative response. Later, after the exile, you have the ways in which Ezra and Nehemiah dealt with people who wanted to co-operate with the returning exiles in the rebuilding of the temple. In both these responses, both negative, there was a fear of syncretism, a fear that the pure worship of God would somehow be mingled with beliefs that were not consonant with God's revelation as it had been given to the Jews.

Against these we have to put some positive approaches, responses and events. Take the response to the Canaanite city states, for example. On the one hand there was the rejection of hierarchy, on the other hand there was a gradual assimilation of the religious symbols of the Canaanites. If you read a description of the building of the temple of Solomon this becomes clear, and the temple itself, as replacing the ark of the tabernacle as a focus for Israelite worship, indicated a shift from being desert nomads to being a settled people (1 Kings 7–9). But think also of Melchizedek encountering Abraham. We have to recognize that the story, as it comes to us, has been edited in different ways at different times in the history of Israel. It is not that there has been no reflection on the story; within the development of Israel itself there has been, and yet what we have clearly is a Canaanite priest king, the very thing that the early Israelites were concerned to reject, bringing bread and wine to Abraham the patriarch of all the faithful, and Abraham making an offering to Melchizedek! (Gen. 14:18-20). Now who was Melchizedek? There is later reflection on him, as I say, not only in the book of Genesis but in the Psalms, 'thou art a priest forever according to the order of Melchizedek' (Ps. 110:4). It is clear that such an order was not Aaronic. What kind of order of priesthood was Melchizedek's? In the Christian tradition, of course, Melchizedek has been seen as a type of Christ himself and the priesthood of Christ, in the Letter to the Hebrews, for example, has been related to the priesthood of Melchizedek (Heb. 7). There is a positive encounter with great potential for reflection by the people of God! Then there are others: there is Balaam, for example, and the fact that he was called to prophesy *for* Israel, on behalf of Israel, in the presence of their enemies (Num. 22–24). It is true that Balaam is shown as coming to rather a sticky end later (Num. 31:8), but that cannot detract from the fact that he prophesied in an authentic way for Israel. In more political terms, there is, of course, the figure of Cyrus and the way in which he functioned as a liberator for Israel (Isa. 45:1–6). In the book of the prophet Malachi, in the first chapter, there is that famous passage where the prophet is comparing the offerings of the people of Israel to the offerings of the Gentiles, to the disadvantage as it were of the people of Israel. There is inescapably some reference here to worship, though there may also be reference to ethical behaviour because the usual words used for the wholeness of sacrifice are not used in the passage; rather, words that are more generally used in the Bible for moral behaviour are used.

But perhaps the most significant aspect of the biblical witness that we need to consider is the developing realization in Israel that their God was the God of the whole world, that he was the God of every nation, of every people. Again, responses to this realization vary in the Bible from a felt calling that God's universality needed to be expressed in terms of judgement on certain peoples. I mean this is, by and large, the witness of the books of Joshua and Judges, though not wholly so. As we have seen, this is replaced then by an approach that regards Zion as the centre of devotion to God, to Yahweh, and the other peoples are seen as eventually coming to Zion to make their submission to the God of Israel. Yes, God is the God of the whole world, but if people want to respond to his universal lordship they must do so in terms of Israel, the way in which Israel has responded must also be the model for them. Later on this becomes known as the Judaizing tendency. If you want to respond to God's revelation, even in Christ, you must do so in the way the Jews have done. Of course, we all know that the early Church rejected such an interpretation but it has been a strong element in the tradition and it affects some of our contemporary attitudes in this area.

The third approach has to do with a growing realization that God, if he is the God of the whole world, of every people, must be working in the histories of those people. Now, sometimes that may be seen as judgement, but on many occasions it is seen as salvation. Sometimes that salvation is projected on to the future, in the great visions in Isaiah, for example, where Egypt and Assyria are seen to be as much, at least potentially, God's people as Israel. It is right to interpret the nineteenth chapter of Isaiah as eschatalogical, to project it into the future, but that is not always the case with other passages. Sometimes God's work among people is about the past, so that in Amos God is shown to have a purpose, not only in the Exodus of the people of Israel from Egypt, but in the histories of the Ethiopians, the Syrians, the Philistines, all the neighbours that Israel had encountered. This is extremely important for our attitude to certain emphases in biblical theology. We are greatly indebted to those who have developed the paradigmatic concept of salvation history, that is to say that God's revelation is not to be understood primarily as propositions about belief, but that God's revelation is about his activity among his people and in the world. The biblical salvation history is very largely about God's action, God's revelation to the people of Israel, that culminates, comes to a climax, in the incarnation, though not of course to an end. But if this is normative salvation history, why is it normative? What is its function? It can be normative only if it leads us to a recognition, to a discernment, of other salvation histories, that is to say, and I believe this to be the teaching of the Bible, that there is a salvation history among every people, every culture. It is not easy of course to discern such a salvation history, it is very problematic, but it is possible for us to discern this salvation history, with whatever difficulty, because of the normative salvation history that we have of the people of Israel in the Bible.

I have not commented particularly on the attitude of Jesus himself, but perhaps one or two remarks are necessary. One is that liberation theologians have underlined the importance of what they call the Galilean option, that is to say the importance of the choice of Galilee by Jesus for his earthly ministry. Their point is that Galilee was *chosen*. It was not an accident that Galilee came to be the focus for his earthly ministry, this was a deliberate choice because Galilee was all that the religious and political and economic establishment was not. Jesus deliberately chose to be among people who were not powerful, who were not wealthy and who were not learned. But from our point of view Galilee is important because Galilee is Galilee of the nations and it is possible to read this choice as a choice for pluralism. Galilee was among the first of the parts of the northern kingdom to be conquered by the Assyrians, depopulated through exile of its original inhabitants, and repopulated by people from different parts of the Assyrian empire. So by the time of Jesus, it had a very mixed population, people of very different beliefs, and some of the encounters in the gospel are about that: 'Many will come from east and west and sit at table with Abraham and Isaac and Jacob' (Matt. 8:11). The Galilean option then is an option for pluralism against the orthodoxy of Jerusalem. Secondly, it is also where the risen Christ is present, ahead of his disciples. In the resurrection narrative in Matthew, the disciples are told to go to Galilee, where Christ will meet them. It is possible to read this in two different ways. It is possible to say that what the risen Christ is saying is that he will *lead* the disciples into Galilee, that is to say, he will go ahead of them. The other is to read it in such a way as to say that he is *present* in Galilee ahead of them, before they get there. However you read it, the point is that when we approach people of other cultures, other communities, other language groups, we can be sure that Christ is ahead of us. Very often the unspoken, implicit assumption in a lot of mission work is that of taking Christ to people, and that expression is sometimes used. Now I know what people are saying and it is not wholly incorrect to speak like that, but we have to be on our guard lest we become, or think that we are, more than in fact we are. Christ is already ahead of us in Galilee.

What then is dialogue in the rest of the New Testament and in the early history of the Christian Church? The words that are used in the New Testament are *dialegomai* and *dialogizomai*. Both mean something like an argument for the sake of persuasion. This is the way in which the word is used in relation to the activity of the apostle Paul in the Acts of the Apostles (Acts 17:2; 18:4 etc.). This is also the sense in which the word is used in Justin, for example, in his dialogue with Trypho the Jew, a dialogue conducted so that the interlocutor may be convinced of the truth of the gospel. Indeed, we find this meaning still in use at the later end of the patristic period, by John of Damascus. Now John of Damascus is a very interesting figure because he came from a family which had opened the doors of Damascus to the Muslim armies. A Christian family, they had done this to get away from the oppression of Christian Byzantium. I think this is, if anything, a matter for profound repentance for Christians. Not only did he come from such a family, but for a while he held very important office under the Ummayad Caliphs. Apart from his great theological work which is the basis for a great deal of the theological method that we still use, he wrote two dialogues, or accounts of dialogues, with Muslims. Now again the word as it is used by John means arguing with somebody, conversing with somebody, with a view to persuading them of the truth of the gospel.

This sense, this meaning of the word dialogue, comes right down to modern times in the way in which Hume uses the word, for example. His *Dialogues Concerning Natural Religion* are about convincing people of certain things that he believed to be true[10].' Nevertheless, in the patristic and perhaps the New Testament sense of the word, there is in the background something about the *dialectical method* that was used by the ancients a great deal to arrive at truth. Think of Plato's accounts of the dialogues of Socrates: conversations which result in a perception of truth that dogmatic teaching does not. The question-and-answer method results in genuine discovery of something new. Now this is very important for dialogue as it is today. While Christians will want to present truth as they see it revealed in Jesus Christ and in the Gospels, there is always a sense in which dialogue with people produces a new kind of appreciation of some aspect of truth, even Christian truth. For me, and this is a personal testimony, my dialogue with Muslims over the years has resulted in a fresh appreciation of the doctrine of the unity of God which in some cases is seriously compromised by certain kinds of Christian trinitarian theology. It is very interesting to me to see how the Western Christian theological tradition, which in the past used to emphasize the unity of God over against the diversity of the persons, has in this century gone completely over to a version of Eastern Christian thinking without the safeguards of classical Eastern Christian thinking. Now that perhaps is another matter, but just to alert you to the fact that dialogue can result in something new when it is conducted in this way.

THE PRACTICE OF DIALOGUE

How is dialogue practised? We have seen that Professor Eric Sharpe, now in Australia, has distinguished four different ways in which dialogue is conducted today. The first he calls discursive dialogue, that is to say when partners come together and exchange information about each other's beliefs. This is a necessary aspect of dialogue. From the Christian point of view it is an aspect of dialogue where Christians must be very attentive to their partners, talk less and listen more; of course, we are not known for this in the world, but when people are telling us what they believe we need to listen very attentively. Then Sharpe talks about dialogue which has to do with a common recognition of our humanity. Again this is a crucial area for dialogue today as we seek to discover each other's commitment to, for example, human rights and the rights of women. In the context of dialogue with Muslims, this is an area that bristles with difficulties. Both sides talk about human rights, but when Christians and Muslims talk about human rights together they soon discover that their perceptions are very different. What are Christian perceptions about Qur'anic penal law, for example, and what are Muslim perceptions? This is a matter for dialogue, and it is something that is not easily resolved. Third, Eric Sharpe refers to dialogue that is for the building up of community: if we are citizens of a particular nation, if we are members of a particular community, we will be committed to the building up of that community. Dialogue is very important to ensure that we are working together for the building up of one community and not engaged in activities that divide communities into Muslim and Christian sectors, Hindu and Muslim and Christian sectors and so on. Finally, Sharpe talks about the sort of dialogue which is about the sharing of spiritual existence. Once again to give an example from Muslim/Christian history, there has been for thirteen hundred years dialogue between Christians in the mystical ascetical tradition and Muslims in the mystical ascetical tradition. Sufism, as a phenomenon in the world of Islam, is glad in many respects to refer to encounters with Christians that have enriched the Sufi tradition. From the Christian point of view, a great deal of mystical terminology that is used by Christians in the Muslim world comes from the Sufi tradition. So this dialogue about the exchange of spiritual experience is important.

The Vatican has recently issued a document which also attempts to classify kinds of dialogue, and once again it seems very like the division that Sharpe made all those years ago. The Vatican's divisions are the dialogue of life, the dialogue of deeds, the dialogue of specialists and the dialogue of the interior life. So you can see how they correspond with Sharpe's division. People, sometimes, do not give enough value to the dialogue of specialists. In some cases this *has* been sterile: where it has been overly concerned with classical issues and there has been a danger in some respects of a merely antiquarian interest. But one way forward which is proving to be quite fruitful is a model which has been taken from intra-Christian ecumenical dialogue. That is a model of dialogue where a group of scholars from each side come together for a considerable period of time, say five or six years, correspond with each other, meet each other regularly, and consider one theme such as the Scriptures in Islam and Christianity – so that they may come to a common mind about the place of Scripture in religion, for example. There has been a fruitful dialogue between French-speaking Muslims and French-speaking Christians in this particular area which has been very revealing about how far the Muslims are prepared to go in their understanding not only of their own Scripture but of the Bible.

DIALOGUE AND MISSION

The Church Missionary Society has been committed for many scores of years to the view that dialogue is the presupposition for Christian mission, for Christian witness. In other words there can be no authentic Christian witness without prior dialogue. Unless we understand people's beliefs, their culture, the idiom of that culture, their thought forms, the intellectual tradition, the artistic tradition, the faith tradition, unless we understand these we will not be able to witness to people authentically as Christians. This is behind the strongly incarnational approach that CMS has taken in the past and continues to take today. Mission is not hit and run. People these days are talking about 'non-resident missionaries'. In some cases these are necessary, of course. But that will never be, I hope, a model for CMS, because mission must be incarnational, and this is why so many distinguished missionaries - Temple Gairdner in Egypt, W. D. P. Hill in India, in our own days people like Roger Hooker and Christopher Lamb - spent years in incarnational situations learning about cultures and languages and peoples before they felt able to witness to them of

Christian faith and Christian truth. This is absolutely essential. So mission cannot be hit and run. It cannot be at a distance. A great deal of time and effort is being expended in the world today in preaching the gospel to people through the mass media. Now in some ways this is necessary, as some parts of the world cannot be reached in any other way. Think of the way in which the Bible was broadcast at dictation speed to the people of Albania. But again it can never be an ideal way, because of the commitment to incarnation and to dialogue as the presupposition for witness.

But dialogue is not only preparatory to witness, *it is also the means to witness*, and here I have been somewhat distressed by the ambivalence in the ecumenical movement on the question. Some documents such as the guidelines on dialogue produced by the British Council of Churches, say clearly that dialogue is a medium for authentic witness. But other documents of the World Council deny this and make every effort to claim that the occasion of dialogue must not be an occasion for Christian witness. I think the concern behind this is that our partners should not see our efforts at dialogue as efforts at proselytization, and that concern is valid. On the other hand, I cannot see dialogue in its fullness without the opportunity for both sides to witness to their faith in trust that the partners recognize each other's integrity. For Christians, dialogue will always be about listening and learning; our partner's faith may shed unexpected light on our own. We must, however, also be committed to let the light of Christ shine through our conversation and reflection. Without that, dialogue remains unfulfilled for the Christian.

20

Accessible Liturgy
Theological and Liturgical Consequences in Therapeutic and Prophetic Narratives in Worship

Jean-Daniel Plüss

*Quod omnes tangit ab omnibus tractari
et approbari debet.* – INNOCENT III

INTRODUCTION

The Christian voices in the New Testament have emphasized in various ways that mankind has found access to God's grace through the life and work of Jesus Christ (e.g. Rom. 5.2; Eph. 2:18; 3:11,12; Heb. 10:19ff). This theological claim, however, is only meaningful if it can be experienced religiously. The liturgies of the Christian churches have traditionally been regarded as the appropriate context for such an experience. In view of the many cultural changes that have taken place through the years, it is legitimate to ask whether such liturgies still represent for the general population in christian cultures a credible invitation to, and a celebration of faith in God.

The aim of this chapter is to tie together the results of the research in the preceding chapters by placing testimonial and visionary narratives into a meaningful liturgical context. Accordingly, the focus will be on the theological and hermeneutical consequences that the use of oral narratives, as they have been described, imply. Three areas where these consequences are of vital importance will be emphasized specifically. First, and perhaps most importantly, a narrative praxis begs for a theology of laity. Second, the nature of the Christian narratives discussed call for a re-evaluation of a theology proper, that is a renewed appreciation of divine activity. The third area relates to the praxis of worship itself. The liturgical activity will first be discussed from an anthropological point of view in a short excursion, and will for a last time pick up the curious relationship between the religious and the secular. Some practical reflections will bring the discussions in this chapter to a close.

THE NEED FOR A THEOLOGY OF LAITY

The attempt to interpret testimonies has shown that the witness does not simply make a religious statement which can be understood as a formulation of his or her affiliation to a certain group or institution. The witness, claiming an experience of self-transcendence, makes a theological statement. In fact, such a claim is not very different from the propositions of faith at the heart of the making of Christianity, as Edward Schillebeeckx has pointed out.[1] It is inconceivable that in the Christian beginnings there was a strict distinction between a group of official theologians and another group of more or less passive consenters.

The conflict in Corinth, as described in the Pauline correspondence, is a lively example of common theology in the making. The conflict, because it touched the foundation of faith, was wrestled with on all levels represented in the church. Paul acknowledged the valid concerns of the different parties and mediated a consensus which found its expression in the common meal and in the celebration of the eucharist. Historically however, Christianity developed from a charismatic movement in which every believer, by virtue of his or her disclosure of faith in Christ (theologically: baptism with/or fullness of the Holy Spirit) was entitled to participate in the formulation of faith, into an institutionalized religion in which statements pertaining to faith were issued by a specialized minority. Although the protestant reformation emphasized the common priesthood of all believers, both branches of western Christianity found it potentially dangerous to "democratize" the formulation of faith to the extent where it would have a tangible effect on the life of the church. The academic and clerical elite thought their role would be threatened if the "common" faithful had a programmatic voice. They thought that the people should be satisfied with living out what the creeds, the devotional tradition, the doctors of theology, or the magisterium proclaimed in matters of faith and morals. The secularization of the West forced a change of attitude. The "common" person today, if he professes to believe at all, wants to make up his own mind. Having come of age he consents to authority only if it is convincing to him.[2] As a result, a *sensus fidelium* can only flourish if it can be elaborated from the base. A theology of the laity becomes a necessity.[3]

The conviction that theology had to be not only *for*, but also *of* the laity dawned only in the second half of the twentieth century. The ice was broken by Yves Congar's pre-Vatican II publication *Jalons pour une théologie du laîcat*.[4] Hendrik Kraemer reacted to Congar's proposals by approaching the topic from a protestant point of view.[5] Whereas Congar's work is still important in terms of the elaboration of basic ideas, Kraemer's book is worth discussing because of the applications it suggests.

Yves Congar: A Catholic Approach

Yves Congar wrote his book at the beginning of the fifties. It is, therefore, to be considered in a context where the distinction between the religious hierarchy and the laity was still dominated by ontological prejudices; the distinction was stronger than the christian message could warrant. He had to mediate between a *de facto* situation and the *de iure* propositions of canon law and tradition.[6] He nevertheless succeeded in bringing attention back to essentials, namely to that which all Christians have in common.

The Basic Dilemma

The faithful, in view of the problematic gap between the officers and the people of the christian body, became conscious that they organically constituted the church. The clergy as representatives of the hierarchical priesthood, on the other hand, considered it important to maintain an ontological difference with regard to the believers representing the common priesthood. Nevertheless; Congar insisted on theological grounds[7] (the sociological changes were only a catalytic agent) that all believers shared fully in the Christian vocation. Consequently, a new ecclesiology would sooner or later have to emerge where the distinction of the church as a *societas fidelium* and the church as a *Helanstalt* would only be functional. Congar also argued that the church official was first of all a lay person; his fundamental Christian option developed before he was ordained.[8] Without sounding "protestant," he could now develop a theology of the laity based on the common priesthood of all believers.[9] He illustrates his convictions through the threefold messianic ministry of Christ.

The Common Priesthood

The messianic ministry of Jesus Christ is classically described as priestly, royal, and prophetic. Congar discusses first the priestly function. The important areas are moral responsibility, testimonial engagement and liturgical participation.[10] The royal function is second. It is described as a way of life (in the power and in anticipation of the kingdom of God) and as an exercise of power.[11] The third function is the prophetic one. It is the participation through the power of the Holy Spirit in mystical knowledge and in teaching.[12] These aspects of the common priesthood must be mentioned because they also cover central issues which surfaced in the discussion of testimonies, prophetic visions and the hermeneutic activity which they provoke. It is interesting to note that Yves Congar brings these various aspects of lay activity together, not in a postulation of some higher institutional order, but in a hermeneutically significant notion based on communicative harmony.

Sobornost' as Theory of Reception

The French dominican appeals to the slavonic notion of *Sobornost'*, a term primarily used in 19th century Russian literary circles to denote consensus and identity formation in spite of plurality.[13] For orthodox Christians this term became the paragon of communion in Christ (the pancrator) through the participation of all. This idea is important for Congar, because for him it truly reflects the etymological meaning of *ekklesia*.[14] As a consequence of this ecclesiology of all, a door is opened to the theory of reception, a theory in which the "law of faith" is received or suspended through a communal praxis which is the "law of praise" and that of "commitment". To put it differently, Christian truth, because of the itinerant nature of human understanding, is not static but is to be received continually by the community as a whole in view of the past (the revelation of God in Jesus Christ and the lessons of church history), the present (the tragedy of unredeemed life), and the future (the anticipation of wholeness in and through faith in Christ, but also the reservation with regard to projects of human finitude).[15] Another consequence of *Sobornost'* is a renewed appreciation of the history of the church in its pluriformity, and at the same time a deeper sense of ecumenism. But all is subject to the common reception of faith and the simultaneous acknowledgement of Christ's lordship.[16] In other words, the reception of dogma is subject to a common trial and a mythologically celebrated consensus in Christ.

Congar then concentrates his theology of laity in a *sensus fidelium*, a sense of faith shared by all believers which on the one hand aims at the conservation of doctrines and tradition, and on the other hand has the task of developing doctrine. He illustrates this by referring to the various activities of the "Action Catholique".

However, he remains vague as to the development of doctrine, which after all is the key issue for a realistic theology of laity, and the pivotal point for a theory of public interpretation of religious narratives. The ideas of Hendrik Kraemer may be of use here.

Hendrik Kraemer: A Protestant Approach

Kraemer begins his response to Congar's book with a short review of lay influence in church history.[17] He notices a diaconical and charismatic function fulfilled by the laity in various renewal movements, which eventually vanished through the consolidation of new ecclesial structures. In the Anglo-Saxon protestant world various religious communities drew on the resources of gifted lay people and committed to them active ecclesial functions. It was a participation in the spiritual realm. Only in this century, however, has the lay issue been addressed in terms of the worldly realm, i.e. in view of secularization.[18] Hendrik Kraemer suggests a radical theology of laity, not only on basic theological grounds, but also because the process of secularization sheds light on the relative character of history and the prominent role of ethics in public life. It challenges the church to be true to its vocation as an *ek-klesia*.

Accents of a Theology of Laity

Basically, the whole idea centres on lending credibility to the church as an article of faith. Its mission, its worship and its actions should again be recognized as a testimony of christian faith. This testimony is mediated through the church as community to the world in a language understandable to all. It is a language with pragmatic repercussions, born of a sense of responsibility and participation. It is a language of faith because it is not anthropocentric but christocentric.

The first accent Kraemer discusses is the mission of the church.[20] If the church only *had* a mission it could be taken care of by a professional elite. The point, though, is that in Christ the church is a mission in which all believers are summoned to participate. Only the fusion of the mission and the corporate unity of the church brings, according to Kraemer, wholeness, healing, and salvation in Christ. An immediate consequence is naturally of ecumenical significance, i.e. that the mission of the church is only truly lived if the church is one.[21] It is noteworthy to realize that the laity in practical terms is already bound to live ecumenically in various ways,[22] whereas the officers of the churches mainly try to tackle theoretical problems of oneness in Christ.

The second accent is the participation of the whole church in worship and is closely related to the third aspect, namely that of committed action issuing from an awareness of faith. To put it briefly, worship as "ascribing worth to God" is a form of *diakonia*, a service. In a secular context the service of worship, if it is genuine, will have repercussions in the world. The melting of the two aspects is in fact mythologically represented in the incarnation of the will of God in Jesus Christ, whose whole life was an act of diakonia. It is in this sense that Hendrik Kraemer sees the charismatic function of the early church.[23] The liturgical roots of the service of the church make it clear that the church in effect *is* and not just *has* a *diakonia*. But the service in word and deed must be mediated religiously and communicatively. One basic means for this mediation is the narrative participation of the laity. As a royal priesthood they celebrate and invite to wholeness in Christ, as messianic prophets they bring it into the world.

Notes

1   For instance, his description of the Easter-Event (4.3.3.), but also in 'The Teaching Authority of All – A Reflection about the Structure of the New Testament', in Concilium 180 (4, l985), pp.13f.
2   A good example is the practical disregard by western Catholics of the moral unacceptability of contraceptives as taught by Pope Paul VI in *Humanae Vitae*.
3   This is also the logical consequence of Robert Bellah's and James Gustafson's ideas, cf. sections 3.5.1. and 3.5.2.
4   Yves Congar, *Jalons pour une théologie du laîcat*, Paris, 1952.
5   Hendrik Kraemer, *Theologie des Laientums: Die Laien in der Kirche*, Zürich, 1959; originally published as *Theology of Laity*.
6   Only in that light can one understand double affirmations like: "Les laîcs formeront toujours, dans l'Eglise, un ordre subordonné, mais ils sont en train de retrouver une plus pleine conscience d'en être organiquement des members actifs, de plein droit et de plein exercice." (Yves Congar, *Jalons*, p.7). The problem then was obviously how to reconcile the idea of subordination with the theological insights of full integration, full rights and full exercise of being a Christian. A solution was indicated in the Vatican II document *Lumen Gentium* where the "people of God" are spoken of prior to the official leadership of the church. (See also below on the idea of reception.)
7   Yves Congar mentions for instance the fact that the New Testament does not explicitly refer to a distinction between a christian clerus and the laity (*Jalons*, p.20). The strong distinction (from an originally functional ontological difference) between the clerics and the laity took place relatively late, namely between the 11th and the 13th century. Gratian in the 12th century was the first to make a definite distinction, "Duo sunt genera christianorum" (cf. *Jalons*, p.27-36).
8   "Et d'abord, affirmons une vérité très importante et qu'il ne faudrait jamais perdre de vue: le prêtre (l'évêque, le pape) est d'abord un laic" (Yves Congar, *Jalons*, p.234).
9   Congar prefers to speak about a "spiritual priesthood" (*Jalons*, p.242) but his terminology has not found many imitators, perhaps because it is virtually a pleonasm.
10 Yves Congar, *Jalons*, pp.246-308. Liturgical involvement is seen in the participation in the eucharist, in emergency baptism and in lay confession, thus not in the shaping of liturgical content, as for instance in the kerygmatic activity (Liturgy of the Word).
11 Yves Congar, *Jalons*, pp.314-366. The exercise of power relates mostly to the church as an institution (e.g. elections, consultation in councils, executive administration); it is not presented as power to a rightful claim, or as consensus formation borne by faith.

12 Yves Congar, *Jalons.* pp.367-453 "...la fonction prophétique de l'Eglise comprend tout l'activité suscitée en elle par le Saint-Esprit, par laquelle elle connaît et fait connaître Dieu et son propos de grâce..." (p.367). The distinction between mystical knowledge and teaching, although valid because of their different vantage points, is no longer very meaningful to the secular person, for he does not consider subjective experience as such as inferior to generally accepted and taught opinions. The two aspects fall together for many. The same happens in religious narratives.

13 "Il nous semble qu'il y a, dans le *Sobornost*', un grand fond de vérité ecclésiologique... Il est, en sous-sol, de quelques principes généraux qui traduisent des valeurs proprement dogmatiques: celui de l'unité de l'humanité depuis Adam d'abord, dans le Christ et par lui en suite-celui de l'Eglise comme finalisée par un idéal de communion où plusieurs soient un, tout en restant des personnes libres: cette idée d'unipluralité ou d'unitotalité...se retrouve, d'une maniere ou d'une autre, chez tous les auteurs que nous avons cités" (Yves Congar, *Jalons*, pp.381f.).

14 "...l'idee de *Sobornost*' reflète une ecclésiologie construite à partir de la notion d' *ecclesia,* d'unité du corps, et non à partir de la notion de pouvoirs hiérarchiques" (Yves Congar, *Jalons*, p.382).

15 The notion of *Sobornost*' as reception has in fact been integrated in *Lumen Gentium* § 12."The holy People of God shares also in Christ's prophetic office...*The whole body of the faithful* who have an anointing that comes from the holy one (cf. 1 Jn. 2:20 and 27) *cannot err in matters of belief.* This characteristic is shown in the supernatural appreciation of the faith (*sensus fidei*) of the whole people, when, 'from the bishops to the last of the faithful' *they manifest a universal consent in matters of faith and morals.* By this appreciation of the faith, aroused and sustained by the Spirit of Truth, the People of God, guided by the sacred teaching authority (*magisterium*), and obeying it, *receives* not the mere word of men, but *truly the word of God* (cf. 1 Th. 2:13)..." Austin Flannery (ed.), *Vatican Council II*, p.363 (emphasis added).

16 Yves Congar is well aware that this slavophile notion was strongly influenced by German idealistic romanticism and Russian culture (*Jalons*, p.383). An appreciation of *Sobornost*' in light of contemporary critical theory would not invalidate the notion of pluriform unity, but it would take divergence and reflection of unity seriously in their own right. For instance, the bond with tradition would have to be a critical rather than an unreflected one. Furthermore, as Hendrik Kraemer rightly emphasizes, the idea of pluriform unity is not to be isolated as a spiritual notion from its *Sitz im Leben*. Hendrik Kraemer, *Theologie*, p.78.

17 Hendrik Kraemer, *Theologie*, pp.14-24.

18 Hendrik Kramer, *Theologie*, pp.24, 28-36. As milestones promoting an engagement between christian convictions and involvement in the world are mentioned the flourishing of evangelical academies, the "Action Catholique", the introduction of a "Kirchentag" in Germany, the opening of centres such as "Kerk en Wereld" and the Ecumenical Institute in Bossey.

19 Hendrik Kraemer, *Theologie*, pp.71-75. "Erst wenn die Verhältnisse der Welt ganz in den Wirkungskreis einer kirchlichen Doktrin treten, wenn dem anhaltenden Ruf nach einer Erneuerung völlig Rechnung getragen wird und die Direktiven für das kirchliche Leben aus ihrem eigenen Wesen und ihrer Berufung abgelesen werden, und zwar im vollen Bewustsein dessen, was dies für einen wagemutigen Glauben voraussetzt, ist eine echte Theologie des Laientums - als unentbehrlicher Bestandteil der ganzen kirchlichen Doktrin - möglich" (p.73).

20 Hendrik Kraemer, *Theologie*, pp.108-III.

21 It is quite evident that an increased narrative activity will influence the ecclesiological image of the church. In the historic churches, because of their traditional tendency to see themselves as (the) one identifiable church, narrative pluralism could relativize their self-understanding. But also the smaller independent communities and protestant free churches would, through the communication of shared religious experience, suddenly find themselves confronted with questions of ecumenicity and visible participation in the universal church. This happened, for instance, in pentecostal circles when catholic Charismatics began to share testimonies that reflected a compatible faith experience although some theological presuppositions were later understood to be different.

22 Most illustrative are the consequences issuing from inter-marriage, and the religious education of children born into a dual confession. Another example is the cooperation in interest groups pursuing political, moral and/or ecological aims based on common religious convictions.

Part Three

—

Living as Anglicans in a Pluralistic World

21

Reception

Henry Chadwick

In the Book of Common Prayer, the special collect for St Peter's day on 29 June, repeated without change since Cranmer's first vernacular prayer book of 1549, first commemorates the Apostle who was entrusted with such excellent gifts and was commanded to feed the flock of God, and then continues: 'Make, we beseech thee, all bishops and pastors diligently to preach the holy word, and the people obediently to follow the same, that they may receive the crown of everlasting glory...'.

The proper response of the people of God to authentic proclamation of the word of God is obedience. Comparison of Cranmer's collect with that found in the Latin books he wished to replace shows at once that in the Latin prayers on 29 June the theme of obedience is absent. Cranmer introduced it for the feast of the Apostle who received so great a commission. Obedience was not a virtue of which the pre-Christian world had much to say, unless prescribing the relationship of slaves to their masters. But for the Christians it became important; to Ambrose of Milan it was *omnium fundamentum virtutum*[1], and Augustine knew of some who called it the very matrix of virtues, universal in its application[2]. In the New Testament Christians are exhorted 'Obey your leaders and submit yourselves to them' (Heb 13,17). In Ephesians 5,21 the exhortation takes the surprising form 'Be subject to one another out of reverence for Christ'. Romans 15,7 has 'Accept one another for the sake of God's glory, as Christ accepted you'. Yielding ground when there is disagreement is an expression of love between those who are members of the body of Christ and therefore inter-connected with each other. Deviationists at Corinth could be sharply told 'We have no such custom, nor do any of the churches of God' (1 Cor 10,10). Yet diversity of gifts is characteristic of the working of the Holy Spirit, and the Corinthian Church is not to suppose they are the only people to whom the word of God has come (1 Cor 14,36).

Reception is not identical with obedience. The term comes forward when the question concerns the recognition by believers, who aspire only to obey the Gospel, of other believers with other customs who also aspire to obey.

In the apostolic age the most difficult problem of mutual recognition arose between the original Jewish Christians and the missionaries to the Gentile world with their converts. In Galatians 2 the apostle Paul speaks simultaneously in terms of his independence of, and of his dependence on, the recognition granted by the pillar apostles, James, Peter, and John. They first listened to Paul's gospel, and then acknowledged him and his work by giving him and Barnabas their right hands in token of fellowship or partnership in a single enterprise. If they had rejected his preaching and refused recognition to his work, the apostle's labours would have been in vain. He was received. Thereby his Gentile missionary churches were also received, and were soon taught to give concrete and tangible expression to their membership in the one body by their financial support for the mother Church at Jerusalem, 'the collection for the saints'.

That the mutual recognition between Jewish and Gentile Christians was never easy is evident from the second chapter of the epistle to the Ephesians. When the author of the epistle of Barnabas attacked contemporaries who reasoned that if the Old Testament was God's word, Christians ought to keep the Levitical as well as the moral law, was he engaged in polemic against the synagogue or, perhaps more probably, against brother-Christians, whether Jewish or Gentile? In Justin Martyr the question of recognition for Jewish Christians from the (by now) much larger body of Gentile believers had become awkward. Justin acknowledged that, to his regret, the majority of Gentile Christians supposed Jewish Christians to be at fault in observing the Levitical customs, and did not recognise them as full and faultless members of the one body of Christ.

Disagreement between different groups of Christians, separated by distance and after the third century also by language, created new problems of mutual recognition. In the second century the disputes about the date of Easter caused painful relations between Rome and Asia Minor, which the autocratic ruling of Pope Victor did not bring to an end. In 325 the prime cause for the episcopal assembly which became the Council of Nicaea was not Arianism but the need to achieve a universal date for Easter, Rome and Alexandria being out of step with Syria. (Does it not remain a source of embarrassment in the twentieth century that West and East use different ways of calculating the right date for the celebration of the principal festival of the Christian year? The divergence is a public declaration of non-recognition.) Be that as it may, the primary locus of reception is initially local rather than universal. It takes place at the point where the preacher proclaims the word of God and the congregation receives it as such. The Apostle thanked God that the people at Thessalonica received his gospel as what it is, 'not the word of a mere human being but God's word' (1 Thess 2,13). The authentic sermon is a dialogue of mutual giving and receiving. The liturgical exchange "Dominus vobiscum, Et cum spiritu tuo" is indispensable not only to the celebration of the eucharist but to all congregational worship. When one local church acknowledges another local church elsewhere, that act of recognition necessarily implies that both communities are microcosms of the one Church of God. Augustine felt deeply wounded when the Donatist bishop Gaudentius treated the catholic church as 'a merely human creation', dependent for its authority on the imperial government, not upon any divine commission[3].

During the second century the gradual formation of a canon of Scripture strikingly illustrates the process of mutual recognition. The records show some degree of disagreement about the Christian texts being added to the Septuagint translation of the Old Testament to provide a lectionary for liturgical readings. The dissimilarity between the Fourth Gospel and the Synoptics provoked some to express hesitations about the canonical status of St John's Gospel, and Irenaeus had to insist on a four-gospel canon, neither more nor less than four, on the ground that fourness is part of the very nature of things in the order of creation. The Apocalypse of John was not read in all churches. The epistle to the Hebrews was not accepted as St Paul's in the church at Rome, the church with which it had some original connection (Heb 13,25), and was slowly but eventually received as Pauline in the West on the ground of recognition given to the custom of the Greek churches. The way in which a coherent and agreed Biblical canon came to be formed shows reception at work.

Similarly with the calendar of the Christian year in respect of the festival of Christ's nativity. There was a celebration on 6 January during the second century in the Greek East, originating in the Nile valley where it was needed to oust a feast of Isis and Osiris. In the Latin West, the winter solstice was important in the festival of Sol Invictus, the unconquered sun, the cult of which was fostered in the last half of the third century. Should not Christians celebrate the birth of the 'sun of righteousness' at the same time of the year? Could it be purely fortuitous that they met to celebrate the Lord's resurrection on the day of the sun? December 25 was a day that ought to belong to the Church, not to pagan polytheists. Accordingly, by the time of Constantine the Great it was already customary in the West to celebrate the Nativity on December 25. By the end of the fourth century the West had also taken into its calendar the feast on January 6. Augustine could regard it as additional evidence for the schismatic nature of the North African Donatists that they observed December 25 but not January 6; they were in communion with neither Rome nor Jerusalem[4]. More gradually the East absorbed the festival on December 25. It was incorporated in the calendar at Antioch in Syria about 375 (on the evidence of John Chrysostom[5]), but was not observed at Jerusalem or Alexandria until about half a century later.

Other differences between East and West were also matters of mutual reception. The Sanctus in the eucharistic liturgy was virtually universal in the eastern churches by the second half of the fourth century, but remained unusual and rare in the West. (So, explicitly, a late fourth century Latin sermon printed among the works of St Ambrose)[6]. The Sanctus is never mentioned in Augustine, who has much to say about the forms of liturgy in North Africa, so that his silence is significant. *The Liber Pontificalis*[7], in this matter a hazardous ground for confident statement, ascribes to the second-century Pope Xystus I the credit for introducing the Sanctus; if there is any foundation for that report, it has to be remembered that in the second century the liturgy at Rome was in Greek, not Latin. But by the sixth century the western churches had made the Sanctus a regular conclusion to the liturgical Preface.

More remarkable is the reception by the western churches of the *Kyrie eleison* at some time during the fifth century. The pilgrim lady Egeria records the use of the *Kyrie* at Jerusalem in the fourth century, and the *Apostolic*

Constitutions[8] attest it for Syria. It was not known in North Africa, the silence of Augustine being again significant. If the *Deprecatio Gelasii* is a litany correctly associated with the name of Pope Gelasius (492-96), then the Kyrie was used at Rome from his time. The second Council of Vaison in Gaul (529) records its recent introduction at Rome and the Gallic churches. The Kyrie was being regularly used by the monks following the Rule of St Benedict. A famous reference in Gregory the Great's letter of 598 to bishop John of Syracuse shows not only that by his time the Kyrie was entirely established at Rome, but that the Romans did not follow the Greek custom by which the entire congregation said the petition together; at Rome the clergy said *Kyrie eleison* to which the people responded *Christe eleison*, and this last petition was never used by the Greeks[9]. Gregory was protesting against the accusation that, under the influence of his years in Constantinople, he was ruining the Roman liturgy by sponsoring Greek prayers in the Latin mass. His critics thought there should be limits to reception and mutual recognition.

The troubles of Leo the Great with the christological controversy at the time of the council of Chalcedon bequeathed tensions between the Latin West and the Greek patriarchates - tensions exacerbated by the 34 years of the Acacian schism (484-518) during which Rome was out of communion with the eastern Patriarchs, and then by the intricate affair of the Three Chapters when Justinian's ecclesiastical policy seemed to many western bishops to compromise the integrity of the Chalcedonian definition of 451. Against this background, recognition became uneasy and distrustful, not indeed for the first time in the relation between East and West, but in a degree and with a depth of feeling that was greater than at any time in the past. Justinian's Greek bishops were putting a gloss on the Chalcedonian 'in two natures' which felt forced and unfamiliar to western minds, though in time they came to accept the decisions of the fifth general council (553).

The problems begin when reception is a term for the recognition of declarations or actions by communities other than that to which one already belongs, when language or customs or ways of worship which are unfamiliar and distinct are acknowledged to be authentic and valid expressions of truth. As the example of Jewish and Gentile Christians in the apostolic age sufficiently shows, reception of what seems different and even alien does not come easily.

In modern times theologians have borrowed the term 'reception' from German historians of Roman law, especially Rudolf Sohm (1841-1917), who wrote on the impact of Justinian's Corpus of civil law upon Germany in the age of the Renaissance and the Reformation. But the wide and broad sense in which the civil lawyers have used the term offers all too little help to theologians in their endeavours to analyse the use of the concept in areas where precision is required. The legal analogy is illuminating to the degree that those who have written about the reception of Roman law have stressed the role of the commentators; that is, what mattered to them was not merely what the original texts meant but, even more, how the commentators understood them as they sought to apply the principles and practices of ancient documents to their own time. To that extent the usage of the lawyers is a pointer for the theologian. In the Church the reception of a theological definition is directly concerned with the way in which, at a later time in a very different context, the definition in question is interpreted. It is coherent with this that most of the writing on the problem of reception has concentrated on the debate following the decisions of Councils. But the issue is in another dress the same question as that of the relation between the biblical text and later interpreters.

St. Augustine observed that the interpreter can be confident of being able to expound the text correctly when its meaning is obvious. Indeed when the text is perfectly clear, an interpreter is superfluous.[10] But if the text is obscure, the interpreter has a difficult and even dangerous task - *periculosum onus*[11]. Different exegetes offer widely divergent expositions, and the reader may be bewildered. But even when the interpreter feels uncertain of the original intention of the biblical author, he can nevertheless offer an exegesis which contains no error in itself. That will be so when his interpretation in no way diverges from the apostolic tradition of faith and causes no offence to the intuitive sense of the faithful. In the *sensus fidelium* Augustine often sees a major criterion of right belief. There are several places in his writings when Augustine regards 'offence to Catholic ears' as a sufficient sign of improper deviation from authenticity. Therefore it is still possible for a preacher who cannot feel utterly confident of the intentions of Moses nevertheless to expound Genesis in a way which will be accepted by the people of God.

In writing polemical tracts against the Manichees or the Donatists Augustine had little difficulty in deploying an arsenal of biblical texts in ways that the Catholic community of Africa and elsewhere found congenial. By definition his opponents were non-Catholic, and were foot-faulted from the start. It is baldly stated, with all the force of a self-evident axiom, that 'one separated from the Church cannot avoid saying false things'[12]. More effort and far more emotional stress were required by the controversy with the followers of Pelagius. Until the vindication of Pelagius at the Palestinian council of Diospolis, Augustine had no worries about the need for canonical verdicts from councils or even primatial action by the Roman see. The synodical acquittal of Pelagius in the East required rectifying action by synods at Carthage and Milan, and by a declaration on the part of Pope Innocent I that Pelagius must disown the heretical notions ascribed to him by the African bishops. But even in the Pelagian controversy it was not natural or instinctive in Augustine to appeal to canonical verdicts by councils. When the Pelagians demanded that the Augustinian rejection of their affirmation of free will should be subjected to review at a general council of both East and West, Augustine significantly averted this plea by the reply that for the Church to protect the faithful against the dangers of Pelagian heresy, no formal decision by any conciliar act was required. The entire body of the faithful would know without any pronouncement from synodical authority that Pelagianism could not be authentic orthodoxy.

When Julian of Eclanum wanted to justify the doctrine of Pelagius by appealing (with some reason) to authorities of the Greek churches, Augustine sharply insisted that there was no division of opinion between the eastern and western churches. Granted that Augustine could speak of *ecclesia occidentalis* and *ecclesia orientalis*, nevertheless it is inconceivable to him that these two traditions might be understood to be different Churches with distinct fundamental beliefs. In both halves of the empire, there is one and the same faith.[13] The division of the empire between two emperors carries no implication that the one Church can be divided: *in utraque parte catholica inveniatur ecclesia.*[14]

Among the ancient 'Fathers' of the Western Church Augustine was no doubt the one who owed least to the reception of Greek theology. Hilary of Poitiers, Ambrose, and Jerome had considerable debts to the Greek theologians. They could all read Greek easily and made use of what they read. Augustine knew from his reading of Jerome that the number of Greek theologians who had expounded the orthodox faith was 'beyond counting'[15]. Although he knew some Greek, the language was difficult for him, and while he would have liked to be able to read more Greek theology, he normally had to be content with works translated into Latin, and moved uncertainly in this area. (He once cites as a work by Gregory Nazianzen a text composed in Latin by Gregory of Elvira.)[16] He knew the Latin translation made by Eustathius of Basil's sermons on the six days of creation, and made some use of them in his Literal Commentary on Genesis. Rufinus' versions of pieces by Basil and Gregory Nazianzen were known to him, and Jerome's translation of Didymus on the Holy Spirit. In the Pelagian controversy, citations from John Chrysostom invoked by the Pelagians needed to be answered to refute the claim that John did not believe in original sin; here Augustine had access not only to Latin translations of some sermons but also to a codex with the Greek original. The harvest of evidence for any deep knowledge of Greek theology is therefore minimal. Nevertheless Augustine never for one moment suggests that the Greek Fathers could have been in error. In controversy his appeal is to the consensus of East and West. He manifests no coolness towards the Greek tradition. Admittedly he felt ruffled when in 420-21 the patriarch of Constantinople, Atticus, wrote to Aurelius of Carthage about Pelagianism but assumed Augustine to be dead[17].

The controversy concerning the *Filioque* has sometimes led to the suggestion or the implication that Augustine knowingly intended to supplement the creed agreed upon by the Greek bishops assembled in 381 at the Council of Constantinople. Without the *Filioque* in some form he certainly believed that Arian infiltration of orthodox communities was inadequately excluded. However, there is no evidence that he had ever heard of the creed of Constantinople. Apart from the bishop of Thessalonica who may have claimed to represent Pope Damasus, there was no western representation at the Council, and the earliest evidence for western recognition of the assembly at Constantinople occurs considerably later than Augustine's age.

Many texts of Augustine attest his conviction that by divinely given intuition all Christians agree in the basic affirmations of the faith. The universal body of believers shares a single faith, *una fides*, transcending the diversity of customs in different parts of the world; it is therefore a mistake when an unnamed writer claims that the custom at Rome of observing a fast on Saturdays is the apostolic usage lost by other churches. In Ps 44, 14-15 the king's daughter is all glorious within, even though on her dress there is external variety[18]. In one of the sermons recently discovered in the city library at Mainz by F. Dolbeau, Augustine writes *varietas linguarum sed non varietas doctrinarum ....varietas locutionis sed unitas caritatis*[19]. The sermon is a partnership of preacher and congregation, not a one-sided relation where the preacher is handing out truths and where the people are passive in acceptance[20]. The bishop is *servus servorum Christi*[21']. In their teaching bishops speak *non tanquam magistri sed tanquam ministri*[22]. Hence Augustine's often repeated declaration *Vobis sum episcopus, vobiscum Christianus*[23]. So in a famous sentence Augustine declared that the ground for his belief in the gospel was the *auctoritas ecclesiae catholicae*[24], not meaning the inerrancy of official organs of teaching but the personal weight of the quality of life lived by members of the Christian community, and the witness they give to the truth of the gospel. Augustine was unsympathetic to the clericalised conception of the Church characteristic of the Donatist schismatics, whose spokesman Parmenianus could make the assertion, 'intolerable to Christian ears', that the bishop is mediator between God and the laity[25]. The Donatist (Maximianist) synod of Cebarsussi (393) likewise offended Augustine by asserting that the *sacerdos* has to be pure ; 'to gain from God for his plebs what they are unworthy to obtain'[26]. Augustine had reservations about the popular usage of *sacerdos* and *pastor*. Christians have only one priest, one chief shepherd, and the clergy are no more than ministerial. Spiritual judgement in the Church is exercised not only by the presiding officers but also by those under their care[27].

On the other hand, Augustine's realism allowed him to acknowledge that in practice the literate and educated clergy were teaching a plebs that was like a mixed comprehensive school, including both sexes and many levels of ability[28]. The Church is like a ship where the laity are the passengers and the clergy the crew[29].

Augustine held a high doctrine of the commission entrusted to the clergy at ordination. But he did not share the opinion (encouraged perhaps by too much sad experience) that the Church is an amorphous and naturally fissiparous body, so hopelessly liable to error and heretical infiltration that only strong hierarchical control from primates, and councils firmly controlled by primates, can hope to keep such a body in the truth of God's revelation. He was content to assert, in many passages, the primacy of holy Scripture and to affirm that, in everything which is necessary to salvation, scripture is clear. There are enough clear texts to provide the key for the interpretation of the many obscure passages. The obscure texts can be expounded allegorically, to the pleasure of the hearer fascinated at the discovery of profound mysteries in improbable places. Allegory cannot be appealed to in polemical theology, since there is too subjective an element in it. Characteristically Augustine insists on the literal character of the essential elements of the Christian story, namely, the birth, life, death, and resurrection of Jesus. Well aware that the Virgin Birth and the Resurrection were widely regarded as incredible by educated pagans, and often interpreted in symbolic terms by believers, Augustine felt bound to be unyielding. Outside the creed professed at baptism there are obscure matters on which ignorance and error are compatible with an essential orthodoxy, but there can be no hesitations about affirming the incarnation and the resurrection[30]. We are to have no doubts *de credendis*, but also *nulla temeritas de intelligendis*[31].

Again in such utterances it is striking that there is no appeal to conciliar or primatial decisions. Yet Augustine was surely optimistic if he really thought that on every element of authentic faith scripture is perfectly clear and unambiguous. *Dogmata* are for him doctrines held by heretics, not by orthodox; he does not use the word in a good sense. But he was aware that in the baptismal controversy in which Cyprian's sacramental theology was a central point of dispute the resolution of the debate had been achieved by the Council of Arles (314), an assembly whose dignity and authority he tended to magnify, but which was certainly of crucial importance for the Catholic communities in North Africa. Doctrinal decisions by great Church Councils would be needless if Scripture were utterly unambiguous. The Council of Nicaea in 325 felt compelled to resort to a non-scriptural term with a strong philosophical pre-history, *homousios*, because the Arian party could appeal to certain biblical texts - selectively no doubt, yet not obviously more selectively than their opponents. On the ground of an appeal to the Bible alone, the grand question at issue was not decidable. So the Council of Nicaea sought to safeguard the mind of the community at large, expressed through the consensus of Greek bishops assembled from many provinces, invested with an aura by the emperor's invitation and personal presence, and with their authority and representativeness enhanced by the presence of two Roman legates. Even so the issues remained far from being conclusively resolved by the Council, and the story of the fourth century Church is largely the narrative of the Council's reception.

There are no great councils in the history of the Church whose decisions have not been subjected to a process of critical assimilation or indeed (as in the case of the Robber-Council of Ephesus, or *Latrocinium*, of 449) rejection. Origen once replied to the pagan Celsus, when he mocked the passionate conflicts between differing Christian groups, that there is no serious subject of human importance which does not provoke disagreement, and the more serious it is, the greater the conflict[32]. The church historian Socrates in the fifth century thought controversy of the essence of church history; were there no disputes, the historian would have nothing to write about[33].

Notoriously the ancient ecumenical councils, shared by both East and West, were all in some degree problematic to the divided Christians of their time. In the fourth century those who accepted the Nicene Creed refused to acknowledge the sacraments of those who did not; and vice versa. But the general judgement that the Nicaenum must become the universal standard of orthodoxy was not achieved in a day. Even at the time of the Council in 325, there were strong opponents of Arius and his friends who were disturbed to find that among those friends there were bishops (Eusebius of Caesarea, even Eusebius of Nicomedia) capable of putting their signature to the creed. The ultra anti-Arians (Eustathius of Antioch) regarded Constantine the Great as responsible for imposing a dangerous compromise for the sake of peace, allowing in bishops with opinions which they wished to exclude. On the other wing, Eusebius of Caesarea found it necessary to assure his own supporters that he had not sacrificed his integrity by signing, and issued an open letter explaining in what sense he construed the creed and its attached anathema.

The fact that the Nicene *homousios* offered cover to characters like Marcellus of Ancyra, with strongly modalist sympathies, produced distrust of the sufficiency of the creed. In the 340s even pro-Nicene supporters did not necessarily think the creed a perfectly adequate statement. A decade later Hilary of Poitiers, defending the Nicaenum, had to concede that unacceptable interpretations could be given to it. The fourth-century controversy engendered a multitude of creeds and councils: how could one be confident that the Nicene creed was right and true, and that the alternatives on offer were less true, less adequate to safeguard the apostolic tradition of faith? The crucial question was not the special or unique authority of the Council in itself, but the correctness of the content of the creed. The simplest defence of the truth of the Nicaenum was to affirm that it enshrined the apostolic faith, the religion for which martyrs had died. For Hilary this was the faith which he held before he had ever heard of the Nicene creed, and he defended the creed because it expressed what he understood to be the faith of the apostolic tradition, but without any implication that it was the only possible way of expressing it or that it possessed an irreformable status.

Because not everyone was convinced of the correctness of the Nicene formula, as witnessed by the impassioned controversy which it provoked, other criteria were needed. At the time of the Council in 325 the authority of the assembly was affirmed to rest on the width of representation, on the number of bishops from far and wide who attended. It was not a local provincial synod, but the largest assembly of bishops that had hitherto met. Those present included not only bishops from Greek provinces where the Church was already strong but representatives from Persia, Scythia (Stobi? or the Cimmerian Bosphorus?), and above all from the distant West, Ossius of Cordoba and two legates sent by Pope Silvester. To Eusebius of Caesarea's panegyric, it seemed a reenactment of the day of Pentecost[34]. Several defenders of the Nicaenum in the 350s, and later, stress the world-wide or 'ecumenical' nature of the gathering.

There were also those who, sometimes as an *ad hominem* argument addressed to the Emperor Constantius, emphasized the sanction of imperial authority imparted by the presence of the great Constantine himself. The political theory formulated by Eusebius saw in Constantine the earthly counterpart of the heavenly monarch. Constantine felt that his mission to reconcile warring factions was strikingly vindicated by the near unanimity of consensus both on the creed and on the date of Easter. For his son Constantius II, the capacity of the Nicaenum to engender urban riots and mutual excommunications seemed to discredit its claims to supremacy among the Councils.

The argument from numbers attending was an appeal to the universality of consent in a world-wide community throughout the *oikoumene*. The numbers took on special significance when from 359 onwards it began to be claimed that the bishops equalled the 318 servants of Abraham in Genesis 14 (318 in Greek being TIH and therefore symbolic of the Cross of Jesus). The assertion (comparable to the legend of the translators of the *Septuaginta*) vindicated the inspired status of the bishops.

In Ambrose's time we meet in Popes Damasus (from 368) and Siricius the affirmation that the special supremacy of Nicaea rests on its confirmation by the Roman See. In its initial and simplest form this affirmation signifies the acceptance of the creed by the senior bishop of the Latin West, an exemplification of the West's reception of decisions made by an almost wholly Greek assembly. The West's reception is grounded on the content of the creed, that is on the awareness (often expressed by Lucifer of Cagliari) that the Greek *homousios* is the equivalent of the Latin *unius substantiae*.

Nevertheless, the Western churches of the fourth and fifth centuries also understood the Bishop of Rome as the principal executive officer for enforcing the canon law enacted by Church councils. Confirmation by Rome therefore had overtones of a juridical and canonical act. The seed is being sown whereby a brotherly exchange of gifts will become a legal verdict. And that shift is naturally enhanced and encouraged by the common assumption of the age that the decisions of a large council also receive ratification and enforcement by the imperial government, which has the strongest interest in reducing Christian controversy to the minimum because of its disruptive social consequences and because the displeasure of heaven is a threat to the Empire's peace and prosperity.

The reception of other great ancient Councils required hardly less time and discussion than Nicaea. The Council of Constantinople (381) had no Roman legates present and did not suppose itself to be providing a creed for the universal Church, though posterity came to think of the creed in that way (thanks to the enshrinement of the creed by the Council of Chalcedon in 451, which needed the Constantinopolitanum to justify its own Definition in face of the decree of Ephesus (431) that no addition may be made to the Nicene creed). Its recognition by the West, implicit in the acceptance by Leo of the Chalcedonian Definition, first becomes explicit with Gregory the Great[35] in 590.

The huge conflagration generated by the christological definition of Chalcedon with its insistence on the preposition 'in' bequeathed a legacy of non-reception in parts of Syria, in Armenia, among the Copts of Egypt and the Ethiopian Church. The fifth Council under Justinian (553) began temporary schisms in the West, but finally achieved reception there mainly by the papal policy of insisting on juridical obedience and giving no reasons. The sixth, anti-monothelete Council of 680-681 also bequeathed complexities of acceptance in the East, and the insistence of the Roman legates on a condemnation not only of the doctrine but of named patriarchs who had advocated it paradoxically led, irresistibly, to the rejection by an ecumenical Council of a Pope - Honorius. The seventh Council of 787 could set aside the iconoclast 'ecumenical council' of 754 on the ground that all the patriarchs (i.e. Rome) had not accepted it, but had the greatest difficulty in achieving reception in the Frankish West.

Of later Western Councils, particular interest attaches to the wide variety of interpretations which subsequent theologians gave to the language about transubstantiation at the fourth Lateran Council (1215), when a change of the substance of the bread and wine was affirmed without an accompanying definition of 'substance', without excluding the notion that with the body and blood of Christ bread and wine remain or that the bread and wine suffer annihilation. The decisions of the Council of Florence, though worded far more loosely than a man like Turrecremata might have wished and in principle generous to the Greek tradition, nevertheless met with non-reception on the main ground that the Greeks thought the western addition of the *Filioque* to the creed to be an act of gross irreverence to authority. In consequence, while the West has looked back on the union achieved at Florence as almost an ideal model, the Orthodox tradition has come to think of Florence in 1439 (not Cardinal Humbert in 1054) as the real moment of decisive estrangement between Rome and Constantinople. The reception of the Council of Trent was not achieved overnight; especially in France there was considerable hesitation to be set at rest requiring some decades of consideration. Many Catholic theologians understood Vatican II not merely as a supplement correcting the balance of Vatican I but also as, in substantial degree, a re-reception of Vatican I, by virtue of the juxtaposition of a koinônia ecclesiology with a 'pyramid' ecclesiology in *Lumen Gentium*. The extraordinary Synod called to the Vatican in 1985 continued to hold these ecclesiologies together, even though it has to be conceded that in practice collegiality has remained a paper idea rather than a reality and that diocesan bishops have continued to feel more *sub Petro* than *cum Petro*.

Since Vatican II with its dramatic decree on Ecumenism, *Unitatis Redintegratio*, the question of reception has been pushed into prominence in the bilateral dialogues, to which it is of crucial importance. That fact is mainly the consequence of the concentration of these dialogues upon fundamental dogmatic questions – a concentration which has seemed to make some of their work marginal to the now universal Christian concern for social issues, for peace and justice, poverty and wealth, pollution of the environment and the accelerating growth of the world population. But the divided state of Christian communions greatly hinders their witness, and where there is division there is no escape from dialogue in the sense of patient, charitable listening.

In ecumenical dialogue there are two particular points where the nature of reception requires careful thought. There are strands of Orthodox theology, notably in Khomiakoff (1804-1860) and his stress is altogether secondary to the truth recognised by the *sensus fidelium omnium*; episcopal councils can promulgate dogmatic statements, the way in which these statements are received by the faithful is the ultimate acknowledgement of adequacy. The stress on the content of the definition rather than the organ is a principle close to the heart of Orthodox and Anglican theologians. In ultramontane Roman Catholic theology the emphasis is made to lie heavily on the organ, namely the *magisterium* concentrated in the bishop of Rome; since 1870 it has to be accepted that without the Pope no assembly of bishops can offer a decisive definition, whereas the Pope has the power to bind the whole Church irrespective of the concurrence of the episcopate - admittedly this fairly extreme position is in practice understood to be subject to conditions and qualifications.

The recent Vatican verdict of December 1991 on the 'final report' of the Anglican Roman Catholic International Commission (ARCIC) published in 1982 exemplified the contrast. A major theme of the verdict is that Anglicans think the truth of an ecclesiastical definition depends on consonance with scripture and accepted sacred tradition, that is, more upon the content than on the organs of authority, though Anglicans fully accept the authority of tradition in determining, e.g. the canon of scripture and the great dogmas of Trinity and Incarnation defined by the ancient ecumenical councils. This is contrasted with the Roman Catholic view that the truth of a definition depends little on the content and primarily on the primate (or the Council ratified by the primate).

The authors of the verdict cannot have been comfortable with ARCIC's dictum that 'The Church's teaching is proclaimed because it is true; it is not true simply because it has been proclaimed'.

The Mariological definitions of the Immaculate Conception and the Assumption are often presented as crucial tests for the recognition of Roman authority, indeed of the power of the Pope to proclaim dogmas without a Council (though it is only fair to add that there was much consultation before the proclamations, and the high costs of general councils make them rare occurrences). The reception of these dogmas would be virtually effortless if the stress were laid on their content. There is no controversy that the mother of our redeemer was prepared by divine grace for her calling of forming and shaping our Lord's humanity, and that whatever the precise honour bestowed upon her in the communion of saints, it is proportionate to the honour bestowed upon earth. Protestants today often appear unaware that at the time of the sixteenth century Reformation the two Marian doctrines were an issue between Dominicans and Franciscans, but not a cause of separation from Rome at Wittenberg or Canterbury.

The last point may serve to illustrate a second point of importance for the comprehension of ecumenical dialogue, too often scorned as either treachery or irrelevance. Reception arises when it is recognised that the partner in dialogue loves God and his Church and seeks to be obedient to the gospel; moreover, that this obedience transcends allegiance to anything sectarian. A true ecumenical dialogue does not leave the participants where they were when they began; they do not shrug their shoulders and expect to end by tolerating ineradicable differences. The ground for this is simply stated. It is not easy to believe that Christ's one, holy, catholic, and apostolic Church can be, or subsist in, a multitude of ecclesial groups, all equally right or equally mistaken, none of which mirrors or even approximates to the intended form of the unique apostolic community. Can it have been the Lord's intention for his community of disciples to have a large number of diverse ecclesial bodies, all of which are equally valid or invalid expressions of his will for his people? Resignation with the discouragements of the ecumenical process can deceive us into thinking that 'reception' has to mean accepting dissension as being for ever, in time, an ineradicable and insoluble cause of eucharistic separation. But in the authentic dialogue reception is quite different. Its basis lies in recognition of where and what the Church is, rooted in scripture and a sacred tradition of faith, proclaiming the whole Word of God, celebrating the sacraments which simultaneously declare the Church's 'memory' of its origins and become the means of God's grace to his people in the present here and now.

Notes

1 Ambrose of Milan, *In Lucam*, v. 82, ed. C. Schenkl (CSEL, 32), Vienna, Tempsky, 1902.
2 Augustine of Hippo, *De bono conjugali*, 32, ed. J. Zycha (CSEL, 41), Vienna, Tempsky, 1900.
3 Augustine of Hippo, *Contra Gaudentium*, 33.42, ed. M. Petschenig (CSEL, 53), Vienna, Tempsky, 1910.
4 Augustine of Hippo, *Sermo*, 202.2, PL 38.
5 John Chrysostom, *Sermo in diem natalem Jesu Christi*, PG 49.351.
6 John Chrysostom, *Sermo*
7 *Liber Pontificalis*, 1. 129 and 56-7, ed. L. Duchesne, *Bibliotheque des Écoles Françaises d'Athenes et de Rome*, 3 (1886-1892).
8 *Apostolic Constitutions*, viii. 6. 9, ed. F.X. Funk. Paderborn, Schöning, 1905-6, 2 vols.
9 Gregory the Great, *Registrum* IX.26 = Ep. ix.12, ed. D. Norberg, (CCSL, 140), Turnhout, Brepols, 1982.
10 Augustine of Hippo, *Sermo*, 32 18, PL 38.
11 Augustine of Hippo, *Epistola*, 29. 7, ed A.L. Goldbacher (CSEL, 35), Vienna, Tempsky, 1895.
12 Augustine of Hippo, *Enarrationes in Psalmos*, 57.
13 Augustine of Hippo, *Contra Julianum*, PL 44.
14 Augustine, *Epistola ad Catholicos contra Donatistas, de unitate ecólesiae*, 13.33, ed. M. Petschenig, (CSEL, 52,) Vienna, Tempsky, 1909.
15 Jerome, *Epistola* 70, to Magnus, ed. H. Hilberg (CSEL, 54–6), Vienna, 1910–18; Augustine of Hippo, *De Doctrina Christina*, II.40.61 (CCSL,4), Turnhout, Brepols, 1962.
16 Augustine, Ep. 148.10, ed. M. Simonetti (CC SL, 69), Turnhout, Brepols, 1967.
17 Augustine, Ep. 6, in J. Divjak (ed.), *Sancti Aurelli Augustini Opera, Epistolae e duobus*.
18 Augustine of Hippo, Epistola, 36.22 (n. 11).
19 F. Dolbeau, 'Nouveaux sermons de s. Augustin pour la conversion des païens et des donatists', in *Revue des Études Augustiniennes* 37 (1991), p. 43,31.
20 Augustine of Hippo, *Enarrationes in Psalmos*, 58, ii.3 (n. 12).
21 Augustine of Hippo, Ep. 217.
22 Augustine of Hippo, *Sermo*, 292.1, PL 38.

23 Augustine of Hippo, *Sermo*, 340.1, PL 38, cf. *Enarrationes in Psalmos*, 126.3, and elsewhere.
24 Augustine of Hippo, *Contra Epistolam quem vocant Fundamenti*, 5.6,ed. J. Zycha (CSEL,25), Vienna, Tempsky, 1891.
25 Augustine of Hippo, *Contra Epistolam Parmenani*, II.8.15. ff., ed. M Petschenig (CSEL,51), Vienna, Tempsky, 1908.
26 Augustine of Hippo, *Enarrationes in Psalmos*, 36.ii.20 (n. 12).
27 Augustine of Hippo, *Confessiones*, XIII.23.33, ed. L. Verheijen (CCSL, 27), Turnhout, Brepols, 1981.
28 Augustine of Hippo, *Epistola*, 138.10, *tamquam publicis scholis*, ed. A.L. Goldbacher (CSEL, 44), Vienna, 1904.
29 Augustine of Hippo, *Enarrationes in Psalmos*, 106.12 (n. 12).
30 Augustine of Hippo, *De gratia Christi et peccato originali*, ii.23.27 ff., ed. C.F. Urba and J. Zycha (CSEL, 42), Vienna, Tempsky, 1903.
31 Augustine of Hippo, *De Trinitate*, IX.l.l, ed. W.J. Mountain and F. Glorie (CCSL, 50), Turnhout, Brepols, 1968.
32 Origen, Contra Celsum, III.12, ed. P. Koetschau, *Die griechischen christlichen Schrift-steller der ersten drei Jahrhunderte*, Berlin, 1899.
33 Socrates, *Historia Ecclesiastica*, VII.48.7, ed. R. Hussey, Oxford, Oxford University Press, 1853, 3vols.
34 Eusebius of Caesarea, *Vita Constantini*, III.7-8. ed. F. Winkelmann, 2nd ed., Berlin, Akademie Verlag, 1991.
35 Gregory the Great, *Registrum*, I.24.

22

The Anglican Acceptance of Contraception

Richard Harries

Before I go on to say something more specific about Anglican approaches I should stress that I will be dealing simply with the issue of contraception. I will not be discussing sterilization directly, nor abortion, to which the Church of England is strongly opposed, except in the most carefully defined circumstances.

From an Anglican perspective birth *control* is unacceptable. It smacks too much of coercion and the developed world telling the developing one what to do. Birth control is out but birth *choice* is in. Indeed, as has been argued elsewhere, 'demographic targets that governments set can in most cases be met or exceeded simply by responding to the *expressed reproductive goals* of individuals. Family planning objectives should be expressed in terms of satisfying *'unmet need'* [for contraceptive provision]' (Sinding 1992).

The availability of contraception enlarges the area of our choice and offers greater opportunity for us to take responsibility for our own lives and those of our offspring, with a view to their well-being and growth under God. From this standpoint the Anglican Church fully supports making the information and technology as widely available as possible. Understandably, however, the Church of England had to move from an inherited position of opposition. The Church of England as such has made no independent contribution to this subject. Rather it has played its part in the formulations of successive Lambeth Conferences, the decanal gathering of Anglican Bishops throughout the world. Resolution 41 of the 1908 Lambeth Conference (R. Coleman 1992) said

> The Conference regards with alarm the growing practice of the artificial restriction of the family, and earnestly calls upon all Christian people to discountenance the use of all artificial means of restriction as demoralizing to character and hostile to national welfare.

Resolution 68 of the 1920 Lambeth Conference revealed a shift away from absolutism. 'The Conference, while declining to lay down rules which will meet the needs of every abnormal case,' it began. However, it continued:

...regards with grave concern the spread in modern society of theories and practices hostile to the family. We utter an emphatic warning against the use of unnatural means for the avoidance of conception, together with the grave dangers - physical, moral and religious – thereby incurred, and against the evils with which the extension of such use threatens the race.

It went on to urge the importance of self-control and to assert that the primary purpose of marriage is the continuation of the race through the gift and heritage of children. The sexual union was not to be regarded as an end in itself.

Resolution 9 of the 1930 Conference showed a much more positive attitude. 'The functions of sex as a God-given factor in human life are essentially noble and creative.' And Resolution 13 began, 'The Conference emphasizes the truth that the sexual instinct is a holy thing implanted by God in human nature.' In contrast to the 1920 Resolution it said that 'It acknowledges that intercourse between husband and wife as the consummation of marriage has a value of its own within that sacrament, and that thereby married love is enhanced and its character strengthened.' Resolution 15, voted on with 193 in favour and 67 against, said:

> Where there is a clearly felt moral obligation to limit or avoid parenthood, the method must be decided on Christian principles. The primary and obvious method is complete abstinence from intercourse (as far as may be necessary) in a life of discipline and self-control lived in the power of the Holy Spirit. Nevertheless in those cases where there is such a clearly felt moral obligation to limit or avoid parenthood, and where there is a morally sound reason for avoiding complete abstinence, the Conference agrees that other methods may be used, providing that this is done in the light of the same Christian principles.

The 1958 Lambeth Conference was less qualified. Resolution 115 reads:

> The Conference believes that the responsibility for deciding upon the number and frequency of children has been laid by God upon the consciences of parents everywhere: that this planning, in such ways as are mutually acceptable to husband and wife in Christian conscience, is a right and important factor in Christian family life and should be the result of positive choice before God.

In 1968 Resolution 22 noted the publication of the Papal Encyclical, *Humanae Vitae* and, while expressing its appreciation of the Pope's deep concern for the institution of marriage and the integrity of married life, went on:

> Nevertheless, the Conference finds itself unable to agree with the Pope's conclusion that all methods of conception control other than abstinence from sexual intercourse or its confinement to the periods of infecundity are contrary to the 'order established by God'. It affirms the resolutions of the 1958 Conference of 113 and 115.

These resolutions show clearly how the Lambeth Conference moved from total opposition, to qualified acceptance, and then full acceptance. My predecessor, Kenneth Kirk, who was Bishop of Oxford from 1937 to 1955, was previously Regius Professor of Moral and Pastoral Theology in Oxford. In a book first published in 1927 but revised for a new edition in 1936 he suggested that the main two reasons for a change in the attitude of the Anglican Church were, first, enhanced appreciation of the value of children, with the implied assumption that it might be easier to express this value if there are fewer rather than more. Secondly, and this is the main reason he gives, the change in the position of women. This, he wrote, 'has led to a natural, proper and wholly Christian demand that the wife should not be forced, by the exigencies of married life, to abandon all the activities in which she found her interests and occupation before marriage.'

All the recent Anglican statements on this subject have set contraception firmly within the context of a loving, stable, and life-long marriage union. It is the importance of this above all that has been stressed. As part of this, as was seen from the changing emphasis in the Lambeth Conference resolutions, there has been a growing appreciation of the value of the marital sexual union in itself, for itself. This change can be particularly clearly seen in the introduction to the marriage service. The 1662 Book of Common Prayer stated that the causes for which matrimony was ordained were:

First, it was ordained for the procreation of children, to be brought up in the fear and nurture of the Lord, and to the praise of his holy name. Secondly, it was ordained for a remedy against sin, and to avoid fornication, that such persons as have not the gift of contingency might marry, and keep themselves undefiled members of Christ's body. Thirdly, it was ordained for the mutual society, help, and comfort that the one ought to have of the other, both in prosperity and adversity.

The 1928 Book kept the first reason, though in slightly different language. The language of the second reason, however, was changed radically.

> Marriage was ordained that the natural instincts and affections, implanted by God, should be hallowed and directed aright; that those who are called of God to this holy estate, should continue therein in pureness of living.

The Alternative Service Book of 1980 has a totally rewritten introduction. It gives the reasons for marriage in these words:

> Marriage is given, that husband and wife may comfort and help each other, living faithfully together in need and in plenty, in sorrow and in joy. It is given, that with delight and tenderness they may know each other in love, and through the joy of their bodily union, may strengthen the union of their hearts and lives. It is given, that they may have children and be blessed in caring for them and bringing them up in accordance with God's will, to his praise and glory.

Here we see that what was traditionally the third reason, mutual society, help, and comfort, has become the first reason. The second reason, relating to the sexual instinct, has become very positive, its purpose 'that with delight and tenderness they may know each other in love', whereas the traditional first reason, the procreation of children, has become the third one.

Professor Gordon Dunstan, one of Anglicanism's foremost ethicists in recent years, reflecting on the process whereby the Anglican Church changed its mind on this issue, has written that the resolutions did no more than reflect 'a moral judgement already made, tested and acted upon by Christian husbands and wives, episcopal and clerical as well as lay, for years before' (Dunstan 1974). He went on to say that:

> It exemplifies an instance in which the *magisterium* of the Church formulated and ratified a moral judgement made by a sort of *Consensus Fidelium*, for which a good theological justification was worked out *ex post facto*. That *Consensus* which, in the history of doctrine, has been claimed as the forerunner of dogmatic formulation, is here claimed as a source of moral insight which a church may, indeed must after testing, properly make its own.

This is a crucial indication of the nature of Anglican moral judgements. They are not simply laid down from on high. The official pronouncements of the Church reflect the tested experience of the wider Christian community, particularly that of lay people. Another good example of change, though one which took rather longer to effect, would be the way the Church, after more than 1000 years' fierce condemnation of usury, accepted that lending at interest for purposes of trade was morally legitimate.

23

Reflection on Biblical Themes of Discipleship

David Bennett

We have identified seven themes that were expressed repeatedly in the terms chosen by Jesus to describe his followers. As we explore the ways in which these terms are used by the writers of the early church, and as we examine the new terms that are introduced, we discover that the same themes continue to recur.

Although the New Testament writings show considerable diversity in style, vocabulary, and imagery, a deep underlying unity becomes evident when we look at the basic ideas about discipleship and leadership that are expressed. We find that we are not listening to new and original melodies, but to variations on a theme. We do not uncover totally new patterns of thought and life, but new perspectives and further insights into teaching already given by Jesus to his followers. Here we will look at some of the ways in which the seven themes are developed.

FUNCTION

The disciple is called to participation in a community as well as to a task.

One cannot read the New Testament letters and the Book of Acts without being impressed by the depth of loving commitment that tied together the early Christian communities. The frequent affectionate references to one another as brother and sister, and the tender parental concern shown by the apostles toward the congregations they established and nurtured, testify to the warmth and strength of the bonds of this new spiritual family. The many appearances of *oikos* (household) and its compounds, descriptions of believers as a chosen people, and the frequent use of images such as the building and the body express the essential unity of the Church.

During the Last Supper, Jesus spoke at length about the love for one another that would be the hallmark of his true followers. In the remainder of the New Testament we see much more about the ways in which that love was expressed. In the Gospels, the competition between the disciples is often more evident than their teamwork; but in the early church we observe numerous *sun-* compounds – fellow-worker, fellow-citizen, fellow-athlete, fellow-soldier, yokefellow, fellow-elder, fellow-member, fellow-heir, fellow-imitator – all expressing a co-operative and sympathetic spirit of oneness. Other images express the bonds that tie believers together as imitators of one another, followers of the same Way, sheep led by the same shepherds, branches grafted into the same tree, and a body that suffers and rejoices with each of its members. Although the differences between believers are acknowledged, images like the body show that there is unity amidst the diversity of gifts.

The community unites, but it also separates. The heavenly citizenship that brings Jews and Gentiles together simultaneously makes them aliens and strangers to their own society. The call to be saints involves separation from the world. As light they are responsible to expose and rebuke the darkness.

The metaphors of the New Testament letters often highlight the privileges that accompany membership in the community – such as the bride's experience of her husband's loving nurture, the slave set free, the son adopted into the family, the temple as the dwelling of God's Spirit, and the church as God's chosen people and treasured possession. The disciples can rejoice not only for all the new dimensions of relationship to one another, but also for the intimacy of fellowship with the Lord who has called them his friend.

Yet, the emphasis on community does not overshadow the importance of the task committed to followers of Jesus Christ.[1] The metaphors drawn from priesthood and temple, including words for 'serve' like *latreuo* and *leitourgeo*, point to the duties of worship, praise, and thanksgiving, as well as the consecration of the entire life as a type of spiritual sacrifice. The church is called to serve and to build up one another through the functioning of the spiritual gifts in the body, through acts of imitating and modelling, and through the nurture of younger believers as parents with children.

The primary focus of the church's service in the world is presented as the proclamation of the good news of Jesus Christ, expressed through the use of terms like apostle, evangelist, herald, and ambassador. Broader dimensions of service and good works are implied in images like light, stars, and fragrance.

This engagement with the world involves conflict. The images of striving as an athlete in competition, and fighting as a soldier with the forces of darkness, appear frequently.

In addition to the tasks to which every follower of Jesus is called, several images accent the specific and different tasks for which various ones are responsible as stewards of different parts of the household, or as different members of the body. In particular, new terms are introduced that apply specifically to leaders within the fellowship: words such as *episkopos* (overseer), *kybernesis* (administration), *presbyteros* (elder), and *prohistemi* (leader), in addition to the further development of terms like *poimen* (shepherd), *apostolos* (apostle), and *hegemonos* (leader) that were used by Jesus. In the Gospels, the main emphasis is on the responsibility of the disciple as servant to follow; but the remainder of the New Testament reveals more of the dimensions of responsibility and oversight to which various servants are assigned.

So then, both dimensions of community and task remain equally prominent throughout the New Testament.

AUTHORITY

The disciple is under authority.

The image of the servant remains a central motif in the New Testament letters. The apostles describe themselves as servants of Christ. Even the freedom of the Christian is seen as freedom to serve, not as absolute autonomy. Terms that imply one who is under authority include frequently used words like sheep, soldier, steward, and apostle, as well as terms like ambassador, pilot, herald, and vessel. Christ is the head of the body, and the cornerstone of the building. He is the chief shepherd of the flock.

A new dimension of living under authority that emerges in the early church is the authority exercised within the community by its human leaders. Believers are called to obey their leaders, to respect them, and to submit to them. To describe elders as shepherds and overseers is to imply that the congregation must follow their direction. The call to imitate Christian leaders is to accept the authority of a pattern of life.

To be a disciple is also to live under the authority of the Word of God. The image of the athlete is associated with the need for strict training and discipline.

RESPONSIBILITY

The disciple exercises authority.

The responsibility of the disciple to exercise authority was implied by Jesus in some of his stewardship parables, in his promises to the disciples about judging the twelve tribes of Israel in the coming kingdom, and in his exhortation to Peter after the resurrection to 'feed my sheep'. Yet, as we have seen, the greater emphasis in the Gospels is on the disciples' need to come under the Lord's authority, rather than on their own exercise of authority.

However, after Jesus' ascension to heaven, the role of leadership in the Christian communiy undergoes considerable development. Prophets and apostles provide overall direction for the church, based on the authoritative proclamation of the Word of God. Various leadership gifts begin to function. Soon elders and deacons are appointed to oversee the affairs of local congregations. Several of the terms used specifically imply the provision of direction and the exercise of authority – especially *apostolos*, *episkopos*, *hegemonos*, *kybernesis*, *oikonomos*, *poimen*, *prohistemi*, and *presbyteros*.

In addition to these specific authority roles, believers in general are appointed to positions of responsibility by the risen Lord. All are instructed to exercise their spiritual gifts as stewards (*oikonomoi*) of the many-faceted grace of God. As a kingdom of priests, all are promised a share in Christ's rule in the coming kingdom. All are invited to represent as ambassadors the King of Kings, proclaiming the message of reconciliation.

DERIVATION

The disciple is one who has responded to the call of Jesus.

The statement of this theme has two aspects. In the first place, it emphasizes that God is the initiator; everything comes from him and starts with him. On the other hand, to be a disciple is to respond willingly to the call, not to be conscripted as an unwilling recruit.

Just as Jesus did, the New Testament writers place great emphasis on the gracious call of God. The very word *ekklesia* (church) pictures an assembly that has gathered in response to a call. Paul describes himself as called to be an apostle, and appointed to be a herald; he says that by God's grace he has been allowed to lay the foundation upon which others are building. The grace, mercy, and love of God are the foundations for our adoption as God's children and his choice of us as a holy nation.

The complete dependence of the church on Christ is expressed in the pictures of Christ as head of the body and cornerstone of the building. The sheep cannot survive apart from the Great Shepherd. Although one plants and another waters, it is God who causes the growth. Every enablement for ministry is a spiritual gift distributed according to God's design. The evangelist, the prophet, and the herald pass on messages given to them by God, not of their own invention. Each believer is a 'new creature', endowed with life that only God can create. Even our very physical existence is like a mist, here only for as long as God's grace allows.

Yet the New Testament images do not express God's initiating role alone. They also indicate the importance of willing human response. The follower of Jesus is a disciple, an imitator, a follower of the Way, a believer.

STATUS

Disciples are on the same level in relationship to God, even though they may have different areas and amounts of responsibility.

Although different levels of responsibility and authority become increasingly evident as the early church develops and becomes more organized, most of the New Testament imagery emphasizes what believers have in common, rather than the ways in which they are different.

On the one hand, there are terms that indicate that no one is higher than anyone else. The ministry of all, including apostles, is called simply diakonia, service as a table-waiter. Even the greatest leader is no more than a servant of the Master. All are children of God, and brothers and sisters to one another. Paul describes himself as a common clay pot holding the priceless treasure of the gospel. Both the one who plants and the one who waters the field are merely doing the task assigned to them.

On the other hand, there are numerous terms indicating the high status that all believers now enjoy because of their union with Christ. Privileges that other societies confer on only a few are now the possession of even the humblest Christian. Each one is a royal priest. Each shares in the rule of Christ's kingdom. Each has been adopted as a child of God. Each one's body is a temple of the Holy Spirit. Each is a full citizen in the new Jerusalem. Each is called saint, chosen, beloved, freedman, heir and treasure.

Yet functional differences remain. Wives are still to be subject to their husbands, children are to obey parents, slaves are to serve their masters cheerfully. Members of the congregation are told to obey and to submit to their leaders, and to keep on paying taxes and giving respect to government authorities. But the one with authority is to remember that he or she is not better than the others, and the one under authority is to remember the dignity and freedom of his or her calling. Whatever may be their differences in social standing in the eyes of society, or their various responsibilities in the church, they are first and foremost partners, fellow-workers, fellow-heirs, children of the same Father.

IDENTIFICATION

To be a disciple is to identify with Jesus, both in his pattern of life and in his suffering.

To follow Jesus is not simply to accept a body of beliefs but to adopt a pattern of life. To be Jesus' disciple is to become like him. This emphasis on life transformation and training through personal identification is continued through the use of terms like imitator, disciple, model, and follower of the Way.

The distinctive identification of the believer with the life of Jesus Christ is implied in the application of the nickname 'Christian', and in the call to behave like an alien and a temporary resident. The child of God is expected to be holy as is the heavenly Father. The fragrance of the believer's life is supposed to make people aware of Jesus.

Identification with Jesus means not only imitation of his character but also participation in his mission, even to the point of suffering and death. Many of the New Testament images are associated closely with the suffering that the believer will experience for Christ's sake. The apostles lead the way into the arena of death, and are seen by many as the scum and refuse of the earth. The saints in the book of Revelation endure through tribulation. The athlete must run the race with endurance, and must wrestle with the forces of darkness. The witness often becomes the martyr. The Christian as soldier contends with deadly opposition, and can survive only as protected by God's armour. To be an alien is to be excluded and sometimes persecuted for one's differences. To serve is to suffer.

The leader is not exempt in any way from these hardships and sacrifices. No, the leader is to be the model of pouring out one's life as a sacrificial offering.

ACCOUNTABILITY

The disciple will be evaluated by the Lord, in terms of his character as well as his service.

Just as Jesus contrasted those who were faithful and effective servants with those who were not, so the New Testament writers speak of vessels of honour and dishonor, fields that produces a crop and others that drink the same rain but yield only thistles, those who have matured and those who remain as infants, those who have become teachers and those who still must be taught. The athletic images illustrate again and again that there is a prize to be won, a crown to be awarded, but that not everyone will even finish the race, let alone be honored as a victor.

Fellow-believers may presume to evaluate one another's performance. But several images suggest caution. The believer is a servant who stands or falls to his own master (Romans 14:4). Paul claims that his faithfulness in stewardship is known only to the Lord, who will make the true assessment at the last judgement (1 Corinthians 4:1-5). He defends himself before his critics by saying that the churches he has planted stand as his crown, his seal, his letter of recommendation.The evaluation for which the believer must prepare is the one that will take place at the judgement seat of Christ (2 Corinthians 5:10).

Note

1   Anderson and Jones, citing images like salt and light, hold that the church differs from other community groups in that it is 'called to be rather than to do' (1978:133). Cedar believes that 'serving as a leader in Christ's kingdom relates to people more than to tasks' (1987:90). Van Engen, however, after reviewing the New Testament images of the church, concludes that 'all of them signal a task to be done' (1981:69). R. Anderson provides a balanced summary: '...Leadership from a biblical perspective is not so much task oriented as it is community oriented, although in many cases it does involve the performance of a task or the enabling and equipping of others to perform tasks' (1986:69).

Conclusions and Implications

We began this investigation with the observation that leadership is a process of influence, and that even though Jesus did not use the words 'leader' or 'leadership', he called his disciples into a development process, through which he prepared them for leadership in the Christian community after his ascension.

Yet Jesus' primary focus in teaching the disciples was not to help them to master the skills often associated with leadership – setting goals, formulating strategies, organizing personnel and resources, exercising authority and discipline. He gave almost no direction about how the early Christian community should be organized, how authority should be delegated, how decisions should be made, how visions should be translated into action, or how others should be mobilized or equipped for the task.

Instead, Jesus showed his disciples how to follow, how to obey, how to respond to the authority and call of God. He knew that the effective leader must first learn how to be a faithful follower. Jesus also knew how destructive the attitudes of pride and ambition could be within the community of disciples. Therefore, he taught them attitudes of humility and self-sacrifice, using the image of the servant, and reminded them of their equal standing before God as brothers. Jesus wanted his disciples to think of themselves as 'among' one another, as brothers, and 'under' one another, as servants, more than 'over', as those in authority.

Jesus was also concerned to help the disciples realize that they were being called to significant relationships as well as to important tasks. They were not just workers; they were also friends. They were not only fishers of men, but also guests at a wedding. Celebration and joy and love were to be as much a part of their vocabulary as responsibiliy and accountability and diligence. They would be evaluated by their love for one another, and their personal commitment to Jesus, as well as by their faithfulness in completing their assigned tasks and investing their divinely-given resources.

Variations on a theme

To impart such lessons as these, Jesus used many images. But the primary images used by Jesus can be grouped into two categories – those that describe the followers as members of a spiritual family (brother, child), and those that picture them as servants (of the Lord and of one another). The first group focuses on relationships. The second group focuses on the task.

These same two clusters of images remain in the foreground throughout the New Testament writings. Some new terms are added, but the essential emphasis remains the same – the Christian has been incorporated into a loving, interdependent family, and has been commissioned to serve the Lord as part of the mandate to make disciples of all the nations.

What it means to be a follower of Jesus remains basically the same. The seven themes discussed in other chapters are revealed in the teaching of the epistles as fully as in Jesus' instructions to his disciples. Implications are spelled out in more detail, and new images are introduced appropriate to new contexts, but we are hearing variations on a theme, not a totally new melody. Even when specific leadership functions are described for the first time in the book of Acts or in the epistles, the underlying concepts echo ideas that Jesus had previously introduced to his followers.

The leader's perspective

How should an understanding of these biblical images and themes influence leadership behaviour in the church? I would like to propose some ways in which reflection on these topics can shape the leader's perspective of his/her own role, and the place of other believers as followers and potential leaders. In this way I will seek to demonstrate the rationale for studying all the biblical terms used for followers of Jesus, rather than simply those that are applied exclusively or at least primarily to leaders.

The leader as follower of Jesus

Again and again in our reflection on the Gospels, we have noted that Jesus focused more of his attention on teaching the disciples how to follow than on giving them instructions on how to lead.[1] The single most important lesson for a leader to learn is that he/she is first a sheep, not a shepherd; first a child, not a father or mother; first an imitator, not a model. Rather than thinking only about those biblical images that set him/her apart, the leader should reflect on the many, many more images that apply to him/her as fully as to any other believer.

The leader is only a mist, mortal and frail; when he/she is gone, God will raise up others; there is no place in the church for the building of dynasties, or the creation of celebrities or personality cults. No matter how grand the leader's title, or large his/her responsibility, he/she is still a steward, not an owner; a partner, not an independent contractor; a fellow-worker, not a boss; a member of the body, not the head; a branch of the tree, not the root; a servant, not a master. The common clay pot must not forget that the treasure is in the pot, not the pot itself.

The leader's view of other followers

Just as the leaders ought not to have too high an opinion of themselves, so should they beware of assuming too low an opinion of the other followers of Jesus. They should remember the terms of dignity and honour by which all followers of Jesus are described. The people they lead are royal priests, precious treasures, full citizens. They have spiritual gifts that are just as essential to the welfare of the body as any exercised by the leader. The leader's role is to equip

God's people, to empower them, to help them to become as effective as possible in the service of the King. Believers are salt, light, the very aroma of Christ; scattered throughout society in their various vocations, they can become ambassadors and heralds, witnesses and fishers of men.

Many have the ability to become teachers and models for younger believers. Some have gifts of administration and leadership that need to be encouraged. Some are still 'newly planted', not yet ready for the responsibilities of leadership, but if given time to mature, they will become able overseers and shepherds.

Many educators have observed that people tend to become what the leader expects them to be. How important it is, therefore, for the church leader to see the other church members as potentially fruitful branches, productive fields, and victorious athletes; as sturdy building blocks, shining stars, and sweet aromas; as beloved brothers and sisters, chosen people, valued fellow-workers, and precious friends. And how essential it is for the leader to help the people to see themselves in these terms as well! When leaders respect, honour, recognize, and affirm those they lead, they will find others far more willing to follow them; and when leaders realize the true worth and dignity of those they lead, the leaders themselves will be more ready to lay down their lives in service for those who are so precious to God.

The leader's special role

Yet neither leader nor followers can afford to lose sight of the particular function and calling that is given to the leader. We have noted the special leadership words like *episkopos*, which means one who oversees, and *kybernesis*, which means the work of piloting a ship, and *hegemonos*, which indicates one who takes charge. One cannot 'go in front' as *prohistamenos* (leader) unless others are willing to come behind; the shepherd cannot lead the flock to pasture if every sheep wanders off on its own path.[2] There can be no teaching without some who are willing to be instructed, and no mature guidance without others being willing to yield to the wisdom of the *presbyteroi* (elders).

An emphasis on the priesthood of every believer and the importance of every gift can become an excuse for diminished respect for the leadership function. The teaching of the headship of Christ must not become the denial of the legitimacy of any human authority within the church. We are not free to focus only on the images of discipleship which buttress the egalitarian spirit of our age, while rejecting the images that point to the need for authority and submission as essential for both order and forward movement in a loving community.[3]

The search for appropriate images

A question which we must ask continually is whether the images we use, or any of the other symbols we employ, 'stir the imagination and the religious feeling of the modern beholder' (Dillistone 1986:217). Sometimes we need new images to stir us from our slumber. Messer reminds us that:

> New metaphors have the power to create new realities. Old images sometimes lose their capacity to empower or to transform because they have lost their original novelty and vitality due to trivialization, habitual

use, or cultural acceptance and assimilation (1989:171).

The search for appropriate terms and images for church leaders today is complicated by the fact that the more exactly suited a certain image is for a particular time and place, the more difficult it may be to understand it in a different context. How do we speak of precious treasure in fragile clay pots to an aluminum and plastic sociey? How do we capture the power of the shepherd image with urban youngsters who have never been to a pasture, let alone a zoo, to see a flock of sheep? How meaningful is it to speak of a 'kingdom' to those living under a revolutionary socialist government, or to use the image of a cornerstone with those who construct their homes from mud and thatch? Some might question why we should start with the Bible at all for our imagery, when our own society is twenty centuries and thousands of miles removed.

I would suggest that the most important reason to begin with the biblical imagery is to identify the themes that underlie the images. Those who believe in the full inspiration of scripture will acknowledge that the images themselves are part of the inspired text, and therefore deserving of our careful study.[4] Once we have identified the basic ideas conveyed by the biblical terms, we can evaluate the extent to which other terms express similar meanings.

For example, we have seen from our study of the biblical terms that the disciple is one who is under authority. If our own society does not have masters and slaves, there may be other useful images that convey an authority relationship, such as an army recruit with a drill instructor, or a soccer player with a coach, or a factory worker with a supervisor. To take another illustration, in order to express the idea of the disciple, who imitates another, we may explore relationships like the skilled craftsman with the apprentice, or the guru with the follower, or the musician with the young student.

Each image will have its own associations within a given cultural context. Our task is to determine whether the ideas suggested by that image correspond closely enough to the concepts of discipleship and leadership expressed by the biblical metaphors.

We would be wise, however, in our search for culturally appropriate terms, to stay close to the biblical images as well. For one thing, the Bible is so full of pictorial and metaphorical language that we cannot teach it adequately without helping people to develop a clear understanding of the biblical images in context. We should not underestimate people's ability to grasp and to apply a biblical image once they have understood its background.

Nor should we overstate our own distance from the biblical images. There are many rural societies in the world today that would have little difficulty understanding the agrarian imagery of the Gospels. Modern societies still have athletes, soldiers, children, resident aliens, and ambassadors. People of all places and times understand light, aroma, and the human body; most know the meaning of letters, trees, and the functions of planting, watering, and harvesting crops. Some of the biblical images like seal, crown, adoption, priesthood, apostleship, and freeing of slaves require more cultural and historical explanation for full understanding, but many of the terms are quite accessible to the modern reader.

The biblical images and the themes that underlie them should also suggest boundaries which will help us to determine which images are not appropriate. As we have seen, not every first-century term for leader was taken into the Christian vocabulary. Most of the terms associated with the synagogue[5] and the pagan religions[6] were avoided. So were the strong authority-laden *arch*-compounds, as well as most other words that denoted ruler and ruled. With images like 'shepherd', which had strong positive associations from the Old Testament writings but unsavoury connotations among the rabbis (who scorned shepherds as unreliable and dishonest), the biblical writers chose the particular aspects of the image that they wanted to emphasize.[8] Perhaps a similar evaluation could be performed with words that may carry either positive or negative connotations when applied to leaders in a Christian community – like 'manager' in industrialized societies,[9] and 'guru' in a south Asian context.[10]

The development of leaders

A study of the biblical images can help present-day leaders of the church to examine their ideas, their attitudes, and their patterns of behaviour. Such a study can also suggest directions for the development of future leaders. How shall we follow in the footsteps of Jesus to nurture leaders for the church of tomorrow?

In the first place, we must develop leaders who have learned how to follow, who see themselves as lifelong students and servants of the Master. Unless one can accept direction cheerfully, one is not ready to give direction to others. Leadership training begins with obeying the order to leave our nets, and cheerfully picking up fragments of food in baskets; it involves patiently lingering to attend to the sick, staying awake for prayer, and humbly washing feet. Leadership training should not be connected with éliteness and special privilege, but with harder work, greater discipline, and more sacrificial service.

Second, leadership training should provide instruction within the context of personal apprenticeship. To be a follower of Jesus is to learn a pattern of life, not simply to give assent to a creed. Such training in attitudes and behaviour cannot possibly occur in a classroom setting alone. There must be opportunities for leaders to live, eat, work, travel, serve, and share with emergent leaders. A life that is not observed cannot be imitated.

Third, the development of leaders needs to involve them in commitment to a community as well as training for a task. The emergent leaders must learn to function effectively as members of a team. They must learn to love their fellow-believers, including other leaders, as members of one family. They must come to rejoice and to suffer with the other members of the body, and to respect the contribution of their fellow-workers.

Fourth, the spiritual aspects of leadership must be stressed. More and more tools of management, planning, and organization are available today. But there is a crying need for leaders who will pray fervently, love deeply, and wage spiritual warfare courageously. Leaders need to be schooled in faith, learning total dependence on the Lord as branches of the vine and members drawing life from the head. They must learn that however much they plant or water, God causes the growth, that he is Lord of the harvest. They must be determined to spread the light and aroma of Christ, not to become well-known themselves. Their message must be delivered as faithful ambassadors and heralds, communicating the words given to them by God's Word and Spirit, not depending on their own intellect or eloquence. In short, they must believe that Christ is everything – *everything* – and that apart from him, they can do nothing (John 15:5).

Yet the ministry of leadership today takes place in a world that is increasingly urban, international, complex and technologically sophisticated. The leader is called to be a steward, a wise manager of all of God's resources – which may include accounting procedures, mass media, computer technology, staff and volunteers with specialized training, and greatly increased knowledge about organizational functioning and cross-cultural communication. Leadership training must include orientation to as much of this modern knowledge and technique as is necessary to foster good stewardship of God's resources. Any tool can be useful in the hands of God's steward, as long as the tool remains the servant and does not become the master.[11]

SOME FINAL THOUGHTS

Images are powerful. They shape what we see, by highlighting certain features and moving others into the background. They dominate our patterns of analysis and reflection. They suggest explanations of why we relate to one another the way we do, or why certain structures exist. They support particular understandings of the past, interpretations of the present, and scenarios for the future. They promote some values and discourage others. They suggest priorities, and awaken emotions.

The choice to emphasize a given metaphor and to put aside another can set the direction of a community and its leadership. Therefore, we must become aware of the images we use, and how we are using them. In particular, we must examine the metaphors we use in the development of our future leaders. For example, what is the balance between our use of 'task' metaphors and our use of 'relationship' metaphors? To what extent do our images reinforce a sense of accountability to God in our future leaders? Do they think of themselves first as 'brothers/sisters' and as 'servants', or as rulers and bosses? Do they speak of their relationships to others more in terms of 'among' and 'under', or in terms of 'over'? Do they understand that there are legitimate differences in responsibility and authority that can be assigned within the community? Or does their emphasis on equality for all in the fellowship blind them to their own need to be willing to come under the authority of a fellow-servant, or perhaps to exercise authority as a fellow-servant?

Our answers to questions like these today will determine the shape of the church in which we serve tomorrow.

Notes

1   Paul Cedar says, '... one of the true tests of our qualifications to be effective servant leaders is whether we are willing to become true servant followers. First, we follow Jesus Christ as Lord, and then we follow those whom God has designated as our human leaders' (1987:131).

2   Michael Harper says: 'If every society needs leadership, and leadership needs to be in the hands of a team, then every team requires a captain' (1977:212). Likewise, Morris observes: 'The minister ought to regard himself as no more than a servant to his people, but his people should regard him as a shepherd over the flock. Great harm is done when the minister thinks of himself as supreme over the flock, or when the people regard him as no more than their servant' (1964:77).

3   Cf. comments by Messer (1989): 'Clergy who think of themselves solely as "enablers" or "facilitators" need to rethink the meaning of ordination and the authority of the clergy. The purpose of theological education is to develop a learned clergy and laity who can give leadership to the church and the world in Christ's name' (p. 73). 'By accenting the powerless servant image to the exclusion of the leader metaphor, people eventually discover that their own self-worth suffers and the church struggles for vision and vitality. Many contemporary churches are hurt more by pastoral default than by pastoral domination' (p.104). The same warnings about the limitations of the 'enabler' ideal are sounded strongly by Wagner (1984:73-106).

4   Not all are willing to agree that the images as well as the underlying themes are inspired. For example, Barbour holds that 'the images themselves are not directly God-given but arise from man's analogical imagination' (1976:18). Similarly, McFague objects to the view that 'the words and images of the Bible are the authoritative and appropriate words and images for God', holding that such ideas are a symptom of the religious literalism of our time (1982:4). The basic issue is whether or not one believes that 'all Scripture is God-breathed' (2 Timothy 3:16).

5   Meeks (1983:79, 81); Stambaugh and Balch (1986:142).

6   Stambaugh and Balch (1986:138).

7   Küng (1967:495–498); Meeks (1983:134); Schweizer (1969:171–180). However, the word *archegos* (leader, in the sense of pioneer or founder) is applied to Jesus in Acts 3:15; 5:31; Hebrews 2:10; 12:2.

8   Cf. Messer (1989:171-174).

9   Richards and Hoeldtke (1988) strongly reject the manager metaphor for the pastor; Hutcheson (1979) and Dibbert (1989) also raise many concerns. In contrast, Anderson and Jones (1978:44) as well as Campbell and Reierson (1981:92) speak of the pastor as 'chief executive officer', and Jones says that 'the biblical roles of ministry and management are essentially just different dimensions of our calling to be pastors and Christian workers' (1988:28).

10 Fernando (1985) is one who uses this image in a positive sense, even though others have used the 'guru' and his disciples as an example of the sort of blind following of authority that should never be found in the church.

11 An excellent theological and practical analysis of the use of management techniques within the church can be found in Hutcheson (1979).

References cited

Anderson, James D. and Jones, Ezra Earl, 1978, The Management of Ministry, New York, Harper and Row.

Anderson, Ray Sherman, 1986, Minding God's Business, Grand Rapids, Michigan: Eerdmans.

Barbour, Ian G., 1976, Myths, Models and Paradigms: A Comparative Study in Science and Religion, New York: Harper and Row (paperback ed.; 1st ed 1974).

Campbell, Thomas C. and Reirson, Gary B., 1981, *The Gift of Administration*, Philadelphia: Westminster Press.

Cedar, Paul A., 1987, *Strength in Servant Leadership*, Waco, Texas: Word Books.

Dibbert, Michael T., 1989, *Spiritual Leadership, Responsible Management: A Guide for Leaders of the Church*, Grand Rapids, Michigan, Zondervan.

Fernando, Ajith, 1985, *Leadership Lifestyle*, Wheaton, Illinois: Tyndale House Publishers.

Harper, Michael, 1977, *Let My People grow: Ministry and leadership in the Church*, Plainfield, New Jersey: Logos International.

Hutcheson, Richard G., Jr., 1979, *Wheel within the Wheel: Confronting the Management Crisis of the Pluralistic Church*, Atlanta: John Knox Press.

Jones, Bruce W., 1988, *Ministerial Leadership in a Mangerial World*, Wheaton, Illionois: Tyndale House Publishers.

Küng, Hans, 1967, *The Church*. London: Burns and Oates.

McFague, Sallie, 1982, *Metaphorical Theology: Models of God in Religious Language*, PhiladelphiaL: Fortress Press.

Meeks, Wayne A., 1983, *The First Urban Christians: The Social World of the Apostle Paul*, New Haven, Connecticut: Yale University Press.

Messer, Donald E., 1989, Contemporary Images og Christian Ministry, Nashville, Tenesee: Abingdon Press

Richards, Lawrence O., and Hoeldtke, Clyde. 1988, *Church Leadership: Following the example of Jesus*, Grand Rapids, Michigan: Zondervan, (Revised edition of *A Theology of Church Leadership*, Zondervan, 1980)

Schweizer, Eduard, 1961, *Church Order in the New Testament*, translated by Frank Clark, London: SCM Press.

Stambaugh, John E., and Balch, David L., 1986, *The New Testament in its Social Environment*, Philadelphia: Westminster Press.

Van Engen, Charles Edward, 1981, *The Growth of the True Church: An Analysis of the Ecclesiology of Church Growth Theory*, Amsterdam: Rodopi.

Wagner, C., Peter, 1984, *Leading your Church to Growth*, Ventura, California: Regal Books.

24

Take Thou Authority
An African Perspective

John S Pobee

This essay is written for a symposium honouring the retirement of Bishop John Howe, the first secretary general of the Anglican Consultative Council. My association with John Howe goes back to the period 1946-1950 when he was chaplain of my *alma mater*, Adisadel College, a secondary school of Anglican foundation in the Gold Coast, now Ghana. He was there a teacher and missionary. In both capacities he was an authority figure. He was a representative of a church which in its history was closely identified with the Crown of England, so much so that although that English Church Mission, as it was then known, was not officially established as in England, it was known as *aban mu asor*, literally the church inside the government castle. Thus in one sense John Howe did represent another face of the colonial authority of the Gold Coast.

Over the years, many African church leaders set me tasks. Almost invariably I learnt that it was John Howe who had in a quiet way put them onto this track. We sometimes had informal discussions about church life in Africa. It may be that it was because the years in Cape Coast, Ghana, had rubbed off on him and he had internalized the good elements of African culture, that he believed there could evolve relevant authority concepts and practice *à la Africaine*, which he could promote to the glory of God.

I remember Bishop John as also a sportsman. His very build was eloquent thereto. But though chaplain, he was also active in training the college sports team. In this regard I recall a particular incident in which at the national inter-college sports, the Adisadel relay team (4 x 110 yards) was disqualified because of something that allegedly went wrong in the change of batons and thus giving advantage to Achimota School, the rival of Adisadel. Bishop John, persuaded that the decision was not just and fair, protested and remonstrated. He respected authority but would neither keep quiet in the face of injustice perpetrated by the lawfully constituted authority, a great lesson in a context which tends to acquiesce in wrongful behaviour of those in authority. All told Bishop John, then Fr. Howe, being in the one person, teacher, pastor and sports master lived a holistic life which endeared him to many a student, if not all. In Africa people who hold leadership in church tend to keep themselves aloof from the day-to-day life of peoples. Perhaps we can do better. Efficient and effective authority can be mediated when the power holders engage members of the community in more than structural ways.

One more point: my mind goes back to a visit he made to Ghana as General Secretary of ACC. When I was a young lecturer at the University of Ghana I recall our having a drink together. Subsequently, we again had drink together at the 1978 Lambeth Conference. That was a significant event: he was allowing for the fact that his past student had grown and come of age and was ready to share drink with him. That simple act is rather unusual. For in Africa, there is a tendency to perpetuate a Peter Pan syndrome, whereby your past student remains a student, with the result that presumed authority becomes a barrier to communion and sharing. Even in world church, so-called younger churches not infrequently are experiencing the Peter Pan syndrome.[1]

With hindsight we can see that something of the Gold Coast's cultures rubbed off on him; he drank, so to speak, of the well and stream of African culture. And so, in celebrating that retirement, it is fitting that something of that culture should be recalled.

NEW CONTEXT FOR REVISITING ISSUES OF AUTHORITY AND POWER

This piece was originally written some ten years ago. While still upholding the general thesis and insights, it cannot stand as it was originally done. For one thing, I myself have grown in the ten years. Whether I have grown wiser or more foolish, more serious or with a greater sense of humour, I dare not say of myself. For another reason, there is a new context in Africa in this lapse of time. Both of these facts compel me to take another look at the original contribution and to make the necessary adjustments.

NEW SITUATION IN AFRICA FOR SEARCH FOR RENEWAL AUTHORITY PATTERNS

Permit me to delineate in broad strokes some of the elements of the new context in which we are talking about authority. First is the shift in the centre of gravity in world Christianity from the North and West to the South and East.[2] Does this fact have anything to say to being church, being a communion today and the structures of communion and family life? Or are we happy to live with a disjunction, dysfunction and incongruence of official statements and actual living and existence? In my view this goes to the heart of efficiency, accountability and transparency of the system of authority structures. Second, when Fr. Howe walked the face of the Gold Coast, he lived in the context of a colonial church. Today they are autonomous, autocthonous churches. In Fr. Howe's time, there was one diocese of Accra with an expatriate bishop. Today, there are six dioceses - Accra, Cape Coast, Koforidua, Kumasi, Sekondi and Sunyani-Tamale. As we write, there are plans to split further some of the dioceses. Each has a native bishop. The dioceses are in the business of trying to develop their African identity. What does all this mean for authority patterns? Besides, the dioceses of Ghana belong to the Province of West Africa, together with the Gambia, Guinea, Sierra Leone (2 dioceses), Liberia and a developing missionary diocese of French Western Africa. These are authority questions *ad intra* and *ad extra*.

Third, one of the significant developments of the African church scene is the rise and proliferation of African Instituted Churches.[3] Some of them like the Church of the Lord, Aladura, Nigeria were breakaways from the Anglican tradition. Some of our membership are voting with their feet and joining some of those new churches. Surely, there must be reason for these happenings and where is the issue of authority in all this? There is evidence that the historic churches are taking from the leaf of these AICs, in their music in particular. What of their authority patterns?

The twin facts of African ownership of the Anglican tradition and the rise of AICs are significant as signalling the need for our authority patterns and structures to be consistent with the African expression of the one holy catholic and apostolic church, rather than with the Anglo-Saxon expression of that one holy catholic and apostolic church. It is showing up the very contextual nature of some of our constructs.

Fourth, the issue of authority is tackled today in a context of ecumenism. This situation is making it difficult to live in isolation; we are borrowing and learning from each other, sometimes unwittingly, sometimes without acknowledgement. Some of our Anglican bishops and structures are looking more and more like Roman Catholic ones. But is that semblance only in externals or only in content or both? It is not just the old familiar discussion of high church (Anglo-Catholic) tradition versus low church (Puritan evangelical) tradition. What does the Porvoo agreement mean for Anglican existence in Africa? In a place like Tanzania in which the high church tradition (originating in the work of SPG) and low church (originating in the work of CMS) co-exist, sometimes not exactly happily.

In highlighting these new factors in our study, one is raising a very fundamental issue: in what does fidelity to Anglican tradition, in this case of structures of authority, consist? Is it just regurgitating and enforcing structures minted in another context in a totally different situation? Or does it consist in discerning the spirit and vision behind the particular inherited structures evolved with the aid of scripture and tradition but with sensitivity to the new situation and the questions the new context too is putting to the Word of God and tradition? In other words, in what does catholicity consist when we address the question of authority, for example? And is that catholic expression the same everywhere? Catholicity is defined not so much in terms of preserving cultural categories shaped in the distant past but in terms of the Christian message for the world today.

Our interest in authority in the Anglican Communion is not and should not be just an attempt to do the archaeology of authority concepts and patterns in the Anglican Communion. More important it is because we desire a more efficient working of our life together as a people of God and as a communion. So we have to reckon with the legacy of history and tradition. But we should always ask: authority for whom and for what? In this context we shall broadly answer: authority for African Anglicans who have chosen to live in communion with others while at the same time belonging to the one Church of God and the one human family of God. Second, it is for the efficient organizing of being a community of faith and a communion which desires, therefore, mutuality and participation. But even that is not an end in itself: it is to be a people of God for the sake of the unity, renewal and transformation of the world and all creation. Do the authority patterns facilitate this or hinder it?

Revisiting the topic ten years after it was first written, one cannot be silent on the issue of women and authority in the church. Where do women fit in the authority structures of the church? So far as I am concerned, to take up this aspect is not a matter of political correctness. For not only do women constitute at least one half of the community of faith and therefore, must be there to speak for themselves and not spoken for. For without that the women cannot take ownership of the project of the church. But also as an African Lutheran from Kenya has put it, "despite women's diverse social, economic and political background, by virtue of belonging to the female gender, women constitute an oppressed social group... (Feminist theologies) invite men and women in the church to radically examine our understanding of God and our relationships together... (They) ask the church to be willing to reflect on how gender history in our societies has shaped our spirituality, our sexuality, our worship and our interpretation and understanding of scripture".[4] The particular denomination of the writer is of no consequence in this matter; it is an ethical issue; it is an ecumenical issue; it is an issue of our credibility when we proclaim the Creator God of women and men in God's own image and likeness.

If I am pleading for taking the African context and experience seriously it is not to deny the Anglican elements of Scripture, Tradition and Reason. So in my effort here, I will implement the elements of Anglican method in dialogue with African context.

The word, *authority*, and its cognate, *power*, are familiar and yet troublesome. For most people the two are synonymous. In everyday life we hear of "power to the people", "student power", "political power", "religious power", etc. The press not infrequently carries news of the misuse of power and of *coups d'état* in Africa. In those stories what is at stake is power and authority. People love power, seek power, seize power, and all too soon get overwhelmed by power and become prisoners of power. But what is power?

Power is "that ability of an individual or group to carry out its wishes or policies, and to control, manipulate, or influence the behaviour of others, whether they wish to co-operate or not."[5] In other words, the wielder of power is supposed to have a wish or even a vision, and resources to enforce or prosecute that vision. Such resources are varied: formal authority, manipulations of social norms or morality, exploitation of ignorance, deception, deceit, position, and social relationships. At the end of the day, power is a social relationship whether it be between persons or groups. To that extent even the power-wielder, *ipso facto*, has obligations, commitments, and even some limitations of his or her freedom of action. The Akan, who constitute about forty-four per cent of the population of Ghana, have their wisdom distilled in maxims and proverbs. One such saying reads *Edom anaa nkoa dodow na ekyere ohene tumi*, literally "large numbers and number of servants indicate the power and authority of the ruler". In other words, power and authority to some extent, if not largely, depend on the number of people who so recognize the leader's authority. *Ipso facto* power, like authority, is a social relationship. For that reason, a chief of the Akan, who did not reflect the best interests and wishes of the people, could be removed from office.

The cognate word, *authority*, is only one manifestation and the most effective form of power. It is "power that is legitimized and institutionalized in a society or other social system".[6] With authority goes status and respect. Normally the authority is inherent in the status itself and is normally not exactly dependent on the personal qualities of the holder of authority. That is why, in spite of the foolishness of political leaders and religious leaders, they are still accorded respect – in public at any rate.

THREE TYPES AND PARADIGMS OF AUTHORITY IN TRADITIONAL AFRICA

Three types of authority may be distinguished. First is the traditional ruler, chief, or king. His or her title to authority derives from sanctity of customs and is located in a family to which you must belong to qualify. Second is the charismatic leader who is the hero of the moment, especially in emergencies, e.g., the Führer Adolf Hitler or the nationalist leader and dictator Kwame Nkrumah of Ghana. The credentials of his authority are derived from other than human source, i.e., his authority is "a gift of grace". To that extent he is like the judge in the Old Testament. Third is the leader who becomes a leader because he or she has certain clear skills, e.g., a headteacher of a school or even some politicians.[7] Where the ordained person comes in to all this we shall see in due course.

There are thus at least three types of authority patterns in African societies: the model of kingship (sacred), charismatic authority, and authority that is rooted in and spawned by particular skills. These three models suggest to me that there are at least three paradigms for exploring leadership, authority and power patterns in Africa. We may, therefore, desist from the temptation to take only one model as the only paradigm. Permit me at this stage to state that because African societies have religious epistemology and ontology, without being sacralist, we should in Africa in particular be attentive to charisms and see the issues of authority and power in relation to the varieties of spiritual gifts.

The discussion of authority is taking place in the context of the Anglican communion, a communion of Anglican churches or provinces scattered round the globe. If Canterbury is its spiritual home, today the majority of Anglican dioceses of the Anglican community is outside the British Commonwealth.[8]

For that reason, there is need for clarity on ecclesiology, especially an Anglican account of the nature of Christian community itself. The discussion of authority is to be set in the context of Anglican ecclesiology, if such there is. There is a sense then that the discussion of authority, even the African perspective on it, should be at three levels: the international level, i.e., the communion; the provincial level or the national level; and finally the local level. To the communion level we proceed presently.

As mentioned earlier, the spiritual home of Anglicanism is Canterbury. Anglicans are a communion because they are in communion with each other and especially with Canterbury. But Canterbury, respected as it is, has no juridical authority over any province. Unlike Rome, the Anglican communion has no centralized authority. And, of course, Africans, who have struggled to rid themselves of colonial domination with which rightly or wrongly the Church of England was associated, are not about to have another master. On the Anglican calendar stands the Lambeth Conference which is the ten-yearly assembly of bishops of the Anglican world, which meets at the invitation of the Archbishop of Canterbury. But the Lambeth Conference, representative of the communion as it may look, has no legislative authority; it can only advise.

The Lambeth Conference of 1958 created the post of the Anglican Executive Officer for the Advisory Council on Missionary Strategy set up in 1948. That metamorphized in 1968 into the Anglican Consultative Council, with the aim of helping Anglicans "to fulfil their common inter-Anglicanism and ecumenical responsibilities in promoting the renewal and mission of Christ's Church."[9] But ACC too has no juridical authority. It "can debate, explore, clarify and propose. But each member Church must respond itself if anything is to be implemented."[10] As its very name suggests, ACC's role is consultative.

From the foregoing then, it can be said that at the communion level there is no centralized authority. Any authority that there is, is at the provincial or even diocesan level. Or at the best, it is a binding force flowing out of a sense of belonging to a community. It is that dispersed authority to which Sykes has drawn renewed attention. There is an implied ecclesiology. The church is the people of God in a diocese, gathered round its bishop in worship. Authority belongs to that people of God.

Permit me to make one more point about the fact that we are exploring the issue of authority and power as a communion. That word must be given currency in the exploration. In other words, what does our self-understanding as communion mean for our understanding and practice of power and authority? That word, currently important for ecumenical exploration of ecclesiology, is an important New Testament word, especially in the life of the earliest christian community. For now the important point to stress is that in its biblical usage the basic meaning is participation.[11] There is a sense of communion because individuals had a stake in the being and life of it and they participated in the life of the group and there was freedom of self-expression.

Authority and power seen in the light of this basic self-understanding of the community of believers means they would be participatory. In this regard I must deny the often-repeated claim that African cultures *per se* make for dictatorships. Traditional societies were participatory and those in authority were accountable to their peoples or else faced exclusion from office.

WORD OF GOD AS MEDIATOR OF AUTHORITY AND POWER

But what is it that each diocese recognizes as of a binding authority? First is the word of God, the normative form of which is located in the scriptures. But the baptismal rule of faith of the early church, the Apostles' Creed and the Nicene Creed, are also believed to attest to the same central truth of scripture. Through these, faith is evoked and enlivened. Scripture then is one canon of authority of the communion and for that matter, of Christians as a whole.

However, the Anglican ethos insists that scriptures never speak apart from a context. Scriptures like the creeds are always received as interpreted tradition, a text already in interaction with a context. In that context, receiving scriptures in the vernacular is an important principle. Reading scripture through African spectacles bearing the marks of poverty, degradation, and other cultural traits enables the African diocese to bring to the communion fresh insights which will engage and be engaged by other interpretations in mutual affirmation and correction. For the communion, authority lives in the word of God engaging respective contexts and in mutual engagement.

If the Word of God is to be authoritative, shaping the lives of peoples and churches, then it must speak to the Africans as Africans, engaging them at their wavelength. As an Anglican and an African, I may read Lightfoot, Westcott etc. But these are no substitute for African Anglicans finding the hermeneutics that will make it possible for the Word also "to read me".[12]

SACRAMENTAL LIFE AS MEDIATOR OF AUTHORITY AND POWER

Second is sacramental life, be it Baptism, Confirmation, Penance, Holy Communion, Marriage, Extreme Unction, or Holy Orders. The sacraments are seen as organs in the living body of the church, with special functions to perform for the good of the whole. There is power and authority to a sacrament, though with Anglicanism it needs to be said that "power of the sacrament is not the same as the sacrament itself" (St. Augustine, *Commentary on St. John.* 26, 11). They produce grace in virtue of their own inherent power (cf. St. Augustine, *Contra Donat.* 4, 16). It only needs to be stated that since African societies represent a very iconic, sacramental culture, the sacraments have special force as instruments of authority and power. Let me also add since most of the Anglicans in Africa are non-literate, ritual and sacramental life become key cornerstones of religious life and powerful instruments of communication of faith and tradition.

PRAYER BOOK AND AUTHORITY

Third is the Book of Common Prayer (BCP). It is not without significance that BCP is common to Anglicans all over the world. Despite the heavy marks of English culture on the BCP and despite numerous attempts at local prayer books, the shape, principles, and ethos of Cranmer's prayer book continue to be the paradigm, in short, authoritative. The liturgy has become "the power base for the Christian community as a whole".[13]

We need to mention the Thirty-nine Articles, the domestic creed standard of *ecclesia Anglicana* which, so to speak, sets the authorized standard of doctrine for the English church. In an illuminating study by Philip H.E. Thomas on *The Status and Function of the Thirty-nine Articles in the Anglican Communion Today*, Thomas concludes, "the Thirty-nine Articles, although not completely mislaid are treated quite differently by different provinces of that Communion. Some of the older churches still give the Articles a formal authority in the interpretation of their doctrine – although it is not at all clear how that authority would or should be exercised. Several others give its Articles some prominence as an indicator of their historical origin and development; but more than half the Provinces identify their Anglican heritage without reference to the Articles at all." So then, authoritative as the Thirty-nine Articles may be, they are not authoritative for all the communion and certainly not for the churches in Africa.

Thus at the communion level there seem to me three authority processes to which all provinces, the African ones included, would agree – scripture, creeds, and sacramental life and BCP. These are applicable to the provinces too. So for the present let us turn to the local level.

Earlier the point was made that there is an implied ecclesiology that the church is the people of God gathered in worship around the bishop. Whatever we may say of the people of God, the bishop is an important authority figure even though he is described as shepherd. The sacrament of Holy Orders is one sacrament, although it has three degrees, namely diaconate, priesthood, and episcopate, which correspond to the measure of the priestly power conferred upon the recipient. In the Anglican tradition as of now, power belongs to the fullness of the priesthood, namely the bishop alone. But how does one define this authority of the *sacerdos*?

First, it is authority "to speak God's Word to his people". This is dramatized in the giving of the New Testament or a bible to the deacon and priest respectively. "Receive this Book, as a sign of the authority which God has given you this day to preach the gospel of Christ," the bishop says to the priest. Christianity like Judaism is a religion of the book and, therefore, the Bible features prominently as a symbol of authority. To that extent, as at the communion level, the word of God is a manifestation of authority. The Bible is not only a classic piece of literature, but also the charter document of the Christian church, which, besides whatever comfort, hope, and guidance it gives, also gives a real view of human life: good deeds brought about through faith, bad deeds brought about through misunderstanding, distrust, and utter wickedness. The authority of the priest then resides not so much because the bishop had so wished and declared but because he, the priest, symbolizes the church, the people of God as the conscious agent and messenger of the good news of the kingdom of God and the life of the world in which the church lives. Explained thus, the priest's sacral quality and authority are derived from the sociological fact that he symbolizes the whole society. And in so far as the word of God is a powerful instrument for the transformation of the world, the priest holds authority. But it is important not to forget that the *magisterium*, i.e., the teaching authority, belongs to the whole church, the people of God, even if the priest is a special ambassador.

In the history of the church, this *magisterium* has been variously defined: the authority to expound scripture, the authority to banish an erroneous witness, the authority to preach reconciliation in a very divided world. In relation to the first two, the priesthood has become the great defender of truth which is more complex than is realized. One consequence is that a very intellectual component is brought into the priesthood: selection criteria and training programmes have a heavy intellectual component. And this intellectual component is expressed in a narrow academic sense and bookishness. Is such a bias really relevant to the African context where the ministry is to a largely non-literate society? There is a danger of authority being based on knowledge or academic attainment. Is that adequate or good enough for the African context? To that we shall return a little later.

The second element of authority according to the Ordinal, is "to minister his Holy Sacraments". This is further defined as "to call his hearers to repentance, and in Christ's name to absolve and to declare the forgiveness of sins. He or she is to baptize, and to prepare the baptized for Confirmation. He or she is to preside at the celebration of the Holy Communion. He or she is to lead his or her people in prayer and worship, to intercede for them, to bless them in the name of the Lord, and to teach and encourage by word and example. He or she is to minister to the sick, and prepare the dying for their death." In other words, the authority of a priest consists in faculties to hear confession and offer absolution (cf. John 20:23); to administer baptism (cf. Matthew 28:18-20); to celebrate Holy Communion, which is dramatically demonstrated by the giving of the chalice, paten, and chasuble; to administer Holy Unction and marriage. It is authority to be a cult person. The authority comes by virtue of the bishop on behalf of the people of God commissioning the priest to be a cult personnel. Africans, precisely because of their background, tend to focus on authority in terms of authority for cult function.

The third element of authority is service. The people of God are called to self-surrender not only in terms of interior emotions and feelings but also in terms of outward obedience. "Worship that is consonant with the truth of the gospel is indeed nothing less than its offering of one's whole self in the course of one's concrete living, in one's inward thoughts, feeling and aspirations, but also in one's words and deeds."[14] Beyond cultic religion and pious attitude, the people of God are called to a daily life of brotherly and sisterly love and moral purity (cf. James 1:27). The priest is expected to incarnate that vocation of service to humanity. The priest's authority comes from service.

Here we must take a look at Mark 9:34 ff. and 10:35 ff. There the sons of Zebedee were desirous of chief seats in the kingdom. But Jesus enunciated the principle that power is for service of God and humanity. The paradox is that one who has authority and power should behave as though he or she had no legal rights, indeed like a slave. He or she puts his/her own dignity and legal rights second to the well-being of those whom he/she serves. True power and authority comes from selfless and self-sacrificing service and devotion to humanity. Authority has meaning and relevance only in so far as it is rooted in service of humanity.

True greatness is not grandness but caring for people. True greatness is the ability to sacrifice what is most precious to us for the sake of real life and the good of all, in short to take sides for God. True greatness and true authority is not coercing, tyrannizing, and snatching power; rather it is "giving with such royal bounty that in the end one's very life is given."[15]

The three elements of authority – *magisterium* (teaching authority), faculties to be cult personnel, and service – *prima facie* belong to the hierarchy. But it is meaningless to speak of the didactic, cultic, and diaconal authority without reference to the taught? Thus the didactic authority, for example, has a complement in the people of God. Authority is not a matter of hierarchy or position; it is functional and a matter of relationships in a community. And a good teacher learns as much from his or her people as he or she gives. So even the didactic authority is a communal authority. As happens in African traditional societies, the community takes part in the education of the priests. Similarly, the function of service is not peculiar to the hierarchy; the faithful are actively there. Thus authority is by definition a social relationship and communitarian. Here we come to the matter of charisma.

Authority in the church is derived from sharing in the power of the Holy Spirit. So it is charism, a concrete way of the Holy Spirit expressing himself in the world. But as Paul insists, a charism, a grace-gift, is given for the enrichment of the community of faith and not of the individual who happens to have been chosen to be the receptacle. Besides, charism is not reserved for the hierarchy. Paul asks "Are all apostles? Are all prophets? Are all teachers?" (1 Corinthians 12:29). But each member has a charism given for the common good (I Corinthians 12:7) and, therefore, to be brought within the service of the community. And no charism is inferior and it must be recognized as a contribution of a particular ministry. Boff is right that

> charism is the pneumatic force (dynamis tou theou) that gives rise
> to institutions and keeps them alive. The principle of the structure
> of the Church is not the institution or the hierarchy but rather the
> charism that is at the root of all institutions and hierarchy. There is
> not one group of rulers and another group of those who are ruled,
> there is one group of faith. Those who rule as well as those who are

ruled must all believe. Faith, or the charism of faith is the *prius natura* (basic nature) and common factor giving rise to communication and fundamental fraternal equality among all members of the Church.[16]

The rightness of seeing authority in terms of charisms is confirmed by the fact that the Ordinal invokes the Holy Spirit on the priest-to-be. That is the significance of the singing of the *Veni Creator* and the words accompanying the laying on of hands: "Send down the Holy Spirit upon your servant . . . for the office and work of a priest in your Church." The only word to add is that the Holy Spirit is not the preserve of the ordained, indeed it is believed to be given at baptism to all the faithful so that the priest's charism stands alongside other charisms.

Such a conception of authority accords well with the African world-view; charisms, service, community are very much ideas in the African background. To that we shall turn in a little while.

MINISTRY AS AN INSTRUMENT AND EXPRESSION OF AUTHORITY

Permit me to dwell a while on ministry as an expression of authority in the communion. Anglican Communion speaks of threefold ministry - bishop, priest and deacon. But prior to this affirmation is the commitment to the priesthood of all believers. Without that the threefold ministry loses its real meaning. I dare suggest that against that background, the leadership role of the ordained is about interpreting God's self-disclosure, especially as contained in scriptures; to be enablers and animators of the community of faith; and third to be celebrants of the mysteries of God. Celebrant is not only of the liturgy in the narrow sense of the word. I learn from church history, from John Chrysostom (347–407), Bishop of Constantinople who spoke of two altars, one within the sanctuary, the other outside the sanctuary in the public square and thus signalling the continuity of Christian worship and committed engagement in society and culture. It is the role and function of the ordained to enable the faithful to worship at the two altars.

Sacral kingship of Akan societies lived the three roles of interpreter, animator and celebrant and therefore, African Anglicans have a thing or two to learn from their own traditional culture. At least, let them start with that model and let it be engaged by scripture and tradition. They do not have to abandon their tradition altogether. In any case, when you take seriously the traditional African and Christian resources, ministry is not about position and titles; it is about functions and service.

As regards the ministry of bishop, whatever else may be learnt from African tradition, there is a lesson to be learned from church history. Nicetas of Ancyra wrote of patriarchal functions as follows: "Do not exaggerate the importance of the title of patriarch, which is given to him. For every bishop is also called

Patriarch ... and titles of precedence are common to all of us, since all the bishops are fathers, shepherds and teachers ... For the laying on of hands is the same for all, and participation in the divine liturgy is identical and all pronounce the same prayers.[17] I quote this to underline that we need to think of episcopacy less as a position than as a ministry or sense of parenting, shepherding and teaching. How many of these images be expressed in the African context meaningfully for the renewal of the faithful community?

Permit me to dip into the history of world Christianity to address one particular aspect of the See of Canterbury. Gregory the Great (590–604) attempted to combine the pre-eminent role of the bishop of Rome and the universally held sense of identity and equality of the episcopate. In his letter to Emperor Maurice and Eulogius, Patriarch of Alexandria he counsels against the use of the designation of Ecumenical Patriarch of the bishop of Rome in the following words: "I beg you never let me hear that word again. For I know who you are and who I am. In position, you are my brother, in character my father. I gave therefore no commands, but ... I do not consider that anything is an honour to me, by which my brethren lose the honour that is their due. My honour is the honour of the Universal Church, my honour is the united strength of my brethren. But, if your Holiness calls me Universal pope, you deny that you are yourself what you say I am universally."[18]

Concepts and patterns of authority in the church in Africa today have been inherited from so-called mother churches in the North.[19] But those very Northern concepts and patterns have been accommodated, if not assimilated to respective cultures in the North. There is no doubt that the English bishop has been a religious version of the middle class, if not aristocratic, gentleman of England. Writing of Methodist ministers in Ghana, Dickson has written as follows: "By his training and habits the Methodist minister of today is a fairly accurate copy of the Methodist minister of the time of the first Methodist missionaries in the Gold Coast."[20] This is, by and large, true of all clergy of the historic churches. But even these Northern patterns represent the amalgam of biblical, theological, and cultural insights. None of those insights is ever acultural – even the biblical insights have a large dose of Semitic and Greek culture. Nowhere is this in evidence more than in liturgical vestments and vessels.[21] Therefore, the African churches have no reason to be apologetic for developing an indigenized concept and pattern of authority, negotiating between the non-negotiable insights of the Bible, tradition, and culture sensitively treated.

As one looks at Africa there are two possible paradigms of authority – that of the chief in the traditional political system and that of the priest. To relevant elements of these two let us now proceed.

The political system of traditional Africa, which continues to hold despite the heavy assault of modern political systems,[22] has been variously classified: (a) acephalous societies such as the Dagaaba of Ghana, the Igbo and Tiv of Nigeria; (b) centralized societies, e.g., the Asante of Ghana, the Yoruba of Nigeria, and the Baganda of Bugunda, Uganda; the Swazi, and Zulus; (c) "politics as kingship-writ-large" and (d) age-based society.[23] Authority patterns in each of these are different. Obviously we cannot deal with all the models in one paper. So I wish to take a model of centralized authority, particularly that of the Asante of Ghana with which I am familiar and to which John Howe in conversations tends to refer.

The chief is the zenith of power. The office of a chief is composite: he is at once judge, commander-in-chief, legislator, the executive, and administrative head of the community. But the most important aspect of the chief's office is the religious one.[24] Chieftaincy is a sacred office. The chief then is described as the "double pivot", i.e., he is the political head of the tribe and the centre of the ritual expression. The sacred quality of kingship derives from the sociological fact that he symbolizes the whole society and is for that reason, perhaps, raised to a mystical plane. Further, he derives the title to authority from the sanctity of customs which is located in a family to which he belongs and which entitled him to authority. The only thing to note is that the chief is chosen from royal houses. Eligibility then is determined by belonging to a particular lineage reinforced albeit by election by those to whom custom assigns the right.

The other religious authority is the priesthood which, in fact, is of different classes. There are (a) the *komfo*, i.e., the one who attends to the gods but does not divine; (b) *brafo*, i.e., the special assistant to the priest; (c) *bosomfo*, i.e., the unorthodox priest. But whatever the class, the functions of a priest are multifaceted, involving cultic ministration, prediction, divination, prophecy, and healing the sick.[25] Thus, this one too, like the chiefship, is a composite office, i.e., a priest is as much a ritual specialist as a healer, a powerful person. But he is a holy man who by virtue of being in touch with the spirit-world, is able to divine and prophesy. The priest, like the chief, is also an authority figure in the society. The office is also often located in a family.

I wish to suggest that, in the minds of many Africans, the priesthood in the Christian tradition has been accomodated to the traditional concepts about priesthood and that some of the dissatisfaction with the churches stems from the fact that the Christian priests are not able to live up to expectations. Let us look at some of the elements that will be crucial for evolving a relevant and satisfying religious authority today.

First, authority must be seen as a composite phenomenon and this is to be expected in a society which sees reality in holistic terms, with the sacred and the secular interlocking. Authority is not just to perform a ritual but to make manifest in acts of power the reality of the spirit-world. The very western dichotomy between the sacred and secular, by which the priest belongs primarily to the former, is meaningless in the African context. Religious authority must be visible in the secular life. In other words, a relevant authority of the priest is to some extent derived from his or her ability to achieve results in the activities of the priest as mentioned above. The loss of membership to the African Christian Independency is precisely an issue of credible authority.

Second, authority is community based. The authority is credible and real if it derives from the sociological fact that the priest symbolizes the whole society. Here really is the reason for taking seriously the idea of the church as the people of God. In so many ways in Africa, "the minister of religion (has become) lineage head, the protector and defender of the group both physically and spiritually."[26] The holy man's authority derives from the fact that he is the symbol of the whole society, particularly the Christian community. Even the peculiar African creation called the catechist is a holy man at the grassroots, on whom the rural congregation was focused.

Third, traditionally authority was located in a lineage. A chief was selected from particular lineage; priesthood belongs to a family. Today we live in a world where this is difficult to continue. Here the church cannot but break with African tradition; for in the church God chooses whom he wills and class, colour, race, sex, cannot be a factor.[27] But even in the traditional society it was not any one in the family who would have the authority. Even there, selection criteria for the candidate took particular notice of crisis syndromes such as illness, psychological manifestations, and mystical experience, which is diagnosed as the call of the divinity. In other words, authority derives in part, at any rate, from signs or indications of a call, not just family connections and not just academic attainments.

Fourth, priesthood involved teaching the wishes of the divinity to the people. But such knowledge is not limited to books; knowledge is from the senses, reason, intuition and tradition, experience gained through observation, initiation and participation which presuppose and demand keenness of perception and an alert and adaptive mind. Such qualities make for authoritative leadership.

One last point – contrary to popular ideas, a chief who did not reflect the wishes of his community was removed from office. In other words, the authority was not *ad libitum*: the power was democratized. Where in our churches do we find the right to remove religious authority for misgovernment? A relevant concept of authority in the church must be people-centred and therefore democratized.

Authority is didactic, cultic, diaconal, and democratic. As practised today in Africa these notes are on models from the North. But it is the submission of this paper that from within the African experience there are elements that can be more meaningful interpretations of didactic, cultic, diaconal, and democratic authority in the African context. In any case, authority is a charism which must manifest in everyday life the presence of the Holy Spirit, the author of authority.

Notes

This is a substantially revised and updated version of the article "Take Thou Authority; An African Perspective" by John Pobee published in *Authority in the Anglican Communion* edited by Stephen Sykes, (Anglican Book Centre, Canada, 1987).

1   John S. Pobee, "Mission, Paternalism and the Peter Pan Syndrome" in *Crossroads are for Meeting: Essays on the Mission and Common Life of the Church in a Global Society*, Eds. Philip Turner and Frank Sugeno (Sewanee, 1986), 91-108.

2   A.F. Walls, "Africa's Place in Christian History" in *Religion in a Pluralistic Society*, Ed. John S. Pobee (Leiden, 1976), 180-189.

3   John S. Pobee, "African Instituted Churches" in *Dictionary of the Ecumenical Movement* (Geneva, 1991) 10-12.

4   Kanyoro Musimbi, "Challenges of Feminist Theologies to Ministerial Formation"

in *Ministerial Formation* 74 1996:16; Richard Holloway (Ed.), *Who Needs Feminism: Men Respond to Sexism in the Church* (London, 1991); John S. Pobee (Ed.), *Theology, Women, Culture* (Delhi, 1994).

5 George A. Theodorson and Achilles G. Theodorson, *Modern Dictionary of Sociology* (New York, 1969), 307.

6 Ibid., 21.

7 Max Weber, *The Theory of Social and Economic Organizations*, trans. Parsons and Henderson (London, 1947), 354-360.

8 Tom Tuma, "Direction in Church Growth" in *Today's Church and Today's World*, The Lambeth Conference 1978 Preparatory Articles (London, 1979), 96-102, esp. 96-97.

9 Stephen F. Bayne Jr., *An Anglican Turning Point* (Austin, Texas, 1964).

10 *Anglican Information*, 38, December 1984, 2.

11 J.Y. Campbell, "Koinonia and its Cognates in the New Testament" in *Three New Testament Studies* (Leiden, 1965) 3-28.

12 John S. Pobee (Ed.), *In Search of Biblical Hermeneutics for Mission* IAMS, forthcoming, especially Justin Ukpong, "Models and Methods of Biblical Interpretation in Africa" and Teresa Okure, "Mission as a 'Gathering In': A Key in the Search of a New Hermeneutic for Mission".

13 Stephen W. Sykes, *The Integrity of Anglicanism* (Oxford, 1978), 96.

14 C.E.B. Cranfield, *A Critical and Exegetical Commentary on the Epistle to the Romans*, II (Edinburgh, 1979), 605.

15 C.F.D. Moule, *The Gospel According to Mark* (Cambridge, 1965), 83.

16 Leonardo Boff, *Church, Charism and Power* (London, 1985), 159-160.

17 J. Darrouzès, *Documents inédits d'ecclésiologie byzantine* (Paris, 1966), 222-224.

18 See John Meyendorff, *Imperial Unity and Christian Divisions* (Crestwood, New York), 1989, 59-66; 127-147; 314-332.

19 See M.A.C. Warren, *Social History and Christian Mission* (London, 1967), 33-34; A. Hastings, *A History of African Christianity 1950-1975* (Cambridge, 1979), 19-20; John S. Pobee, "Afro-Anglicanism: Meaning and Movement", paper read at Pan Anglican Conference on Afro-Anglicanism: Present Issues and Future Tasks, Barbados, 17-21 June 1985.

20 K.A. Dickson, "The Minister – Then and Now", in *Religion in a Pluralistic Society*, ed. J. S. Pobee (Leiden, 1976), 179.

21 Rudolf Peil, *A Handbook of the Liturgy* (Edinburgh, 1960), particularly 35-42.

22 K.A. Busia, *The Position of the Chief in the Modern Political System in Ashanti: A Study of the Influence of Contemporary Social Change in Ashanti Political Institutions* (London, 1968); K.A. Busia, *Africa in Search of Democracy* (London, 1967).

23 M. Fortes and E.B. Evans-Pritchard, eds., *African Political Systems* (London, 1940); J. Middleton, *Tribes Without Rulers* (London, 1970); Audrey I. Richards, *East African Chiefs: A Study of Political Development in some Ugandan and Tanzanian Tribes* (New York, 1959); Audrey Richards, "Authority Patterns in Traditional Buganda", in *The King's Men*, ed. L.A. Fatters (London, 1964); J.M. Assimeng, *Social Structure of Ghana* (Tema, 1981) especially 88-112; B.C. Ray, *African Religions* (Englewood Cliffs, 1976), 119-128; J.S. Pobee, *Religion and Politics in Ghana*, Studies Misionalie Uppsalensia XL VIII (Accra 1991) Chapter 2.

24 Busia, *Africa in Search*, 26; Busia, *Position of Chief*, 36-37.

25 J.B. Christensen, "The Adaptive Functions of Fanti Priesthood", in *Continuity and Change in African Cultures*, eds. W.R. Bascom and M.J. Herskovits (Chicago, 1959).

26 J.S. Pobee, "African Spirituality", in *A Dictionary of Christian Spirituality* (London, 1983), 7.

27 In some of the African Christian Independency such as the Musama Disco Christo Church of Ghana and the Eglise de Jésus Christ sur la terre par prophète Simon Kimbangu of Zaire, leadership is located in the family of the founder, a son to be precise.

25

Towards Reconciliation in Rwanda

Emmanuel Kolini

I write as an Anglican Bishop of the former Anglican province that included both Rwanda and Zaire before Zaire became a separate province. Any process of reconciliation will involve a recognition of problems caused both by Protestant and Catholic Churches, and also an understanding of crucial points in the history of the interaction of Church and State in Rwanda.

There are three ethnic groups in Rwanda. The Tutsi, monarchical cattle farmers, were in control of Rwanda; the Hutus were mostly peasants. The third group was the Twa.

After Rwanda became a protectorate of Belgium, the status quo was at first approved by Belgian authorities and the Tutsis were encouraged to receive education.

The Roman Catholic Church, which arrived simultaneously with colonial power, was content to accept the Tutsis' position of leadership. The Church was the main provider of education. The Anglican Church, which was introduced later, was not regarded with enthusiasm by the Roman Catholic Church.

The Protestants tended to think of politics as a dirty game. They did not consider the Catholics to be as Christian as themselves because of their involvement with politics. The Protestants therefore had two stumbling blocks which made them ill-equipped to have practical political judgement: their supposedly biblically-based belief that politics is evil and a low standard of education which reinforced a lack of understanding of political issues.

The consequence was that the Protestants followed leaders who had the wrong motives and whose politics were based on tribalism. They remained a weak minority with no representation within the government.

By contrast Roman Catholics were proactive and used politicians to achieve their own church political aims.

COMMON DISTORTIONS OF HISTORICAL FACT

There are a number of popular misconceptions concerning the past in Rwanda. It is claimed that the monarchy brought nothing good. However, we must note that it brought extension of Rwandan territory; forced labour was abolished in 1950; Rwanda enjoyed good relations with its neighbours; the king achieved independence for the country which cost him his life, and secured religious tolerance especially for the Anglicans.

Secondly, the charge is made that the king favoured his tribe. But, at his enthronement the king in fact automatically lost his clan and tribe so that he could exercise fair justice. "A man of all."

Thirdly, the Tutsi are accused of cruelty. It is important to define who is meant by the Tutsi. The Belgian definition was that, following vaccination which caused many cattle to die, whoever had more than ten head of cattle became a Tutsi: this meant some Tutsi became Hutu and vice versa which distorted the percentages of the population. The census of 1985 showed that Tutsi constituted 30% of population of Rwanda.

The truth is that whoever was in power mistreated subordinates: both Hutu and Tutsi suffered injustice from either Hutu and Tutsi in authority. There was no war between tribes, but between groups or classes or individuals.

My point is that the problem of Rwanda is more political and economic than tribal. The common man from both ethnic groups always suffered and is still suffering. All Tutsi were not rulers. Some were also peasants as well as Masai type, the Gogwe, an exploited people who were wiped out between 1990 and 1992. And all Hutu are not *Interahamwe* (militia) or extremists, but they are in camps simply because they bear the name.

With these points in mind, we turn to consider the problems of the Church in Rwanda.

THE CHURCH IN RWANDA

Problems caused by the Roman Catholic Church

The Roman Catholic Church bears much of the responsibility for Rwanda's conflict between the extremists from both ethnic groups, Hutu and Tutsi.

1.   The King Musinga was exiled to Moba-Congo, because he believed in Imana (a Kinyarwanda word meaning God), while the Roman Catholic bishop believed in *Mungu* (a Swahili word for God). The bishop therefore persuaded the Belgian authorities to send the king into exile, seeing him as a stumbling block to Christianity.

2.   The Administration School run by the Brothers of Charity, Frères de la charité, Butare, the former Astrida, was for sons of chiefs and sub-chiefs who would succeed their fathers. Few ordinary Tutsi and Hutu went to that school. The main purpose was to gain influence over these young chiefs and sub-chiefs who eventually rebelled against the king even though they were Tutsi.

3.   The young king was in disagreement with the Tutsi chiefs when he put an end to forced labour. The church then turned against him and eventually against the Tutsi in general, although they had baptized them. The oppression of the Hutu was their excuse, calling it social revolution, or, as the former governor called it "Revolution assisté", that is, assisted revolution. This so-called "social revolution" was actually supporting one tribe at the expense of the other.

4.   The Catholic church had attracted Tutsis into the seminaries to nurture leaders. Now Tutsi seminarians were expelled and a number of Tutsi religious men and women fled in 1959, 1962 and 1973.

5.   In 1973 there was a coup d'état because of the problem of regionalism, in the south and north. The Roman Catholic archbishop from the north became a member of the ruling party until the Pope wrote a strongly-worded letter demanding that he choose between the church and politics. There was no Protestant minister because the Roman Catholics in power did not want to upset their spiritual father.

When the war broke in 1990 the Roman Catholic archbishop told a foreign journalist on video that the President had done nothing wrong in his seventeen years in office. In 1994 a good number of his priests as well as other religious people were killed, but still he said nothing. Even so this does not justify his murder, along with other bishops and priests, by angry and undisciplined RPF young soldiers.

Problems caused by the Protestant Church

1.   Leaders of other churches were elevated to positions of significance when the colonialists and First Republic left. This, I believe, was the reason they did not challenge evil, since they were indebted for their advancement to the government. Some church leaders were even used to speak on behalf of the government, nationally and internationally.

2.   Within the Anglican Church there were power struggles among the Hutu. This diverted their attention from tackling social injustice: the Tutsi had already become marginalized anyway.

3.   In October 1990, following the incursion of the RPF, one of the Anglican bishops congratulated the then Rwandan army for their supposed victory by sending Psalm 109 as a message. It gave encouragement to the victors and cursed the "false accusers", the RPF.

4.   In my opinion, missionary societies held back, like Peter, to see what might happen, hoping that events would resolve themselves. Their timing was miscalculated. I do not suggest they denied the problems, but that they delayed their challenge. Sometimes evasion of responsibility can become a liability.

The Church leadership, I am afraid to say, betrayed the church they were called to serve.

REVIVAL

The 1930s

The Revival of the 1930s touched individuals in all churches but did not reach society in general. Those it did reach were mainly the lower classes: the illiterate Anglican minority. The individuals affected continued to witness to their faith during the thirty-five years of struggle.

Questions concerning the relationship between Gospel and culture came up amongst the people and they were not equipped to resolve these tensions.

For example, at marriage it was the custom for the bride to sit on the lap of her mother-in-law and father-in-law symbolizing that she was then born into the family. There was a feeling that such rituals were pagan in origin and therefore contrary to the Gospel.

It took a long time for people to accept the Revival because it broke cultural taboos. Barriers of status and between white and black were challenged. When finally church leaders and society began to accept the value of the Revival, political upheaval began interfering with its natural progress.

The 1970s

The Revival in the 1970s was cross-denominational and involved mostly young people. There was much spiritual experience but little teaching. The generation gap may have caused the churches to leave the young too much to their own devices. They were content merely to see them embracing Christianity in its more lively form.

There was little interaction amongst the churches. The established churches resisted the movement because they suspected the doctrines of what they saw as its Pentecostal orientation.

The movement also involved increased social awareness. It would mean challenging the policies of the government, particularly over events concerning Tutsis and the southern Hutus. Avoidance of social issues reflected the attitude of much of the church around the world at the time.

THE AFTERMATH OF REVIVAL

When the Tutsi and missionaries left, they left behind a church with no mature leadership because energies had been concentrated simply on spreading the revival rather than ensuring that it would endure. There had been inadequate teaching to consolidate people's conversion and equip them for leadership, particularly in the midst of political turmoil.

RECONCILIATION:
WHAT DOES IT REALLY ENTAIL?

After such horrible events we face a great challenge. The fear, guilt and mistrust are enormous. However the grace of God is greater than those huge sins. Isaiah 1:18: *Even if your sins are red as scarlet they shall become as white as snow.* It is vital to understand that the verse begins *Come and let us reason together.*

1. Assumption of responsibility

Roman Catholics put it, in Latin, *"Mea culpa, mea culpa, mea maxima culpa"* "I am at fault". That personal conviction is so vital. There must be awareness of God's mercy and of the cross where all our sins were assumed and forgiven. This must be realized by whoever has sinned against God and their fellow man, without any reservation.

There is a saying in Kinyarwanda *"Akamuga, karuta agaturo"*: "A disability is better than a grave". One life is more important than all the houses in Kigali because if there was only a single sinner, still Jesus had to die. Life should be taken seriously. It is very hard to be a refugee, and those who are now back in Rwanda have been refugees for more than thirty years. But those who were mercilessly killed can never come back to Rwanda. They are with their God to whom they cried in those churches, sanctuaries which became butcheries.

There needs to be blame, admission of sin, and grief, the sincere acknowledgement of the burden, confession, cessation of all such acts and the payment of the penalty. Zaccheus said: "I shall pay back four times the amount." Jonah allowed himself to be thrown into the sea; the criminal on the cross next to Christ said: "We deserve it." This is the first step of reconciliation.

2. Justice must be exacted

God is the God of justice. He will not let the sin go unpunished. Justice is required from those who say they love their country, those who claim to be the patriotic. *Ukiza abavandimwe, arararama:* "If you want to help brothers in conflict do not be sentimental". Again, *aho abagabo bali, abandi ntibapfo:* "Where wise men are, justice is exercised". Those who are concerned for justice for Rwanda need to know that the Hutu and Tutsi are brothers. The world should look for wise men within the country along with friends from the international community and wait on their wisdom for Rwanda.

Once justice has been exacted fairly, it will be much easier to talk about forgiveness and reconciliation. Again the Banyarwanda tradition has *inzoga y'icyiru*: "a cow of atonement". Once the case was assessed and sentence was passed, as a sign of atonement the offender paid the *y'icyiru*.

Kabili gatatu rekada! Three times: that is enough! There were killings in 1959, the 1960s and 1970s and now the 1990s. Still the world community kept quiet. Yet here in England people protest that animals which are taken to Europe are badly treated. Were not those Hutu and Tutsi created in the image of God as we all have been and are they not worthy of protest?

SIGNS OF HOPE

A world of hope

There are so many signs of hope around the world: the unification of Germany; the end of apartheid; the collapse of communism; restored Arab-Jewish relationships; steps towards reconciliation in Northern Ireland.

A nation of hope

There are so many factors to unite the Rwandans, Hutu and Tutsi.
- Their culture, language, Christian faith and civilization.
- The seven thousand people who have not worshipped the ethnicity idol. Some are in refugee camps and others have stayed or gone back to the country.

Hope: in Christian doctrine

When the disciples, who were to become leaders, ran away from Jesus, women continued to follow closely, weeping. The unknown witnesses are there today too.

ANGLICAN LIFE AND WITNESS

"The arm of the Lord is not too short to save" (Num. 11:23). The blood is still there to cleanse those who come to reason with Him. The world will not come to an end before the one who is to repent repents. We sow in tears. We shall reap in joy.

Hope: in shared experience

The three ethnic groups who went into exile together: Tutsis, moderate Hutus, and Twa, together form the RPF with a Hutu leader.

The sharing of the experience in refugee camps should be a balance between the two groups; those who have been there before and those who are there now.

The gun is not an answer, as those who have tried this method have discovered. The gun is certainly not a tool for reconstruction. Nor is the weapon of majority effective. I would like to think the shared experiences may bring the former enemies to sit together and settle their differences and live together.

Hope: in the compassion of the religious and secular world

Why cannot the church and the world have compassion on these innocent people who suffer because of national and international political manipulation?

Hope: in international policy

Finally may the superpowers, by the mercy and grace of God, unite and not divide, construct not destroy. The international community should not exploit the situation for their own gain. Building either a Francophone or Anglophone empire has been proved shameful: there is no other word to describe it.

Postscript

"A person heaps up wealth, not knowing who will enjoy it" (Ps. 39:6). Whoever makes wealth more important than human life should remember this, "What you want others to do to you, do the same to them" (Luke 6:31).

The sister church should not only pray, but speak out to their governments to bring to their attention what can be done for the powerless. The church worldwide should join the faithful of the Gospel in central Africa to put an end to what I will call the spiritual genocide which has been encouraged for thirty years by the preaching of hatred on their part.

"By this the world will know that you are my disciples: if you love one another" (John 13:35).

Let us do that.

Part Four

—

Seeking Full Visible Unity

26

Evangelical Mission Societies and the Church in India

Vinay Samuel

Evangelical growth in India is reflected principally in the rapid growth of indigenous missionary societies during the past twenty-five years. Over fifty of them have substantial ministries. The Evangelical Missionary Movement uses the description missionary for cross-cultural work. A majority of such societies are based in South India and send South Indian missionaries to communities and regions in the north, central and western parts of the country. The significant cultural and linguistic differences between the regions mean that missionaries have to learn new languages and adapt to new cultures. It is estimated that there are more than three hundred indigenous missionary societies, with about 4,000 missionaries involved in ministries of evangelism, church planting, medical work, child care, education and vocational training. A significant number of the well established missionary societies are led by lay members and/or pastors of mainline Protestant churches. They have developed a network of support groups among local churches. Their lack of relation to denominational structures introduces a tension between their commitment to independent missionary activity and their obvious commitment to the church. This paper explores the way in which evangelical missionary societies have handled that tension. It also identifies the missiological and theological issues that arise from such a context.

EVANGELICALS AND THE CHURCH

Evangelicalism as a theological and missiological movement gathered momentum after India gained independence in 1947. In 1951, church leaders from evangelical denominations such as the Free Methodist Church, The Christian and Missionary Alliance, The Conservative Baptists etc. joined with leaders from mainline churches such as the Methodist Episcopal Church (now the Methodist Church in India), the Church of South India, The Mar Thoma Church, to form the Evangelical Fellowship of India (EFI). From the beginning, evangelicalism included individuals from mainline churches in its leadership. The EFI's institutional membership consisted of evangelical churches and missions but individual members came from different church traditions. Commitment to an evangelical basis of faith, fundamentals that needed to be conserved and passed on, priority of sharing the gospel inviting people to a personal faith in Christ and a passionate desire to pray for the revival of the church, united people in the EFI.

Evangelicalism saw itself as an interchurch movement. In 1962, when the Evangelical Fellowship in the Anglican Communion was founded, attempts were made to bring Indian "Anglican" evangelicals together. It was discovered that "Anglican" evangelicals were active in the Evangelical Fellowship of India and did not see the need for a denominational evangelical fellowship. Co-operation was a key component of evangelicalism's self-understanding. Co-operation in working for the survival of the church and in evangelistic activity was based on a deep sense of unity as God's people. A statement of faith summarized fundamental faith commitments common to evangelicals. Added to commitment to a doctrinal basis was the shared experience of having experienced Christ personally as Saviour and Lord. Unity was based on common doctrinal commitments and a common experience of salvation.

Evangelicals worked hard for the first visit of Billy Graham to India in 1956. Its impact was dramatic. Church leaders from different traditions were involved in the planning and were visible on the platforrns during the "crusades". Large crowds attended. Significant numbers of people came forward to accept Christ. Those who were converted included people from other faiths. A study done on the impact of Billy Graham meetings on the churches in Madras City showed beneficial effects on the local congregations. Over sixty-five percent of those who responded at the meetings became faithful and active members of local congregations. Evangelical initiatives among youth, children and college students received much encouragement. Evangelical seminaries and Bible schools began to expand rapidly.

The entire exercise confirmed the nature of evangelical identity and the priorities of the evangelical movement. Evangelicals identified themselves as those committed to historic Christianity particularly expressed in a statement of faith. Their church affiliation was secondary to their principal identity as those who had personally experienced Christ as Saviour and Lord and were committed to the fundamentals of the faith. They could relate to one another as "believers" rather than through their denominational identities. They could cooperate as believers in revival meetings, evangelistic efforts and mission endeavours. Confirming the evangelical credentials of individuals and organizations continues to have a major role in evangelical movements. This is related to evangelical stress on identity, assurance concerning an individual's status as a believer and an organization's commitment to evangelical fundamentals of the faith.

The overwhelming response to the "simple" preaching of the gospel during Billy Graham's visit also confirmed the priority of proclaiming the gospel for the evangelical movement. In a land where most people did not have an opportunity to hear the gospel, it was seen that proclaiming the gospel and inviting people to personal faith in Christ must become the dominant objective of Christian mission.

Evangelicals developed a pattern of local church cooperation for evangelism. City penetration plans and city-wide evangelistic rallies were organized with a wide cross-section of local churches cooperating. Revival prayer groups also started, with Christians from different church traditions praying together for the revival of the church in their area and throughout India.

The need to take the gospel to unreached people beyond local communities began to capture the attention of Indian evangelicals in the late fifties. A missionary consciousness developed, and challenge to be a missionary to tribal communities in the central part of India and to places in the north of India having only traces of Christian presence began increasingly to be heard in evangelical conventions in South India. Leadership came principally from younger evangelicals from the Tirunelveli region of Madras State (today's Tamil Nadu) in South India. A predominantly Anglican area, Tirunelveli has a unique tradition of founding the first two indigenous missionary societies in the early part of this century. The first Indian bishop of the Anglican Church in India, V.S. Azariah (1874–1945), was passionately committed to missionary work and helped to found the National Missionary Society and the Indian Missionary Society. That tradition of Tirunelveli was carried on by evangelicals such as the Rev. Dr Sam Kamalesan and the Rev. Dr Theodore Williams, both with Tirunelveli Anglican roots but now ordained ministers of the Methodist Church in India in Madras. Both provided leadership to the growing evangelical missionary movement. Theodore Williams helped found the Indian Evangelical Mission and Sam Kamalesan the Friends Missionary Prayer Band.

From the beginning, indigenous evangelical missionary movements drew on the prayer and financial support of local churches from a variety of traditions. They saw themselves as the missionary outreach of these local congregations and local Christians. They recognized the need for Indian Christians to take increasing responsibility for cross-cultural missionary work. This was against the background of the rapid decline in the number of foreign missionaries in independent India.

EVANGELICAL MISSIONARY SOCIETIES AND THE CHURCH

A brief description and analysis of the Friends Missionary Prayer Band (FMPB), the oldest evangelical missionary society, illustrate the nature of the relation of indigenous and independent missionary societies to the churches in India.

The FMPB grew out of the tradition of evangelistic bands common among Christians of Madras State since the early part of this century. It was not unusual for youth, factory workers, church groups, women's groups to band together for evangelistic activity and go street preaching, especially during weekends. The Friends Missionary Prayer Band was probably the first to develop the missionary prayer band tradition. It was a group of young Christians who banded together primarily to pray for the unreached people of India. They were ready and willing to obey any call that came through such activity of prayer.

The FMPB was founded in 1966 and held a passionate concern to reach the unreached people of North India with the gospel.

C.B. Samuel, who has known this movement from its early days, writes that it was a movement for verbal communication of the gospel with the motto to "go or send".[1] People were invited to become missionaries and fulfil the "go" part of their mandate or get involved in sending people to the mission field. The FMPB decided to depend only on local Indian financial support, a policy that it has maintained faithfully.

C.B. Samuel identifies the stages in the development of the FMPB. The success of the evangelistic phase resulted in groups of believers gathered into worshipping communities. By 1991, approximately 27,500 people had become believers and were baptized, 648 worship groups were formed and 182 church buildings were constructed.[2] As churches got planted, the FMPB in its church planting phase committed itself to work with the Church of North India. As they became established, the worship groups became recognized congregations of the Church of North India (CNI). Some FMPB evangelists, who were responsible for evangelism and church-planting, were ordained as presbyters of CNI and assigned to pastor the new churches.

This infusion of growth through evangelism among unreached people brought encouragement and renewal to some dioceses in the north of India that had struggled to survive for many years. The bishops and diocesan leaders took a bold step in accepting the ministry of the FMPB without attempting to bring it under the control of the diocesan structures. In its mission work, the FMPB sought to maintain a relationship and commitment to the diocese. The churches planted became fully-fledged diocesan churches over a period of time. In its church-planting phase, the FMPB demonstrated commitment to church planting and also to the local established church. The dioceses of CNI, which welcomed the work of the FMPB, showed their willingness to work with mission organizations they did not control.

The care of baptized believers not only led to a commitment to the established church in the area, it also challenged the FMPB to recognize the socio-economic needs of the converts. A separate ministry, called *Navajeevan Sewa Mandal* (NSM, meaning new-life service association), was created to respond to such needs of the new churches. C.B. Samuel describing this phase writes:

> This called for a totally different approach to resource input needed for the work. FMPB prayer groups were challenged to provide technical skills if possible and also look for alternative and creative ways of funding (such as micro and macro enterprise programmes). This has brought into being other smaller units such as SCAN, FES etc.

The response to the socio-economic needs of new churches soon led to the recognition that such needs were inseparable from the needs of marginalized communities. Socio-economic transformation, not just of believers but of the entire marginalized community through which the believers come, is increasingly finding a place in their agenda for action. A network of marginalized communities to facilitate a people-owned programme of transformation is beginning to emerge. The FMPB, in its silver jubilee year, is at a critical stage of involvement in Christian mission. New directions in mission involvement have in no way reduced evangelistic effectiveness. In the State of Bihar, long known as the graveyard of Christian mission, five hundred people join the church each month. A tribal group on the verge of extinction has begun to find new life. 474 missionaries and 144 local evangelists work in 99 mission fields. The entire work continues to be supported by Indian Christians and local churches.

The FMPB showed significant sensitivity to the culture of a people in their practice of evangelism and nurture of the converts. The recognition of people's cultural needs enabled it to note the needs of the total context in which people lived. This openness to culture and the context of the people impacted its theology and practice of mission. It helped develop a wholeness in the relationship between their evangelistic/church-planting activities and their response to the socio-economic needs of marginalized people. In contrast, some other indigenous evangelical missionary societies exhibit an uneasy relationship between their evangelistic activity and their response to human need. The FMPB's financial independence, its awareness of the needs of the context and its commitment to the local churches enables it to respond contextually while maintaining faithfulness to biblical authority and teaching.

C.B. Samuel notes[4] that the FMPB gives low priority to its institutional growth. All important decisions continue to be made by representatives of the prayer groups that constitute the FMPB. The field missionaries and representatives of new churches provide the major input for decision-making. A democratic, congregational polity loosely structured but strongly bonded together by a common commitment to prayer and mission activism is a distinguishing mark of the organization. The organization's commitment to train local leaders has enabled it to meet the leadership needs of its new churches and socio-economic programmes.

ISSUES OF MISSION AND CHURCH

Indigenous evangelical missions begin with the assumption that evangelism is the responsibility of every individual Christian. Church structures are not seen to be necessary to define or confirm the individual's evangelistic mandate. Missionary work is a distinct activity focused on evangelism and church planting in cross-cultural and often geographically distant contexts. Missionary work is seen as an extension of the evangelistic mandate. So, missionary responsibility is given to each individual Christian and does not require authorization from ecclesial structures. The focus is on an individual Christian fulfilling his/her missionary responsibility, supported by a group of Christians who, while they fulfil their evangelistic responsibility through local evangelism, fulfil their missionary calling through "sending" one of their number. Evangelism and mission are primarily the calling of individuals.

It is my contention that such an individualistic understanding of mission responsibility shapes the ecclesiology of evangelical mission societies. The church is viewed as the institutional structure for nurturing Christians and empowering them for mission. Its own role in mission is to enable the individual Christian to fulfil his/her mission calling in the world. The church in its institutional form is not seen as receiving the mandate for mission, identifying God's mission for a particular context and time, and engaging in mission through its members. It is true that the church has often been preoccupied with the nurture needs of its members and the needs of its own development as an institution. Mission responsibility is hardly central to its life. But the detachment of mission responsibility from the church to individual members continues to widen the gulf between nurture and mission in the institutional church.

The indigenous missionary society recognizes that the domain of the institutional church is the nurture and development of the worshipping congregation. New churches that are planted are handed over to church denominations. It is only among a few missionary societies having no link with local indigenous churches that we find new churches continuing to be independent or part of the work of the society.

The FMPB and other such evangelical societies demonstrate a clear commitment to established local churches. However, the independence of mission activity from the nurture life of the institutional church cannot contribute adequately to the renewal of the church for mission and congregational life. It must be noted, however, that where local congregations are actively involved in missionary support and prayer, the congregation's own life is renewed and deepened. Evangelical ecclesiology focuses on the local congregation. The essence of the church and mission is sited in the local congregation. Evangelical missionary societies point to their partnership with local congregations as a demonstration of their commitment and accountability to the church. Evangelical missionary societies develop relationships of accountability to local churches, prayer groups and support groups. The calling and commitment of their missionary candidates is tested and confirmed by these groups.

Evangelical preoccupation with evangelism determines its practice of unity. Unity is often viewed as cooperation for mission rather than competition. Evangelicals place a high priority on doctrinal unity. A commitment to a statement of faith that covers the fundamentals of Christian faith ensures doctrinal unity. Such unity in the area of faith is seen as adequate to express the unity among Christians that the Bible enjoins. With its orientation to a congregational understanding of the church, it prefers democratization and plurality as the movement of the church's institutional development. Evangelical movements are networks of individuals and local churches. Even evangelical denominations often become part of such networks. Evangelicals assume that the visible unity of the church in faith and order is not a prerequisite for unity in mission activity. On the contrary, mission cooperation reflects the nature of our unity as churches.

Indigenous missionary societies are becoming increasingly responsive to the socio-economic challenges of the context in which they labour. The political aspects of the context are still seen as out of bounds to Christian activity. But, there is some convergence between the work of evangelical social activists and indigenous missionary societies. The FMPB increasingly works with the EFICOR (Evangelical Fellowship of India Commission on Relief) in addressing the total needs of a community, as in the case of the Maltos tribe in Bihar. Such relationships will undoubtedly influence indigenous missionary societies in being open to involvement for community transformation and not remaining content with church planting.

It is in the area of other faiths that there is little change in attitude or strategy among indigenous missionary societies. Other faiths are often viewed as enslaving people to hopelessness. There is strong disapproval of anything that is considered idolatrous. A more positive appreciation of people's religious culture without blunting the sharp edge of evangelism appears distant.

CONCLUSION

The experience of indigenous evangelical missionary societies in India confirms that a significant number of apparently independent evangelical bodies are closely related to local churches and denominational structures that are themselves part of the ecumenical movement. The experience of the FMPB with the Church of North India illustrates the mutual benefit of such a relationship. I believe the time is right for further study in this area.

Notes

1   C.B. Samuel, "Friends Missionary Prayer Band", unpublished paper, New Delhi, 1992, p.1.
2   India Mission, *Quarterly Bulletin of India Missions Association*, Jan–March 1992, p.7.
3   C.B. Samuel, *op.cit.*, p.2.
4   *Ibid.*